*The Boy King*

Edward VI, *c.* 1551: *an official image of the King. Small pictures like this, now in the Hermitage Museum, St Petersburg, would be presented to visiting diplomats.*

DIARMAID MacCULLOCH

# The Boy King

EDWARD VI AND THE
PROTESTANT REFORMATION

UNIVERSITY OF CALIFORNIA PRESS
Berkeley · Los Angeles

University of California Press
Berkeley and Los Angeles, California

First Paperback Printing 2002

THE BOY KING
Copyright © Diarmaid MacCulloch, 1999.
All rights reserved. No part of this book may be used or reproduced in any
manner whatsoever without written permission except in the case of brief
quotations embodied in critical articles or reviews.

Reprinted by arrangement with PALGRAVE

ISBN 0-520-23402-2 (pbk. : alk. paper)

Library of Congress Cataloging-in-Publication Data available
at the Library of Congress.

First published in Great Britain by Allen Lane, The Penguin Press 1999

Printed in the United States of America

08  07  06  05  04  03  02  01
10  9  8  7  6  5  4  3  2  1

The paper used in this publication meets the minimum requirements of
ANSI/NISO Z39.48-1992 (R 1997) (*Permanence of Paper*). ∞

For Simon White

# Contents

# List of Illustrations

# *Acknowledgements*

The basis of this book is the series of Birkbeck Lectures which I delivered in the University of Cambridge in Lent Term 1998. I must thank the Master and Fellows of Trinity College, Cambridge, for doing me the great honour of inviting me to give the Birkbeck Lectures for 1997–8, and for their warm welcome and hospitality while I was delivering the lectures. My four visits to Cambridge were a thoroughly enjoyable experience. My colleagues in the Theology Faculty of Oxford University and the Master and Fellows of St Cross College kindly afforded me a term of sabbatical leave in order to research and write, and during that time I was particularly assisted by the helpfulness of the staff of the Bodleian Library. Subsequently, Bodleian staff, especially Mrs S.C.N. Harris, and Mrs N. Collyer of the History of Art Library of the University of Oxford, have given cheerfully of their time in helping me track down illustrative material. I am also much indebted to the kindness of Mr Nick Mayhew of St Cross College and Dr Catherine Hall for particular illustrations.

Many friends have generously shared their knowledge with me during the course of my research. In particular, I am very grateful to Lisa Richardson for permission to quote from her thesis, to Margaret Aston for allowing me to use illustrations from her book *The King's Bedpost*, and to Ethan Shagan and Richard Hoyle for their invaluable part in pointing me to important manuscript material, while Norman Scarfe's gift of a first edition of Sir John Hayward's biography of Edward VI was an act of princely generosity. Robert Baldock provided advice and guidance at an early stage of this project, and he will know how much I appreciate his help. Penguin have made the production stages of this book a pleasure rather than a trial, and I am especially thankful to Stuart Proffitt for his friendly interest in it. As ever, I owe a great debt to Mark Achurch for tolerating the obsessions, chiefly with Tudor England, which went into creating this book.

All quotations in the main text have been modernized; as in previous books, I have adopted the spelling 'Strassburg' for the modern Strasbourg, given the overwhelmingly German character of the sixteenth-century city. Original spelling is retained in notes.

Diarmaid MacCulloch
*St Cross College, Oxford, December 1998*

# *Abbreviations used in the text and bibliography*

All primary and secondary works cited in the notes are abbreviated with reference to the bibliography, by title, author or editor. Likewise, see the bibliography for full bibliographical descriptions of specific works mentioned in the table below.

| | |
|---|---|
| *APC* | Dasent, ed., *Acts of the Privy Council*, with date |
| *ARG* | *Archiv für Reformationsgeschichte* |
| *AST* | Strasbourg, Archives Municipales, Archives du Chapître de St Thomas de Strasbourg |
| *BIHR* | *Bulletin of Historical Research* (see also *HR*) |
| BL | British Library |
| Bodl. | Bodleian Library, Oxford |
| CCCC | Corpus Christi College Cambridge Library |
| *CPR* | *Calendar of Patent Rolls* |
| CS | Camden Society |
| *CSP* | *Calendar of State Papers* |
| CUL | Cambridge University Library |
| *DNB* | *Dictionary of National Biography* |
| *EHR* | *English Historical Review* |
| *ET* | *Epistolae Tigurinae* |
| HMC | Historical Manuscripts Commission |
| *HJ* | *Historical Journal* (formerly Cambridge Historical Journal) |

| | |
|---|---|
| *HR* | *Historical Research* (formerly *Bulletin of Historical Research*) |
| *JEH* | *Journal of Ecclesiastical History* |
| *JTS* | *Journal of Theological Studies* |
| LACT | Library of Anglo-Catholic Theology (Oxford: J.H. Parker) |
| Lambeth | Lambeth Palace Library |
| NS | New Series |
| *OL* | *Original Letters* |
| PCC | Prerogative Court of Canterbury wills, P.R.O. |
| *PP* | *Past and Present* |
| PRO | Public Record Office, London |
| PS | Parker Society |
| RHS St. Hist. | Royal Historical Society Studies in History |
| *RSTC* | Pollard and Redgrave, eds., *Short Title Catalogue* |
| ser. | series |
| *St. Ch. Hist.* | Ecclesiastical History Society *Studies in Church History* |
| *Tr. R.H.S.* | *Transactions of the Royal Historical Society* |
| UP | University Press |

# I

# Dramatis Personae

Edward VI came to the throne of England on 28 January 1547, a boy of nine fathered in middle age by a king who died still middle-aged, before his son had the chance to grow up and observe his father's style of governance. This may not have been entirely a disadvantage: Henry VIII had become an increasingly capricious and dangerous man. His judgement – at the best of times directed by egotism and a considerable opinion of his own abilities – had grown impaired by years of continuous pain from ulcers in his legs (probably the long-term result of injuries sustained while jousting). On his accession in 1509, Henry had been a relief to the kingdom after the increasingly gloomy and paranoid rule of Henry VII, his father: he had been a handsome, highly educated, ebullient late teenager, a symbol of change and renewal. He had indeed brought plenty of change, especially in the religious life of his subjects: some would think of this change as renewal indeed, others would find less positive ways of viewing the result. Henry had broken his kingdom away from its near-millennium of association with the Bishop of Rome, the Pope, head of the Western Christian Church. In a search for cash for the defence of the realm, only fitfully justifying his drastic action in terms of religious reform, he had closed all the religious houses of England, leaving hundreds of monasteries, friaries and nunneries as empty shells to be sold off, torn down by speculative builders, left to rot in remote countryside or converted into country houses for wealthy gentlemen. He had encouraged some limited measures of liturgical experiment, and thus he had begun to change the way in which ordinary people experienced their encounter with God when they entered their parish churches; yet he had not given a decisive signal as to what his future plans would be.

Henry's quarrel with the Pope and his destruction of the monastic way of life took place against the background of a European-wide movement of reform which convulsed the whole Western Latin Church. Without considering this wider Reformation, it becomes impossible to understand the events of his son's short reign. In the years after Edward's death, that is from the mid-1550s, English people would become used to calling this movement by a newly coined German word: Protestantism. The word had started life merely describing a political accident: at the meeting of the Diet (Assembly) of the Holy Roman Empire held at Speyer in 1529, a group of German princes who supported religious reform had drawn up a protest – a 'Protestatio' – when the majority of the Diet's members had made decisions favourable to traditional religion. Two decades later in Edward's reign, like 'glasnost' or 'perestroika' in the England of the 1980s, 'Protestant' still remained a foreign word to describe the doings of foreigners, even among those who felt enthusiastic about their opinions. Thus in the preparations for the old king's funeral at Windsor in 1547, provision was made for the diplomatic representatives of the reformist German religious alliance (the Schmalkaldic League) to attend if they wanted to, and a few days later, they were given an honoured place in the coronation procession for the new king in London. In both cases, they were simply called 'the Protestants'.[1]

It is therefore premature to use the label 'Protestant' for the English movement of reform in the reigns of Henry and Edward, even though its priorities were intimately related to what was happening in central Europe. A description more true to the period would be 'evangelical', a word which was indeed used at the time in various cognates.[2] It went to the heart of Europe's religious divisions, because the reform movement represented itself as a faithful return to the true spirit of Christ's Gospel, the good news or *evangelium*. It was a restatement of Christian faith, an attempt to return to the supposed Gospel shape of the Church in its first

1. *Henry VIII in his last years. The engraving by Cornelius Matsys pitilessly reveals the deterioration which illness wrought in the king.*

generation of existence. Martin Luther, Huldrych Zwingli, Martin Bucer were only the most prominent names among a group of European preachers, pastors and writers who shaped evangelical agendas: they were mostly clergy who had repented of their calling to ministry in the old Western Church, had found a new vocation and now raged against the style of devotion which medieval religion had created.

In the context of this Continent-wide struggle, the religious outlook of the king who plunged his two realms of England and Ireland into traumatic change much puzzled his contemporaries, and remains a complex problem to unravel.[3] Henry loved to present himself as occupying the middle ground in the turbulence of the European reformations. When making a keynote speech to Parliament in December 1545, an occasion which proved to be his swansong on the public stage, Henry denounced both those who 'be too stiff in their old mumpsimus' and those who were 'too busy and curious in their new sumpsimus', and he was so overcome by his own plea for his subjects to unite in religious harmony between the two extremes that he dissolved into tears. His devoted if not uncritical servant Archbishop Thomas Cranmer admired the king precisely because of such sentiments about the middle way, although the two men were not entirely in agreement about where that middle way might be found.

In fact, by his last decade of life, a chasm had opened up within Henry VIII's own religious opinions, making his middle way a distinctly precarious path which few others seemed capable of treading without his imperious guidance. He had jettisoned much of the old church's ways from his thoughts. Crucially, the idea of purgatory – a middle state between heaven and hell, a time of purging after death – which had been central to the thought and devotional practice of northern Europe for centuries, had ceased to hold him in its grip. His final official doctrinal statement (the so-called 'King's Book' of 1543), more conservative in many respects than its predecessors, reduced purgatory's sway over humanity's future fate to the vaguest of propositions, and the book even forbade people to use the word. Henry also distrusted the power of clergy. Admittedly, so had many of his medieval predecessors, but, stimulated by the example of evangelical theological opinion abroad, he was now able to crystallize this anticlericalism, using the definitions provided in the King's Book to downgrade those of the traditional church's seven sacraments whose administration might be seen as unnecessarily emphasizing clerical mystique: confirmation, unction and ordination. Additionally, he remained convinced that he had done God's work in destroying shrines and images which were the objects of devotion and pilgrimage, and he annotated his personal copy of the psalter with self-congratulatory notes when he felt that the Psalms of David were endorsing his action.

In contrast with Henry the radical reformer was Henry the pious son of traditional religion. Despite all the efforts of Archbishop Cranmer, patiently trying to persuade God's anointed to take the evangelical view of God's purposes, the king never accepted the Reformation view of justification by faith alone: the doctrine that all salvation was an act of God's grace, conveyed to a helpless and unworthy humanity by the divine gift of faith in Christ's saving work on the Cross, and not the result of any human initiative or good work. Henry felt passionately that this approach to the problem of salvation destroyed all incentive to do good, because it detached human salvation from human virtue; after all, he was the guardian of his kingdom's morality. So he had lost his hold on the central organizing principle of traditional theologies of salvation – the doctrine of purgatory – without finding his way to a coherent replacement doctrine in the mould of Martin Luther. Given this void at the heart of his religious opinions, it was hardly surprising that the structure of ideas which he gathered for himself had the quality of a theological jackdaw's nest. In particular, his strong opinions about marriage – not a sacrament which he was prepared to downgrade – were linked first to his passionate hatred of divorce, for he never divorced a wife, merely declared that certain of his 'marriages' had never existed and should therefore be annulled (Cranmer obliged three times – Catherine of Aragon, Anne Boleyn and Anne of Cleves). However, his convictions on marriage also related to his equally emphatic traditionalist maintenance of clerical celibacy: after his Six Articles Act of 1539, all

2. *The four evangelists stoning the Pope, together with Hypocrisy and Avarice:*
*a picture by Girolamo da Treviso the Younger, commissioned by Henry VIII in the*
*last decade of his life, and hanging at Hampton Court at his death.*

his clergy had to remain celibate or at least, like Cranmer, send their
wives out of the realm – even the monks, friars and nuns whose way of
life he had destroyed must observe their vows of celibacy to their dying
day. To describe this religious mixture as theologically ambiguous is to
indulge in courtier-like understatement. The spiritual portrait of Henry
VIII would have been a mask of Janus.

Given these personal contradictions, it is hardly surprising that all
through the 1540s Henry VIII had encouraged a seesaw in the fortunes
of evangelicals and traditionalists around him, although the general pattern was that each fresh lurch ended up with religious conservatives in a
weaker position than before. This was only to be expected, for although

conservatives occupied high places in government, the people closest to the old king in his everyday life and in his private apartments – even his doctors – were mostly evangelical in sympathy. For three years after 1543, Henry gave up burning evangelical heretics. Perhaps he was temporarily disgusted by the manoeuvres of leading traditionalists who had tried to extend their heresy-hunting as far as his Archbishop of Canterbury in the so-called 'Prebendaries' Plot': in the end the king decided that this was an unwarranted assault on a faithful servant, and in 1544, he executed a few conservatives instead, before diverting himself with the joys of fighting the French. However, as his illness and physical agony grew in 1546, his savagery returned in even more erratic form, first to the benefit of traditionalists, then of evangelicals.[4]

After the lapse of three years, that summer of 1546 saw a crop of burnings at the stake: the victims were evangelicals who were labelled 'sacramentaries' because they denied that the bread and wine of the eucharist could become the body and blood of Christ. Meanwhile Gurone Bertano, a freelance Italian envoy, made a quixotic but determined bid to persuade Henry back into the papal obedience, an effort which was taken surprisingly seriously by the small group at court who knew of the initiative. However, only a few months later, the flamboyant heir of the Howard family, Henry Earl of Surrey, was brought to the scaffold because of his supposed ambitions for the throne. This spelled disaster for Surrey's father, Thomas Howard Duke of Norfolk, the most powerful and implacable conservative among the leading lay nobility; Norfolk was thrown in the Tower, himself only saved from execution by the death of the old king, and his estates lay ready to be divided up among his enemies. So by the end of 1546 and the beginning of 1547, despite all previous hazards to the cause of reformation, the king had left evangelical politicians in an unassailable position to take over at his death. Edward Seymour's colleagues on the Privy Council helped him consolidate his position by recognizing him as Lord Protector, and by confirming his promotion to be Duke of Somerset (amid a general shareout of honours, together with estates, mostly from the Howards, which it was said that the old king would have authorized had he but lived). Norfolk

7

remained a helpless and bewildered prisoner in the Tower; the Lord Chancellor Thomas Wriothesley was the only prominent conservative on the Council prepared to make any trouble for the new dispensation, and he was quickly elbowed out.

Now Edward's reign was on course to be directed by a closely knit group of his father's advisers and servants. They had been given their chance of power in the last weeks before his accession by the deliberate design of a king who was acutely ill but still in full possession of his life-time's accumulation of political skill; Edward Seymour's assumption of the Protectorate was a natural outgrowth of the arrangements which Henry had made for government in his last months of life. He was sur-rounded by a group of like-minded politicians – notably John Dudley, William Parr, Thomas Cranmer and William Paget – who constituted the leading voices of the Privy Council. Straightaway we can describe them as heading an evangelical establishment, which also included cer-tain leading reformist churchmen like Nicholas Ridley and Thomas Goodrich, plus those chiefly responsible for the king's education, the Oxbridge dons Sir John Cheke and Richard Cox. Through the reign, one or two people joined the group, like William Cecil and some associates of John Dudley; one or two, notably the two Seymour brothers and cer-tain of Somerset's clients, were subtracted, with the aid of an executioner. But the evangelical establishment remained small and closely knit.[5]

So this evangelical establishment shared an agenda which would have been difficult to hide from Henry VIII. They were determined to join the religious revolution in the rest of Europe: to destroy the old world of devotion of the English Church, which, as a result of the political seesaw of Henry's thirty-eighth year, now lay helpless before them, a severed limb of the Western Latin Church. Edward's leading political advisers were poised to implement the alternative programme for religion which evangelicalism promised. They could not have failed to notice that a programme of religious change also gave the possibility of diverting some of the old Church's huge wealth to their own pockets. At such a distance of time, it is difficult now to disentangle sanctity from selfish-ness in their motives.[6]

We are beginning a consideration of this religious revolution with a cast list, since we are to be spectators at a drama: a drama of six years' span. Edward's reign and the Reformation which it encompassed is a story of adventure. It has often been viewed as a tragedy: but there are utterly opposed readings of what the tragedy was about. It might have consisted of the spectacle of destruction, attacks on beauty, refined spirituality and a widely loved way of life, a senseless waste of resources sacrificed to greed and ambition. Or it might be seen as a noble experiment in transforming a nation, prematurely brought low by the inscrutable providence of God, or by the inadequacy of Tudor medicine, which was helpless after the onset of Edward's final illness.[7]

The play is indeed an epic contest between polar opposites. It lacks the nuances of the official Reformation which came about when Edward's half-sister Elizabeth I ascended the throne in 1558. In the years after 1558, the royal purpose centred on defence: creating a polity which would stand against all comers. Elizabeth's favourite, Sir Christopher Hatton, an enthusiast for her strategy, said in a parliamentary speech of 1589 that she 'placed her Reformation as upon a square stone to remain constant'.[8] Nothing could be more remote from the tone of policy under Edward VI. The Reformation of 1547 to 1553 carried out in his name was a revolutionary act, a dynamic assault on the past, a struggle to the death between Christ and Antichrist. John Foxe's illustrator summed up Edward's reign in a picture for *Acts and Monuments*, Foxe's classic epic of the struggle to establish God's kingdom in history (better known by its nickname 'Foxe's *Book of Martyrs*'). In the foreground, he portrayed a peaceful pair of scenes: the young king presides over the ordered hierarchy of the royal court, while in the reformed house of God there is godly preaching and the austere but reverent performance of the two biblical sacraments, baptism and eucharist. But the tranquillity of the new order is placed against a background of purposeful turmoil: a church building is being stripped of popery ('the Temple well purged'), a bonfire is consuming images, while the agents of the Bishop of Rome are fleeing to the English coast to take sail for abroad, clutching whatever paraphernalia of their errors they can salvage – 'Ship over

3. *An allegory of the reign of Edward, introducing John Foxe's account of the reign of Edward VI in* Acts and Monuments, *1570.*

your trinkets and be packing ye papists!' the artist cries in triumph.

Such histrionics embarrassed the later leaders of English established religion; so the play of King Edward has constantly been rewritten to make more sense of its unlikely sequels. We must now try to see the original shape of the drama, as well as seeing how it was re-scripted to suit later needs. We will find that the play had many versions so, following the example of Christopher Haigh's survey of the religious history of the period, we must frequently talk of Edwardian Reformations, rather than the Edwardian Reformation. There was an official Reformation in England: indeed more than one official Reformation, for largely beyond the concern of this study are the Reformations of Ireland, Edward's other kingdom, and of certain outlying and semi-detached Tudor territories besides, like the Channel Islands.[9] There were Reformations by self-help, not all of which coexisted very happily with the government's plans. There was another Reformation waiting in the wings, whose plot would be written by Roman Catholic Queen Mary and Cardinal Pole.

Is Edward's reign a drama worth observing? Often it has been treated as a rather confused entr'acte for the two set-piece spectaculars of Henrician and Elizabethan England. To view it thus is a mistake. These six years reshaped the culture which the union of the English, Scots and Irish crowns later exported to the rest of the world. They saw the first officially backed moves to turn English maritime strength to ventures of world exploration, as expeditions set off for Africa and Muscovy.[10] They also began with a spirited attempt by the first Edwardian government to unite the whole British archipelago under one crown: different initiatives were undertaken in Scotland, Ireland and Wales, which bore contrasting fruit. Somerset's regime invaded and devastated Scotland in order to secure the marriage of the boy Edward and the even younger Mary Queen of Scots, but it also sought to charm the people of Scotland into a union, using a newly coined rhetoric of British identity. The effort was inept and in the short term a spectacular failure, but it had a lasting effect. By 1603, a union of crowns seemed a natural outgrowth of the religious links set up in the Edwardian era, instead of the bizarre mismatch of ancient enemies which it would have been a century before. In Ireland, it was Edward's government which first planned the fatal policy of planting settlers from overseas in colonies, and Britain still struggles with the consequences of that scheme.[11] In Wales, the first faltering efforts were made to establish a Welsh evangelical culture which began achieving notable results in the reign of Elizabeth, and which later became central to Welsh identity.

The English returned to the Edwardian evangelical adventure when, in 1558, Queen Mary's stomach cancer brought a very different religious experiment to a premature end. Now, under Queen Elizabeth, the kingdom began an uninterrupted journey into a Protestant national experience. Yet Edwardian government decisions moulded the church settlement restored in 1559, equally in liturgy, theological confession and church polity. Elizabeth I put Edwardian structures to rather different uses to those originally intended, but even so, the Church of England is the Church of Edward VI more than it likes to admit. Thomas Cranmer, that editorial genius, bequeathed Elizabeth the *Book of Common Prayer*, which (perhaps against her personal inclinations) she restored in its more radical version of 1552, virtually unaltered. This was the prose sequence (only slightly modified by revision in 1662) most regularly given public performances in England and Wales over the next three centuries. It was used more relentlessly even than particular passages of the Bible, and at least up to the Stuart Civil Wars of the 1640s, it was complemented by regular use of the official homilies pioneered in Edwardian England.

Unlike all other key books of the English Reformation down to Bunyan's *Pilgrim's Progress*, one heard and spoke the Prayer Book and the homilies, rather than read them. They were experienced from an early age primarily through the ear, not through the eye, and so only the Bible heard in the household from infancy exceeded their influence in shaping the English language. For three centuries the Prayer Book was supplemented by another dramatic public performance, the singing of metrical psalms – the songs of King David turned into Tudor rhyming verse – which were first championed by the Edwardian Church, which were said to be particular favourites of the young King Edward and which were perhaps the single most effective weapon which the English Reformers possessed.[12] In this universally performed theatre, the

4. *The title-page of Thomas Sternhold's metrical psalter of 1549; this was the ancestor of the long series of 'Sternhold and Hopkins' psalters which remained bestsellers into the seventeenth century. The book contains a dedication to Sternhold's master King Edward, which refers to the king's enjoyment of Sternhold singing the psalms*

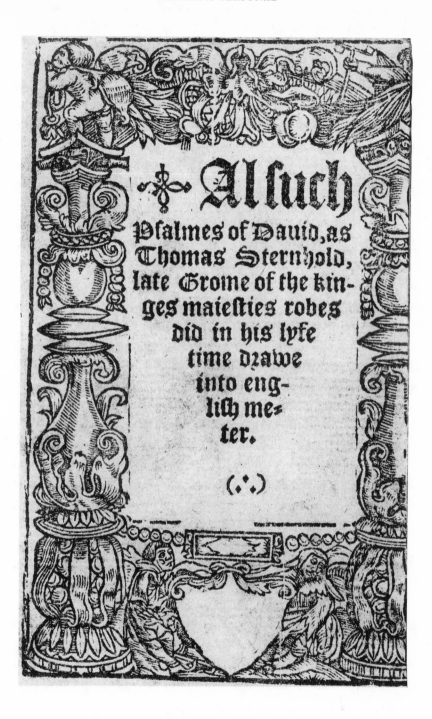

Al ſuch Pſalmes of Dauid, as Thomas Sternholo, late Grome of the kinges maieſties robes did in his lyfe time drawe into engliſh meter.

(.∴.)

Edwardian Reformation lived on, in uneasy relationship to the more urbane impulse of a later Anglican tradition. If we neglect it or misunderstand it, we will miss a vital stage in the fashioning of a nation and a culture.

The dramas of the Edwardian Reformations were biblical in more senses than one. The rebuilt Church was evangelical in essence. The assignment for evangelicals was a treasure hunt for the *evangelion*, the good news to be found in the New Testament, and the excavators were impatient of the centuries of church experience which overlay it. Yet spokesmen for the Edwardian revolution were also drawn to the Old Testament, where they could view other kingdoms battling against great odds to hear the message of God. Henry VIII had already enjoyed posing as one or other of the two great success stories in Israelite politics, David and Solomon. However, in the turbulence of his son's revolution, other kings of Israel and Judah entered the stage, because they were more urgently scripted to act as warning or encouragement.[13] Some, like King Manasseh or King Ahab, had strayed from God's truth. Ahab had done so with the encouragement of his lascivious wife Jezebel, who had her own possibilities as a negative exemplar, and who excited sixteenth-century reformers a good deal more than her husband. Other kings, chiefly Hezekiah and Josiah, had done the right thing. And right and wrong, in Israel and Judah just as in Edwardian England, were measured in terms of destruction: destroying that which stood as an obstacle between humanity and the truth of God. For the Church of Edward VI, this meant holy statues and pictures, and indeed a high proportion of the other fittings and decoration of sacred buildings.[14]

Much has been written about this destructive side of Edwardian Reformations, usually in blanket condemnation. In a series of recent studies, Margaret Aston has brilliantly helped us to understand it, even if we find it unappealing, and she has made a particular point of exploring that common identification of Edward with Josiah: both boy-kings who purged their land of idols.[15] The work of Josiah, purifying, tearing down, remoulding, is the theme of Chapter 2 below. But Old Testament events and Edwardian England melted into each other in different ways for different purposes. It is sometimes forgotten that Edward was never exclusively King Josiah. He was also King Solomon, an image which had deeper resonances than the clichéd connotation of Solomon's wisdom.[16] Edward was more fully Solomon than his father Henry had been, because he was allowed to build the Temple of Jerusalem, the privilege denied to Solomon's father King David. The nobleman-scholar Henry Lord Stafford made a slightly clumsy attempt in 1548 to pay courtly tribute to the late Henry VIII, claiming in a dedicatory preface to Protector Somerset that the temple 'was begun by David, and finished by Solomon'.[17] However, this was to improve on what the Bible actually said, and such equivocation would soon be made terminally unconvincing by the rapid process of Edwardian change, which by 1553 had outstripped anything which Henry VIII might have contemplated. The temple-builder of godly religion was Edward alone. Chapter 3 below explores this constructive side of Edward's Reformations: what they could offer the English people, while they destroyed so much of England's past.

Implicit in setting up Edward as Solomon the temple-builder against Henry VIII's David were some significant loose ends. One might speculate whether Henry VIII would have wished to build an evangelical temple in the design chosen by Edward's regimes, a question which is still controversial, and which was the subject of much debate at the time between reformers and traditionalists. But a further relevant implication of the David–Solomon relationship would quickly have occurred to those immersed in a biblical culture. Early Stuart commentators could put into words what it would have been tactless to say in the mid sixteenth century. For instance, in 1627, the writer-clergyman Christopher Lever delved into Reformation history in order to call Charles I to his Protestant duty, and his solemn historical platitudes are all the more revealing for being so commonplace. He commented on the building of English Protestantism's temple that 'God would not King Henry to effect it, because he had been in blood, and war, as was David Solomon's father, but he reserves it for King Edward.' The courtly Calvinist clergyman and propagandist Dr George Hakewill had spoken similarly of David and Solomon in 1616, though he was concerned to point out that

15

the English version of Jerusalem's Temple was built over two reigns of Henry's children: both in 'the peaceable time of his son Edward, and Elizabeth his daughter, whose hands were undefiled with any blood, and life unspotted with any violence or cruelty'.[18]

Edward, indeed, could have claimed this lack of defilement rather more plausibly than his middle sister, who was responsible for the deaths of a large phalanx of Roman Catholics, let alone a number of enthusiasts for Reformation who had also fallen foul of the official Elizabethan church. By contrast, magnanimity and the seeking of peace were important in the self-image of Edward's regimes. People were indeed put to death, ranging from the Duke of Somerset himself to two unitarian radicals, but it was remarkable that no Catholic opponents of the regime suffered execution; Henry's murderous religious ecumenism was out of fashion between 1547 and 1553. And if Somerset specialized in ostentatious personal clemency, his successor in power, the Duke of Northumberland, deserves to be remembered as one of the great peace-makers of the century, bringing to an end in 1550 wars against Scotland and France on terms which consciously risked major public disapproval.

Solomon had seven years for his temple-building, Edward less than six. As he grew fatally ill, his Reformation was in mortal danger from his traditionalist half-sister, and if there was any hope for the future, yet

5. *The title-page of Christopher Lever's* The history of the Defendors of the Catholique Faith. Wheareunto are added Observations Divine, Politique, Morrall . . . *(1627). In this work, heavily dependent on Foxe's Book of Martyrs, Edward takes his iconographical place amid a succession of great names designed to call Charles I to a sense of Reformation duty. Henry VIII tramples on the Pope and a friar, with confounded papists on the right (mostly clean-shaven), bearded Protestants on the left, and Cromwell and Cranmer (both bearded) receiving the Bible – below, Edward VI and Mary (excused in her Latin motto from being cruel by nature) bear banners respectively showing a church being purged with crosses being shipped overseas, and Protestants being burned. Underneath, Elizabeth has a cartouche of the Armada, to the left, James I carries a picture of Guy Fawkes creeping into the Parliament House, and in centre Charles I is credited with an army and navy to defend the Protestant faith.*

another Old Testament story must merge with sixteenth-century events. Solomon must give way to Hezekiah, whose Jerusalem came under siege from Assyrian armies, and who was only saved at the last minute by divine intervention. This was the analogy desperately brought to God's attention in the official prayer for Edward's recovery, said in the Chapel Royal during the last month of his life, and published for general use:

as thou didst most favourably deliver King Ezechias from extreme sickness, and prolongedst his life for the safeguard of thy people the Israelites, and defend-edst them and the city from the tyranny of the Assyrians, so we most entirely appeal to thy great mercies graciously to restore the health and strength again of thy servant Edward our sovereign Lord.

This identification of Edward as a second Hezekiah was echoed in praise of the boy by Archbishop Cranmer's evangelical emigré chaplain Pierre Alexandre, but now with a dying fall, as he brought to a close his divinity lectures in Canterbury Cathedral in the weeks after Edward's death.[19] For no miracle came that summer. Hezekiah faded away, a Catholic Jezebel occupied the throne, and Edward's career as Josiah was posthumously confirmed. John Foxe made much of that image in his pioneering history of the reign, and the identification was given official status when in 1570 it was deployed to make a point in a new Homily against Rebellion.[20]

Carrying this weight of symbolism, heavier than the adult crowns which he had briefly endured at his coronation, was a boy nine years old at his father's death, and fifteen at his own death. Can he really bear the burden of the central role in our play? At the beginning of his reign, such a child could only expect to be a symbol of policies determined by the adults around him, yet, as we shall see, his views and his personality were already becoming significant factors in official religious changes as he entered his teens, and that significance accelerated as year succeeded year. His youth was, of course, both his asset and his disadvantage. He was a symbol of change and hope, in the way that the young are always the focus of that irrational adult belief that the next generation will

6. *The future King Edward, painted* c. *1546, possibly by William Scrots.*

avoid the mistakes of all generations past. But his youth also raised a question already relentlessly posed in 1547 by the champion of traditional faith, Bishop Stephen Gardiner of Winchester: should not religion be left as it was until the boy reached years of discretion? 'I think silence best, with reverence to the authority of our late sovereign, whose soul God pardon, and therein to remain, till our sovereign Lord that now is, come to his perfect age, whom God grant then to find such people as his father left, not altered with any innovation.'[21]

Gardiner's stance was alarmingly plausible. Evangelicals could comfort themselves with their usual resort to the Old Testament; the fiery clergyman John Hooper menacingly listed the kings whose youth had not spared them from God's wrath when they had pursued the wrong religious path – twelve-year-old Manasseh, eight-year-old Jehoiakim.[22] The refugee Italian apologist for the regime, Peter Martyr Vermigli, equally creatively drew attention to the wrath of God which would descend on those who oppressed young orphans, that is Edward VI, but no one else seems to have taken up this ingenious if strained line of argument.[23] Such strategies, or the positive example of the image-smashing Josiah, would not cut much ice with the likes of Bishop Gardiner. Conservatives were more likely to turn, discreetly if riskily, elsewhere in the Bible to highlight the text 'woe to you O land, when your king is a child'. Quoting this text raised obvious dangers of being accused of sedition, but its very existence caused evangelicals some embarrassment of exposition. The best way out for them, and an escape route which several chose, was to redefine the text as referring to childish kings, rather than kings who were children. This carried the additional advantage of being a perfect springboard for praise of the exceptionally adult qualities of the young King Edward.[24]

Fortunately for the regime, Edward's qualities really were exceptional, and they shine through the flattery which inevitably came his way. We have an extraordinarily rich archive of the boy's own writings, which cry out for detailed study simply as a rare corpus of material on how a de luxe education was conducted in Renaissance Europe: for instance, there survive of his essays (what were then called *orationes*) fifty-five in Latin and fifty in Greek.[25] He was a talented member of a talented family; given every opportunity that England's best teachers could put his way, he was energetic in study. Yet contrary to the image of a sickly boy, he was also a keen sportsman who enjoyed deer-hunting, and he filled his personal journal or chronicle with enthusiastic detailed descriptions of military display.

A school report would have complimented Edward on all-round promise. It would probably have singled out his competence in handling rhetorical argument. For instance, at the age of eleven, he spent two successive weekly essays considering two rival classical proverbs, the first week glorifying a military death and the second condemning the horrors of war. One admires his tutors' sense of topicality in late July 1549, at a time when the government was frantically calling together troops to put down popular commotions throughout southern England, and only a week before the long-expected confirmation that France was declaring war. This was a perfect demonstration of the humanist ideal of applying the craft of rhetoric to statecraft; one would expect no less from the principal royal tutor Sir John Cheke, who in a letter only two months before to Protector Somerset had stressed the need to balance theoretical instruction of the king with discussion of practical politics. Edward's twinned essays, fair copied in his best italic hand (his penmanship was excellent) went beyond a wooden recital of classical examples, for they brought in present-day concerns. His advocacy of war pointed out the particular glory of fighting to defend religion, 'as often happens in contemporary wars'. His attack on war, on the other hand, was interestingly a more elaborate effort, and it stressed the appalling destruction wrought in the wars of the 1540s by the French in the Isle of Wight, by the English in France and, especially regrettable, the wrecking of Scotland by English armies – this at a time when his own forces were still causing havoc north of the Border.[26]

The balance of entries in Edward's personal Chronicle makes it fatally easy to argue for his possessing a 'cool and secular spirit', as did the Chronicle's modern editor, W.K. Jordan. Jordan saw the king as not much concerned about religious matters 'save as they touched his

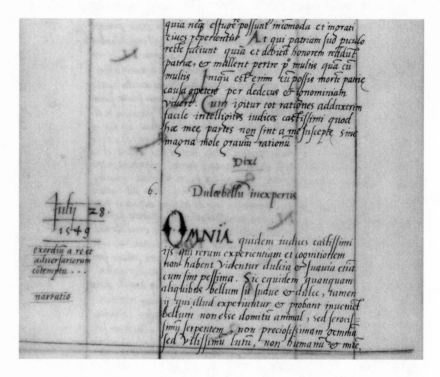

7. *A page from an 'oration' (essay) written by Edward VI on 28 July 1549 on the horrors of war ('*Dulce bellum inexpertis*').*

supremacy and his ultimate sovereignty'. To imply that the royal supremacy might be a secular notion is in any case a strange judgement, for in the England of the 1550s the supremacy was a profoundly religious concern. Nevertheless, Jordan might at first sight seem to have a point in observing that there is little material in Edward's Chronicle on religion. It is true, for instance, that the king never describes a sermon in detail in the Chronicle. So when John Foxe and others enthusiastically stressed the king's evangelical piety, were they merely indulging in wishful thinking? Were his real loves the tournament field and the hunt?[27] Before we rush to assume that we know better than those who knew Edward personally, we must realize how easy it is to be misled by an archival accident. The essential parallel to the Chronicle has been lost:

Edward's notebook of the sermons he heard, carefully noting the preacher's name, time and place. Some time before 1616, Bishop James Mountague saw this book, which was then in the King's Library under the care of the librarian Patrick Young, but since then it has disappeared.[28] This book would have complemented what the young king wrote in the Chronicle, so the loss accounts for the Chronicle's apparent lack of interest in evangelical preaching: Edward was too tidy-minded a boy to duplicate effort.

In April 1550 the ambassador of the Holy Roman Empire, a good Catholic who had no reason to add to myth-making about an evangelical paragon, noted the king's enthusiasm for taking notes on sermons, and he added that Edward was particularly insistent on inviting the most extreme preachers to court.[29] These court sermons had their effect on official action. We have the Protestant publisher and chronicler Richard Grafton's story of one occasion in 1552, at which the king was moved by a sermon from Bishop Ridley to add a dramatic bonus to a major initiative of social policy. For more than a decade, the city authorities in London (Grafton prominent among them) had been lobbying the Crown in an effort to systematize London poor relief in a series of new hospitals and institutions; now the king gave away the royal palace of Bridewell to be converted into a central workhouse and detention centre for those labelled social undesirables.[30] At the end of the reign, as we will see, the effect of such sermons was much less positive, although even more dramatic, as preachers angrily confronted the secular leaders of the regime about their shortcomings (below, pp. 154–5).

Because of the importance of court sermons, we should qualify an observation by the historian of Tudor ceremonial, Sydney Anglo, that court revels under Edward 'veered away from blatant politico-religious propagandizing'. If they did, this was because a parallel development in court life meant that there was less need for them to play such a role. Henry VIII, probably in the last decade of his reign, had built a new open-air pulpit in the Privy Garden of his palace at Whitehall, where the preacher 'might be heard of more than four times so many people as could have stood in the King's Chapel'.[31] Henry had intended this

8. *Edward VI granting the charter to the governors of Bridewell, 1553: a grateful seventeenth-century re-creation of the scene.*

primarily for the course of sermons in Lent which had been customary at court for more than a century, but from April 1550, Henry's son ordered that regular preaching at court should be very greatly extended: from now on, there would be weekly sermons. Many of them must have been in the Privy Garden pulpit. It had been built in an enclosure which continued also to host animal-baiting and wrestling matches.[32] The combination might seem ludicrous and distasteful to our refined age, but it underlined the fact that preaching was drama and entertainment.

Sermons complemented other court theatrical performances with the peculiar drama of the preacher's one-man show, providing more than enough political or religious propaganda for the regime's concerns.[33]

What emerges from the king's writings apart from the Chronicle is the consistent fervour of his evangelical commitment. In 1545 Bishop Gardiner took a premature pleasure in recalling that in 1538 the one-year-old prince had been terrified by the beards of the German Protestant ambassadors, but this is Edward's only recorded rejection of the Reformation, and a pardonable one.[34] Some of the most striking evidence comes from his French schoolwork, which may indicate that among his tutors he was given particular encouragement in evangelical enthusiasm by his French master, Jean Belmain; however, Belmain was

9. *Bishop Latimer preaching in the Privy Garden pulpit, as portrayed in* Foxe's Acts and Monuments. *The king and various courtiers in the galleries had the advantage of shelter, a useful privilege since many sermons were preached in winter or early spring.*

nephew by marriage to the principal tutor Sir John Cheke, so we need not consider that this represented any special division of policy among Edward's schoolmasters.[35] During 1548, for instance, Edward spent some time collecting and translating into French two sets of scriptural passages as a present for Protector Somerset. One was on the subject of justification by faith, and it began with a lip-smacking assault on the enemies of God, with their diabolic or papistical superstitions. The other, predictably, formed a collection on idolatry.[36] Edward was perhaps being encouraged to imitate the filing system of his godfather Thomas Cranmer, Archbishop of Canterbury, whose topically arranged collections of quotations from scripture and the fathers were the foundation of his own two-decade war against Antichrist.[37]

By themselves, these bible-text collections need not have been anything more than dutiful school exercises, although one can see that the labour might appeal to the sort of schoolboy who in the twentieth century would be an avid stamp collector. One also has to admit that Edward quickly gave up a further attempt to imitate Archbishop Cranmer in a topically arranged collection of Latin biblical extracts; he got no further than entering his headings and trawling through the first seven chapters of Matthew, the first Gospel.[38] However, this may be because he had something altogether more creative in mind. Most remarkable of all Edward's boyhood religious compositions is his extended treatise in French on the papal supremacy, started on 13 December 1548 and finished on the last day of August 1549, once more with a dedication to Somerset. The work is arranged in four parts and rounded off with a conclusion. Edward marshalled a variety of arguments for and against (mostly against) papal supremacy, and then turned to more detailed consideration of whether the apostle Peter had ever actually visited Rome, before discussing the gradual build-up of papal power and the nature of Antichrist, that impersonator of Christ who (in Edward's opinion) could be identified as well with the Pope as with Mahomet. So, as he triumphantly summarized his argument in a neatly argued conclusion, the Pope is 'the true son of the devil, a bad man, an Antichrist and abominable tyrant'.[39]

The text of Edward's treatise was sufficiently coherent and well-argued to be published in English translation 'by a Person of very great quality' in 1682, in the wake of the Exclusion Crisis, which involved the attempt to prevent the popish James Duke of York from succeeding to the throne. The treatise could then serve as a piece of propaganda which would confound both Roman Catholics and Anglican High Churchmen, and which might suggest to Charles II that English monarchs should be godly rather than merry.[40] The originality of Edward's composition is not only suggested by the fact that the draft autograph manuscript is corrected throughout in another hand, which may be Belmain's, but also another contemporary hand has added a note confirming that the treatise was the eleven-year-old king's own work, even if it was based on his conversations with different people and on the books at his disposal.[41] One of those helpful books is clearly traceable in Edward's text: John Ponet's English translation of *A dialoge of the uniuste usurped primacie of the Bishop of Rome* by the maverick Italian refugee Bernardino Ochino.

Ochino dedicated his translated book to the king in early 1549, and the second of its two editions survives from Edward's library, signed presumably as a presentation copy by Walter Lynne, its printer, himself an enthusiastic evangelical.[42] It is quite possible that Ochino's patron, Archbishop Cranmer, encouraged him to write the work, knowing of the young king's project. It is framed in a series of conversational playlets explaining how the centuries-old papal plot for world domination was now being foiled by a syndicate of God, Henry VIII and Edward himself. So the young king could savour the prospect of reading about himself and people he knew personally in the framework of a cosmic drama; Ochino had created the ancestor of the interactive computer game. The combination of Ochino's wit and Ponet's racy English prose flags only in a turgid speech put in the mouth of Archbishop Cranmer explaining why the Pope is Antichrist. This is by far the longest piece of uninterrupted text in Ochino's work, utterly different in texture from the rest, and it is stuffed full of historical and biblical references, very much in the manner of Cranmer's private theological source collections. I strongly suspect that it was written by Cranmer himself, and

that it represents an offer of help which Ochino was unable to refuse.[43]

Edward was already familiar with his godfather's didactic ways, and at one point in his own treatise, probably via Ochino's book, he seems to have benefited from Cranmer's concern to refute the pseudo-Clementine epistles – ancient ecclesiastical forgeries – because of the misleading claims which they made on behalf of the apostle Peter.[44] Yet the boy did not mechanically copy out passages in sequence; he redeployed significant ideas and historical details as the dynamic of his own argument required them. The most distinctive link between his work and the Ochino *Dialoge* is that he follows Ochino's somewhat eccentric choice of the obscure Pope Boniface III to be the chief villain of the papal plot.[45] Other motifs also appealed to him: for instance, Ochino's question as to who held the keys to heaven when the Pope died. Like Ochino, he made a contrast between God, forbidding adultery, and the Pope, who supposedly ordered his clergy to take concubines, forbidding them marriage.[46] But combined with this were personal touches: particularly Edward's remarkable references to religious persecution and Henry VIII's Act of Six Articles which, when passed by Parliament in 1539, had represented a dire moment of defeat for evangelicals and which had led to many burnings at the stake. On these subjects he got quite carried away, to the extent that his tutor felt compelled to tone down the king's prose draft.

Edward, King of England, was indignant on behalf of what he described as the poor lambs of God. 'If they do not do the Pope's bidding, that is to offer to idols and devils, he burns us, and makes us bear a faggot.' His tutor decided that it would be more suitable as well as more

10. *'The downfall of the Pope', from Ochino's* Dialogue: *monks are fleeing and a cardinal wails in grief; the papal ass is fallen. The vengeful God appears without any superstitious representation of his likeness, but simply as a word, his name in Hebrew (the 'tetragrammaton'). This picture was reused by the printer Walter Lynne from one of his books published in 1548; it occurs only in Ochino's second edition of late 1549, and was introduced to cover up the alterations in the text made by removing the first edition's references to Protector Somerset, after the coup against him led by John Dudley.*

grammatical at this point for a reigning monarch to write less personally: so that phrase was altered to read 'if they do not do the Pope's bidding ... he burns them, or forces them to make honourable amends'.
Edward then pursued the theme nearer home. 'In my father's days,' he
said – his tutor, worried at the informality, made him correct this phrase
to 'in the time of the late king my father' – 'when [the Pope's] name was
struck out of books, he stopped the mouths of Christians with his six
articles, like six fists'. The young king should be given credit for trying
out a pun in a foreign language, for he seems to be making the six points
of the Six Articles into six papal fists or '*poings*'. One also notes that the
attentive reader might not be quite clear as to what Henry VIII was up
to while the Pope slipped the Six Articles past him; evidently Edward
was disposed to let his father off the hook for this crime against the poor
lambs of God. But, in any case, it is remarkable to hear the young king
identifying himself personally with those who suffered death for refusing idol worship. Perhaps prompted by Belmain, he went on to note the
refinement of cruelty practised by the authorities in France against
evangelicals: they cut out the tongues of heretics just before burning
them, to stop them testifying to their faith.[47] Altogether, Edward's passionate identification with the Pope's victims is hardly the voice of a
cool secularist concerned only with the royal supremacy – and, in any
case, the supremacy was a matter which was a profoundly religious concern in the England of Edward VI.

This was not merely a passing burst of early adolescent emotion. In
the next few years we can observe Edward expressing his religious feelings in a matter which clearly fascinated him: the remodelling of the
statutes of the Order of the Garter.[48] E.M. Thompson, the Victorian editor of some of the documents involved, had mixed feelings about them:
'Is it not with a feeling almost akin to pity that we regard the young
Edward's painful tinkering of these ordinances, and conclude how much
better it would have been for himself, and perhaps we may add, for his
country, if he had given the hours thus spent to something better suited
to his youthful years?'[49] It is ironical that Thompson posed his question
in that late Victorian era which Eric Hobsbawm has characterized as at

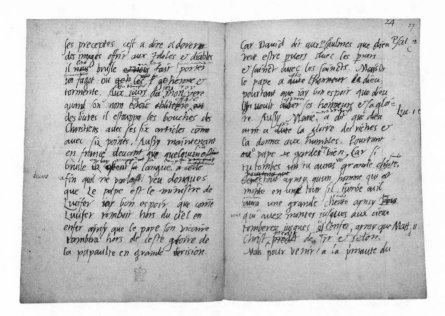

II. *A page of Edward VI's draft version of his treatise against the papal supremacy (1549), showing his tutor's amendments to his text discussing the burning of heretics and the Act of Six Articles.*

the heart of the 'invention of tradition'; as an antiquary, he was showing notable insensitivity to the significance of Garter statute revision. The Knights of the Garter were of prime concern to any English monarch, but in a kingdom where the royal supremacy was the central principle of the reformed Church, one could regard a reformed chivalric Order as the highest expression of what this reformation was about. The Order had always been a sacred organization; a variety of super-guild. In it, the monarch met his companions in arms in ceremonies which were both formal and an intimate religious expression of their comradeship; moreover the Order had a foreign membership extending to fellow-monarchs or figures of international chivalry. In 1548 the government had destroyed thousands of guilds throughout the land, and thereafter, without radical change, the Order looked especially anomalous in the

Edwardian Church. Worse still, it was intimately linked to the cult of St George, a saint of decidedly legendary character whom most reformers treated with frank contempt, and whom Edward himself ridiculed at the Garter ceremony of 1550.[50] It was vital to make the Order send out the right message about the character of England's Reformation at home and abroad. After some characteristic hesitation in the first three years of the reign, plans were made for this, although they only reached completion on 17 March 1553, to be swept away by Queen Mary six months later. Edward played a major part in the drafting, and as the king, he was the ideal person to do so.

Edward's successive autograph redrafts, like his treatise on papal supremacy, are shot through with teenage evangelical fervour tempered by adult second thoughts, no doubt largely those of his collaborator, the government servant and future Elizabethan minister, William Cecil.[51] Each in the king's sequence of three surviving drafts, dateable between late 1550 and mid 1551, is more moderate than the previous one, and the final statutes more moderate again. Nevertheless, after all this toning down, the Order still severed all connection with St George. To begin with, Edward had disapproved even of the connection with the Garter, and wished to rename the Order rather clumsily as for 'defence of the truth wholly contained in scripture'. In a vision of Tudor sacral monarchy and with an egotism worthy of his father, his first thought for a badge for members to wear at their necks was a picture of himself as supreme head of the Church: 'a king graven, holding in one hand a sword and in the other a book, and upon the sword shall be written *Justitia* [Righteousness], and upon the booke VERBUM DEI [the Word of God]'.[52] Second thoughts about a device for the order were for a shield incorporating a red cross on a white ground, and Edward produced a flurry of excuses for retaining without superstition this former

12. *The medieval stalls of the Knights of the Garter in the choir of St George's Chapel, Windsor, with the knights' banners hanging above. At the north-east corner of the choir is the tomb of the founder, King Edward IV, which was drastically simplified during the reign of Edward VI.*

symbol of St George. He was thus revealed as deeply unhappy with even this simple survival of the old world's imagery. The end result was the adoption of a safely anonymous armed knight on horseback.[53]

Significant features of the king's over-excited first draft which would disappear later, besides a battery of scriptural texts on idolatry to emphasize his detestation of St George, were some interesting characterizations of the corporate communion service. Here was the chief area of contention between the old religious world and the new. Communion would act for the Order as a 'token that in the defence of Christian doctrine, wholly contained in God's word, they are so united that they will defend it even to the death'. In an interesting dialogue with the text of the communion service in his own first Prayer Book of 1549, he described the communion as 'the supper of our Lord'. Clearly this was his preferred term, for he then struck out his addition of the second alternative which the 1549 Prayer Book provided and which was normally used in official public statements: 'otherwise called the communion'.[54] There was, of course, no question of him using the 1549 Book's already grudging third alternative 'commonly called the mass'; elsewhere in his draft, Edward classed the mass, along with prayers for the dead, as superstition. What would the king say about the vexed question of God's real, corporal or spiritual presence in or absence from the elements of bread and wine? In another place of his text, the Lord's supper was for him 'the remembrance of Christ's death', and he thought better of adding to this the phrase 'and his body and his blood spiritually by some mystery . . .'; perhaps he feared the danger of getting over-elaborate and letting in by the back door an idea of eucharistic real presence. Earlier, his emphasis had been on communion as 'the faithful remembrance of Christ's death, which was once offered up for all, and dwelleth not in man's temples'. It might be reading too much into these brief phrases and erasures to posit that an emphasis on remembrance meant more to Edward than the nuanced language in Cranmer's eucharistic writings about the spiritual presence of Christ in the eucharist. Nevertheless, his radically minded admirer (soon to be one of his bishops), John Hooper, described the boy as disapproving of a

Lutheran discussion of the eucharist presented to him in spring 1550; Edward knew that he was in the Reformed camp in eucharistic matters, and he had no truck with Martin Luther's obstinate defence of the idea that the body and blood of Christ were present in consecrated bread and wine. And we can certainly say that this was a king who in late 1550 had bade goodnight to the 1549 Prayer Book; he was well prepared for the 1552 revision.[55]

So here is Edward as King Josiah the purifier and King Solomon the builder; but were these images of any further contemporary significance? How far did the teenager's influence extend beyond the confines of St George's Chapel, Windsor? In the years when Edward Seymour was Lord Protector he was too young to do more than absorb the surrounding atmosphere of revolution from above. However, even then the brothers Edward and Thomas Seymour struggled over his favour, and significantly he revealed no especial affection for the Lord Protector. In autumn 1549, when the Protector was overthrown in a bloodless coup by his colleagues in the Privy Council, the success of this putsch was partly dependent on persuading the king that all was still as it should be, despite Somerset's departure. Moreover, Edward's religious enthusiasm may already have been significant in deciding the outcome of those events, which (at first sight surprisingly) confirmed evangelicals in their control of power. One historian of the English court, John Murphy, has suggested that a clinching factor in evangelical political success during that autumn turbulence was the boy's unwillingness to be served by traditionalist gentlemen in the Privy Chamber, so it was impossible for religious conservatives to take advantage of Somerset's fall.[56]

But it is in Edward's thirteenth year, in 1550, that the first sure signs of independent initiative begin, and one should note that they are primarily in the religious sphere. In a remarkable scene at the official confirmation of the aggressively advanced reformer John Hooper as Bishop of Gloucester, the king personally noted that the oath of supremacy which Hooper was about to swear was still in the form devised for his father, including mention of the saints, placed in association with God in offensively traditional fashion. This was just a few months before

35

Edward would eject St George from the Order of the Garter and, in similar spirit, he now struck out with his pen from the oath the offending words about the saints, much to Hooper's delight. The adults let him get away with it; there was to be no waiting for Parliament to confirm this unilateral ejection of the holy company of heaven. By this single act on impulse, he had altered the theology of the English Church and had shown more emphatically than Henry VIII or Elizabeth ever did what Tudor royal supremacy was about.[57]

Edward's most high-profile intervention in 1550s politics was in the struggle to force his half-sister, the Lady Mary, into conformity with the reformed church. This was potentially the most important issue to face his government, involving as it did a coincidence of dynastic, diplomatic and religious policy. Mary's closeness to her cousin the Holy Roman Emperor, the pious Catholic Charles V, meant that the issue could never simply be a domestic one; the English government's refusal to let Mary's religion alone became inextricably and contrarily entangled with their efforts to persuade the Emperor to give English diplomats free exercise of evangelical religion on embassies to the imperial court. In all this, the king was the most aggressive advocate of trying to pressure Mary into obedience. All the predictable tensions between a teenager and his much older sister were added to their intense religious differences. Normal rules of behaviour were complicated by the anomalous relationships of power between them: here were two people by definition marginal to Tudor hierarchies of command, a single woman and a male who was not an adult, but they found themselves with no appropriate adult in a sufficiently authoritative position to spell out the rules, and with all the formal authority in the hands of the much younger boy. Mary, who had taken refuge in the illusion that Edward would see sense as he grew more mature, seems to have been particularly upset at Edward's first undeniably personal intervention, a partly autograph letter to her about her religious nonconformity, on 24 January 1551. Small wonder that the end result of this family row was messy and indecisive.

During this involved story, one crisis point in March 1551 is particu-

13. *Mary Tudor as Queen, 1554,*
*by Hans Eworth.*

larly striking because it involved Edward in a double confrontation, first public intransigence towards his sister, face-to-face with her, backed up by his councillors, and then in private, strongly reacting against the caution of those same councillors. Against Mary, the thirteen-year-old Edward emphasized that only within the last year had he become an active participant in negotiations, the implication being that all previous bets were now off. Mary succeeded in leaving the meeting on a high note: she declared her willingness for death, to which her brother could only decently respond with a hasty expression of shock, and she signed off with the unanswerable if not wholly compatible declaration that she would always remain his humble, obedient and unworthy sister.[58] Two days later, the stand-off became even more serious, because of a diplomatic row which had already broken out in the imperial capital at Brussels. The Emperor was furious with Sir Richard Morison, the English ambassador, an outspoken evangelical, with whom he had a bitter spat about religion. Now the imperial ambassador in London came to the English Privy Council to threaten war if Mary was not given free exercise of the mass; this threw the Council into a panic. An eye-witness account, probably given later to Morison by that increasingly important royal servant William Cecil, makes clear that it was Edward who most strongly resisted compromise. By itself, this might be of no more significance than the natural tendency of teenagers to see matters in starkly simple terms and to be passionately partisan. However, the story also illuminates the councillors' evolving relationship with their king.[59] Some of them were repeatedly disconcerted by his precocious grasp of events: 'because his talk was always above some of their capacities, they therefore thought it rather stirred up in him by gentlemen of his privy chamber than grown in himself'. The narrator says that they tried to prevent him being briefed in advance by bringing him to the Council Chamber without telling him what business was to be discussed.[60]

The strategy for winning the king round was first to get an opinion on the matter from Archbishop Cranmer and Bishop Nicholas Ridley, who had been given the most pessimistic briefing possible about the Emperor's hostility. Suitably alarmed, the bishops still did their best to preserve a hard-line affirmation that 'to give license to sin was sin', while they drew on a Council statement from the previous Christmas to recommend continuing a strictly temporary concession to Mary. Next the whole Council must impress Edward with the gravity of the situation; they all went down on their knees, and the Marquis of Winchester, a veteran of hard-headed political pragmatism, outlined how dire things were.[61] But even temporary concessions were now too much for the king. Significantly, he was prepared to follow Council advice and replace Morison as ambassador to the Emperor, but he would not give way on a matter which more personally touched his honour as head of his family. He was left alone to argue with the bishops. Characteristically in the Edwardian Reformation, it was a competitive swapping of situations in the Old Testament, and the king's knockout blow was a quotation from the psalm which they had heard at evensong a few days before on the subject of God's wrath at Israel's unfaithfulness.[62] The bishops retired discouraged. Now it was once more up to the rest of the Council to urge realpolitik on the king, who threatened to burst into tears at the thought of climbing down. Richard Morison, who transmitted the story of the incident, represents it as a defeat for Edward, a young giant among pigmies, since the whole point of Morison's discourse was to stress how unworthy England had been of its king. In fact, that was not the result.[63] Over the next few months Mary got no concessions, quite the reverse: pressure on her household now increased, and indeed broke the morale of the distinguished poet Alexander Barclay, one of her senior chaplains, who left her service and accepted a comfortable benefice in London under the benevolent eye of Archbishop Cranmer. Throughout the next few months the Council continued obstinately to confront the Emperor on the twinned issues of Mary and their ambassadors' religious privileges, and the king's continuing hard line was clearly a material factor in stiffening official resolve. It may be significant that he was given real access to decision-making just at the moment of the Council's next major confrontation with the Emperor over Mary in August 1551.[64]

Edward grew up very fast. Less than two months after that incident in March, he took part in his first tournament, the sign of imminent adulthood.[65] Moreover, during 1552, he stepped further up to the threshold of power with detailed briefings on the acute financial crisis which the government faced, and its drastic measures for rescue. From 30 May 1552 there survives the evidence that he had stepped right over the threshold, directly participating in everyday financial affairs: on that day we have the first of a number of extant signet warrants for payments bearing his sign manual rather than the collective signatures of the Council, and the warrants multiply from 19 February 1553.

The final example is from 14 May.[66] After this, his health was collapsing and he needed all his strength for the one last audacious move of his life: the attempt to exclude his sisters from the succession and leave it according to his own 'device' to a reliable evangelical dynasty. There can be little doubt of the king's central determination in all this. Perhaps

14. *Sign manual (signature) of Edward VI on the last of a series of routine though*
*very substantial warrants for payment: this is an order to deliver £1647.19s 2d*
*to Northumberland's son Sir Andrew Dudley, to be kept in the privy coffers,*
*14 May 1553. No later warrants survive to indicate Edward's involvement*
*in ordinary administration.*

Northumberland did provide the initial suggestion, but it seems out of character for a man who was temperamentally a taker of small steps and a reviewer of all options to come up with such a bold idea.[67] In any case, once the first move had been made, surviving paper drafts show the teenage king laboriously but determinedly working out the different phases of the scheme.

Amid the increasingly panic-stricken bustling of his councillors, it was he who personally faced down the doubts of Cranmer and other waverers to create what seemed like a watertight consensus. He knew that he had nothing to lose. He had a chance of making sense of his short

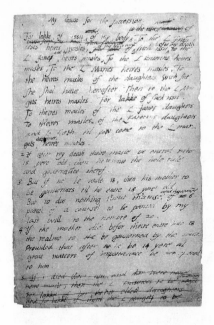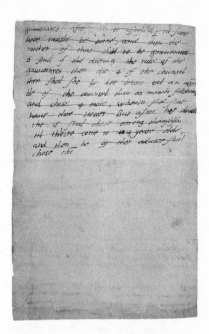

15. 'My devise for the succession': one of Edward VI's drafts of his
proposed arrangements, altered to allow the direct succession of Lady Jane Grey.

life with a last decisive act to outshine his grandfather's seizure of the
throne, in a coup against his own unsatisfactory family and in a final act
of rebellion against his father's plans for the future. Only when we leave
his sickbed for the more complex, untidy world of adults outside the
Privy Chamber, do we find incompetence, hesitation, lost opportunities
and the wrecking of his teenage dreams of founding an evangelical
realm of Christ.

Edward's reign is often seen as twofold: the Duke of Somerset's Protectorate from 1547 to 1549 and thereafter the regime which, in October
1549, deposed Somerset and gave John Dudley ascendancy, first as Earl
of Warwick and later as Duke of Northumberland. Undeniably, there
were clear contrasts between these two phases and the policies which
characterized them. Some of these differences can be attributed to
changing pressures, domestic and foreign, particularly the greater

degree of stability brought by the end of war against France and Scotland in 1550. However, it is impossible to ignore the contrast in personality and agendas between the two dominant politicians, and the nature of that contrast is still controversial. Early Protestant tradition, stemming from the propagandists John Ponet and John Foxe, saw Somerset as 'the good duke', a phrase apparently invented by Ponet in 1556 in his angry political tract *A short treatise of politike power*. Twentieth-century historiography was kept on this path by the powerful advocacy of that accomplished Tudor biographer, A.F. Pollard, echoed later in the work of W.K. Jordan. It followed that if there was a good duke, the man responsible for his removal must be a bad duke; this was also a stance which Ponet had pioneered, styling Dudley equally snappily 'the Alcibiades of England' – spoilt, flashy, cynical and treacherous, an authoritarian and unprincipled politician.[68]

Particularly in the portrait painted by Jordan, Somerset became not so much as a good duke as a goody-goody duke. When Jordan wrote (as he did at length, in many variants) of 'the pervading gentleness and idealism of [Somerset's] nature', one feels his prose begging for the revisionist equivalent of a good kicking.[69] Over the last quarter-century revisionists have closed in on the Pollard/Jordan thesis. In a highly influential and meticulously researched book of 1975, M.L. Bush portrayed a Somerset whose whole range of policy was geared to one aim: winning the war with Scotland – a soldier who otherwise was entirely unoriginal and conventional in his attitudes. In Sir Geoffrey Elton's accurate as well as gleeful summary of Bush's arguments, '[Somerset's] mind was never out of step with those of his colleagues in government, though he had an unfailing knack for alienating people'. This amounted, in the title of Elton's review of Bush, to 'the demolition of the good duke'. Naturally, if Somerset's stock slumped, Dudley's would rise, and we have seen essays in balanced sympathy, particularly in the recent biography of Northumberland by David Loades.[70]

Bush did not underestimate or distort Somerset's evangelical religious commitment. His picture of Somerset's religion is a good deal more accurate than Jordan's, who bizarrely managed to find in the duke

and historians have also caught glimpses of the array of pardons and monetary gifts with which the regime neutralized much of the trouble throughout the country. The nine letters reveal Somerset spearheading an astonishing series of concessions to the July 1549 insurgents. These concessions are easy to dismiss or minimize in other surviving sources; they are to be found most explicitly in the charges laid against the Protector by his fellow-Councillors after his fall in October 1549, and hence they have often been dismissed as hostile propaganda.[74] Now, however, we can see just why the Councillors were so angry.

The various letters used a traditional rhetoric of hierarchy and obedience, and they said much about the monstrousness of rebellion, yet this rhetoric was in fact radically redeployed to provide boundaries for a constructive dialogue between the Crown and its people. Dialogue involved the presentation of lists of grievances from the various camps. We have always known of the Mousehold articles from Kett's Norwich camp; now we have evidence of many more sets of articles. When the Suffolk commotioners sent up their demands, Somerset replied in almost chatty and confidential mode, 'indeed we will not dissemble with you, we see them for the most part founded upon great and just causes'; he even claimed that he had already thought of most of the demands himself.[75] Given this robust affirmation that the insurgents had a point in their protests, another central feature of the dialogue was Somerset's insistence that the commons amply deserved pardon for their risings. As Dr Shagan points out, this was not the disingenuous offer of pardons made by Henry VIII back in 1536–7 in the Pilgrimage of Grace; that had been the prelude to betrayal by government. Now the reality of the pardons was an urgent, even obsessive theme of the letters. The commons of Oxfordshire had already received a pardon under the Great Seal carried by one of the king's guard; only a few days later, Somerset's letter offered them a second pardon just in case the first had not arrived, and told them to arrange a day to receive it at the hands of the local gentlemen commissioners bearing the letter. A collective Privy Council letter offered Suffolk camps the option of an extra pardon just in case they did not disperse by the date stated in their first pardon. This was of particular significance, because it was precisely the technicality which had enabled Henry VIII to justify much of his punitive cruelty in the north in 1537, and the implication is that there was a widespread popular memory of that betrayal. Some of the Hampshire insurgents were nervous because there were rumours that their collective pardon did not cover them individually. Somerset reassured them in the most extravagant language: 'if his Majesty might gain a million of gold to break one jot of it with the poorest creature in all his realm, he would never' – 'million' was not a common word to use at the time. The Protector promised a twenty-crown reward for the arrest of any rumour-bearer.[76]

One might dismiss this as window-dressing by a politician who liked to talk a lot. But there was much more than simply pardons: there was new direct action to meet the issues raised by the demonstrators. One would expect Somerset to show sympathy with grievances about agricultural enclosures of arable for pasture, since for the past year he had been making much of investigations by an enclosure commission in central England. However, he went further than simply feeling the people's pain. It was precisely now, at the beginning of July, as the letters flurried out from the capital to the rebel camps, that a new enclosure commission was created with real powers. The previous commission had merely been inquiring about violations of previous parliamentary enactments against enclosure: it had no power to hear and determine. Now, on 8 July 1549, the final clause of the new commission's inquiry articles gave it the power directly and immediately to 'reform' any enclosures of commons and highways, and this was duly pointed out to the camp of demonstrators at St Albans three days later.[77] Concession piled on concession. To the commotioners at Thetford, Somerset promised to restore the lordship of the town to the Crown, so that the townsfolk could lease the profits of tolls once more: this was especially remarkable, since the present lessee of the manor who had caused the grievance was the duke himself.[78] The Thetford camp was also dissatisfied with the make-up of the local enclosure commission: after a snarl at their 'obstinacy', Somerset suggested that they forward 'such names as be required

46

17. *An annotated page of Alexander Neville's Latin history of Kett's rebellion,* De furoribus Norfolciensium Ketto Duce (1582). *An Elizabethan schoolboy has added the English translation of unusual words in the Latin, witnessing that Neville, far from providing an objective account of the rebellion, has turned the story into the basis of a Latin textbook. The rebels are seen through the eyes of a schoolmaster, and treated with little sympathy.*

... either to be added to the others or put in stead of their places'. We had always known that the Mousehold rebels had asked for a commission under the Great Seal 'to such commissioners as your poor commons hath chosen'. Now we can see that this was not just some hopelessly idealistic rustic pipedream, but a reflection of what the government had actually been doing. This cannot but increase our respect for the rebels in the face of the unsympathetic portrait which survives of them in most contemporary narrative sources; and certainly Somerset treated them with a respect unusual among his colleagues.[79]

In the most dramatic of all the concessions made in the nine letters, Somerset promised to bring forward the calling of Parliament by a month, from 4 November to 4 October, so that all the rebel grievances could be discussed quickly; the king was made to ask the Norfolk com-motioners to choose four or six shire delegates to present new bills of grievance to the Protector in preparation for it.[80] One wonders at what stage this plan was abandoned; for in the end the Norfolk men would lie dead at Dussindale rather than electing a parliamentary delegation. It is tempting, though perhaps too neat, to see this looming October deadline for Parliament as a trigger which in late September made it essential for the Councillors to launch their action against Somerset. For what all this re-emphasizes, and what Bush was concerned to minimize, was the deep rift in political outlook by summer 1549 between the Protector and the other members of the Privy Council and of the evangelical estab-lishment. It was there for us to see in the extraordinarily candid letter which William Paget wrote to the Duke at the height of the negotiations with the camps, on 7 July 1549: he told Somerset bluntly that although the poor loved him, the policy of pardoning them was folly – most importantly of all, none of his Council colleagues agreed with what he was doing, and thought that he would bring them all down with him. 'Alas! Sir, how can this gear do well? I know in this matter of the com-mons, every man of the Council have misliked your proceedings, and wished it otherwise ... I believe if anything chance amiss, wherefore a reckoning shall be asked by the King ... that not only your Grace shall give the account, which have authority in your hands, but also such as did first consent and accord to give you that authority.'[81] Those who knew that they had thus 'consented' back in 1547 were unlikely to allow themselves to be dragged down to disaster with their over-mighty fellow-Councillor.

Protector Somerset had isolated himself from all those who mattered in English high politics, and Paget was in effect prophesying that they would seize back the power which they had surrendered to Somerset back in 1547. So forward an evangelical politician as the Provost of Eton, Sir Thomas Smith, writing in a state of sleepless despair to William

Cecil in the middle of the July commotions, was at a loss to understand what the duke was up to.[82] Two months later another loyal servant of the regime, Sir Anthony Aucher, was not just baffled but angry when he contemplated the results of Somerset's policy in Kent: 'To be plain, [I] think my Lord's Grace rather to will the decay of the gentlemen than otherwise.'[83] It is remarkable, and a tribute to the force of Somerset's personality, that the bewildered politicians of England let his plans go ahead for so long. Gentlemen ran errands back and forth to the camps throughout July; Privy Councillors put their signatures to excitable letters which embodied his policy. Somerset divided gentleman against gentleman, allowing the commons to decide who they thought was suitable to be in commission for the king, recognizing the ability of ordinary people outside the charmed circle of the gentry to make moral and political decisions. It nearly worked; after all, every commotion in the south, east and midlands dispersed without much bloodshed, except the Mousehold camp. The Protector might indeed have got away with the whole great gamble if the Marquis of Northampton had not blundered when he led his expeditionary force from London into Norfolk, combining lack of local knowledge with political ineptitude: his mishandling transformed the Norwich encounter from negotiation to bloody battle. Once Norfolk exploded into really murderous violence, Somerset's strategy came crashing down, and the Privy Councillors could vent their feelings on him and on the commons of England.

Who is the Somerset that we now meet? The character of his regime is marvellously summed up in the words of his royal nephew's letter to the Norfolk commotioners on 18 July: 'We have always shewed ourselves by the advice of our dearest uncle Edward Duke of Somerset, Governor of our person and Protector of our realms, dominions and subjects, and the rest of our Privy Council, most ready and willing to provide for your ease, quiet and comfort as much as ever prince hath been for his subjects, as the multitude of things reformed in the short time of our reign well declareth to the world.'[84] What comes across here through the mouthpiece of the king is the Protector's brash self-advertisement which so angered his fellow-councillors ('the rest of our

18. *Wymondham Abbey, Norfolk: the government hanged William Kett, brother of Robert, from the west tower of the church.*

Privy Council'!): a claim to be uncle not just to the king but to the whole realm. His regime was hyperactive and gloried in the fact: no single area was immune from alteration. And this was because everything was linked: all the fuss about enclosures merged with the issue of religion. Somerset's evangelical client and publicist, the government servant John Hales, spelled that out when, in embarking on the enclosure commission of 1548, he connected the enclosure issue intimately to the furtherance of godly reformation: 'If there be any way or policy of man to make the people receive, embrace, and love God's word, it is only this, – when they shall see that it bringeth forth so goodly fruit, that men seek not their own wealth, nor their private commodity, but, as good members, the universal wealth of the whole body.'[85]

We do not have to restore the good duke to his pedestal to find here a politician with a style of government unique in Tudor England: personal, autocratic, increasingly contemptuous of his actual partners in government and with a compulsive urge to reach beyond them, explain himself and win the approval of the wider population.[86] Even after his fall, he was insistent on living his life in a curiously public, confessional way. Otherwise it is difficult to explain how he allowed Peter Martyr Vermigli's letter to him commemorating his release from prison to be translated into English by Thomas Norton, a member of his household, and published in 1550: the letter is a rather schoolmasterly mixture of congratulation and exhortation which does not make the duke out to be a super-hero.[87] Somerset uneasily combined the reforming zeal of Thomas Cromwell, the *chutzpah* of Cardinal Wolsey and the flashy populism of Queen Elizabeth's doomed Earl of Essex. Amid the various dramatic styles of the Edwardian Reformation his regime must have seemed like Barnum and Bailey's circus to his fellow-Councillors. More charitably, we can see a leader of English high politics paying an extraordinary degree of respect to the concerns of the world of low politics; or at least that section of low politics which shared his own evangelical enthusiasm.[88]

This idiosyncratic strategy was admittedly more than just a matter of temperament: as Ethan Shagan has observed, it was almost a political necessity – a consequence of the Protector's decision to step beyond the status of first among equals which the Council had ceded to him in government. He had injured his colleagues' self-esteem; his formal authority came from his relationship to a boy whose future attitudes were an unknown quantity; where else could he turn but to the people? He persisted in the same course after his fall: during his attempted fightback against his fellow-Councillors in their coup of early October 1549, he appealed directly to the commons. Several of the surviving handbills which sought to recruit a people's army for Somerset around London breathe open animosity to the gentry and nobility, as having indulged in extortion and murdered the king's subjects. One handbill, particularly singled out by the Privy Council for condemnation, specifically praised the duke's policy of issuing pardons during the summer.[89] Even when Somerset's fellow-Councillors had humbled him and admitted him back to their ranks on sufferance, they still paid him the grudging

compliment of trading on his popularity, for it was he who was selected
to ride off as a roving trouble-shooter to tame the commons over the
next two summers, when there were further threats of insurrectionary
trouble in the south and midlands.[90] And when Somerset's increasing political inconsistency and folly finally made him too dangerous to
tolerate, his execution in January 1552 was an extremely difficult affair
where crowd hysteria came close to a disastrous explosion.[91]

What are we to make of John Dudley, the man who filled Somerset's
place with a good deal less flamboyance? If Somerset talked too much,
Northumberland comes across in his surviving writings as strikingly
inarticulate; perhaps this is what attracted his fellow-politicians, though
it may also have something to do with his frequent bouts of illness
during Edward's reign. In religious terms, he has often been seen as an
enigma, compounding confusion by his spectacular last-minute conversion back to traditionalist Catholic faith in the last days of his life, facing
the scaffold after his failure to convince the realm that its queen was
Jane Grey. We should not take too seriously this declaration at a
moment of dire personal crisis and defeat. Even then, in that final public
statement, he frankly painted a picture of his conversion to evangelical
views in the 1530s, a conversion which had remained constant all
through the alarms of Henry VIII's reign. John Dudley had not just been
a fair-weather sympathizer with the evangelical cause. He affirmed from
the scaffold in summer 1553 that he had not been a Christian, in other
words he had not been a traditionalist Catholic, for sixteen years; that is
since about 1536-7.[92] In an emotional letter a few months before, while
he was still in power, in December 1552, he had extended back the
period of his evangelical faith slightly further to the beginning of the
Anne Boleyn era, declaring that he had stood in one kind of religion for
twenty years.[93]

Certainly by the mid-1530s Dudley was part of that fashionable evangelical circle at King Henry's court whose identities and close links can
be traced in the Latin poem dedications of the French poet Nicholas
Bourbon.[94] In 1551, among the various books for pleasure then owned by
Dudley's eldest son Lord John, was an array of evangelical literature,

19. *A seventeenth-century impression of the Duke of Somerset's execution on Tower Hill: the executioner holds up the severed head.*

most notably the *Dialoge of the uniuste usurped primacie of the Bishop of Rome.* This was the same book by Bernardino Ochino which had so fascinated King Edward when compiling his 1549 treatise on papal supremacy, although one suspects that Lord John's copy was the second edition, which censored out the flattering references to Somerset and replaced his character (significantly) with a personification of the whole Privy Council.[95] And it is worth taking seriously the testimony of John Bale, a connoisseur of evangelicals who was not inclined to suffer hypocrites gladly, however highly placed. In dedicating one of his vintage anti-papist diatribes to Northumberland in 1552, Bale ended up with testimony which is specific beyond mere flattery: 'I have always known the same a most mighty, zealous, and ardent supporter, maintainer, and defender of God's lively word.'[96]

John Dudley also won Edward's approval by treating him seriously; he punctiliously gave the boy a place in Council meetings from the age of fourteen, although this was not without sensible calculation. Given their good relations, freedom and greater initiative for the king was to

20. *John Dudley, Duke of Northumberland.*

Dudley's own advantage. Yet Dudley did not alarm his fellow-Councillors as Somerset had done. His style of politics was consensual: the title he took in government was Lord President of the Council, avowedly identifying himself as the first among equals whom politicians had hoped for in vain when creating the Protectorate back in 1547.[97] Dudley was a politician who traded on normality, and the keynote of most aspects of his policy was achieving stability and reconstruction. He gloried in having suppressed those same Norfolk commotions for which Somerset had shown such sympathy: when he was created Duke of Northumberland, the suppression of Kett's Norfolk rebellion was given as one of the reasons for his promotion, and on the wall of his London home hung a map of his 1549 expedition to Norwich, just as there were maps of his other military campaigns in Scotland.[98]

Yet we should never judge Dudley simply as a ruthless and ambitious politician. Central to his strategy of restoring normality was making peace with France and Scotland to stop a ruinous drain of money, and the price which he was prepared to pay for peace was a good deal of personal unpopularity: he gave Boulogne – old King Henry's glorious prize, virtually all England had to show for all those wars in the 1540s – back to the French. There was widespread public anger at the loss of face; but the cession of Boulogne did bring peace.[99] At home, Dudley sponsored reforms of central administration and rather clumsily began to end the policy of debasing the coinage, which had earned the government easy money but which had sullied England's financial reputation abroad, and brought misery to most of the nation. Churchmen, evangelical and traditionalist alike, loathed him for plundering the Church, but they may not have realized just how dire was the financial crisis which faced the Dudley regime.[100]

All this indicates idealism of a sort, an idealism without fireworks – much as it may seem strange to attribute idealism to a nobleman who undoubtedly feathered his own nest, and who came to quarrel bitterly with like-minded evangelical leaders of the Edwardian Church. When all that is to the Dudley regime's discredit has been taken into account, the fact remains that the Dudley years were the beginning of a period of

21. *An example of one of the new coins minted by the Dudley government in its effort to restore the standard of English coinage: a fine silver shilling of 1551–3, with the tun mint-mark of the mint at the Tower of London.*

painstaking reconstruction, a different variety of reconstruction from that of the Somerset years, with a different rhetoric. Notoriously, Mary's regime had no problem in carrying on with much of Northumberland's reform programme without any sense of incongruity. The one exception was of course religion. Only in that sphere did Dudley's government, when compared with Somerset's, deliver more of the same: evangelical revolution. Here was continuity, indeed an accelerated and more relentless pace of religious change. This anomaly needs explanation, but so far, our cast list has described merely those at the top of the bill, and we have said little about one very important actor, Thomas Cranmer. We must go on to meet him, and many of the supporting cast, as they pursue their crusade against the forces of Antichrist.

# 2

# King Josiah: Purifying
# the Realm

The leaders of the Edwardian regimes set out to destroy one Church and build another. This is the most important continuity between the ascendancies of Seymour and Dudley. Yet the story contains a good deal of hesitation, and most of this hesitation is to be found during the time of the more demonstrative evangelical leader, Protector Somerset: the period 1547–9. Does this then indicate that the official Edwardian Reformation was a series of haphazard steps or that, particularly in its first phase, it reflected an ideology of moderation and compromise? To provide answers, we must consider how the old Church was pulled down. The whole process can be traced through a detailed consideration of Edward's first regnal year (January to January 1547–8), which reveals a consistent strategy which went into creating King Josiah's purified Church.

The Church of England inherited by the evangelical establishment around Lord Protector Somerset in 1547 reflected the old king's eccentric mélange of religious opinions (above, pp. 1–7). In presenting religious policy over the next year, the new rulers sheltered behind Henry's ghost: they claimed that his unstable theology had been about to change direction once more. When the imperial ambassador expressed his concern about what was happening to the English Church during the summer of 1547, Somerset and his devious adviser William Paget blandly told him that their policies were merely what Henry VIII had been planning just before his death.[1] In the immortal phrase of Mandy Rice-Davies, they would say that, wouldn't they – but there is enough evidence to give their claim some substance: detailed and circumstantial statements (made at much the same time) from Archbishop Cranmer and from the Strassburg reformer Martin Bucer that if Henry had lived, the mass and clerical celibacy would have gone.[2]

The most realistic assessment of Henry was nevertheless that of an evangelical outside government, John Hooper, writing to his admired friend the leader of the Zürich reformation, Heinrich Bullinger, just before the old king's death. Hooper was speaking from the comparative safety of exile in Strassburg, where it was possible to be frank about England's alarming monarch. Hooper pointed to the international situation and to the Schmalkaldic War in Germany, where the two religious parties of central Europe had finally squared up in a war inspired by ideology. He suggested that the outcome of the fighting between Charles V and the German Lutheran princes of the Schmalkaldic League would decide matters in England: 'the king is adopting the gospel of Christ, if the emperor should be defeated in this most deadly war: should the gospel sustain disaster, then he will preserve his ungodly masses'.[3]

Hooper had rightly sensed the instability of Henry's thinking. The king was facing increasingly polarized religious choices as he unravelled more and more of the old system. Deeply felt as his theology was, its radical incoherence – stranded between his loss of purgatory and his rejection of justification by faith – meant that he needed some external criterion for making theological choices: the criterion was likely to be the balance of diplomatic advantage for his kingdom in a divided Europe. By contrast, the clique around Somerset unhesitatingly adopted the more radical of Henry's stark alternatives, and for all its hesitations, it would not thereafter be diverted for long by diplomatic embarrassments from moving towards its aim. Yet all the while the Edwardian evangelical establishment had the advantage of the ambiguity of Henry's last years; it could keep opposition within bounds, as long as it could put out enough contrasting signals to reflect the old king's diverse views.

The constraints both overseas and at home remained. The Emperor

Charles V's attitude to the new regime was very dangerous; he regarded the Lady Mary as the true heir of Henry VIII, and if Charles's agents could have detected any groundswell of English support for putting her on the throne, the Empire might well have withheld recognition from Edward. Even when it quickly became clear that there was no internal challenge, England's tense relations with France and eventual slide into war meant that Somerset could never ignore Charles's feelings.[4] Four years later in a review of policy, William Cecil was still suggesting a worst-case scenario in which a furious Emperor combined with English conservatives to bring down the regime.[5] For at home, the evangelicals were considerably more nervous about public opinion than Henry had been after his flamboyant thirty-eight years on the throne. Archbishop Cranmer felt the need to justify to Ralph Morice, his trusted secretary, the slow pace of change in Edward's first regnal year: 'if the king's father had set forth any thing for the reformation of abuses, who was he that durst gainsay it? Marry! we are now in doubt how men will take the change, or alteration of abuses, in the church.'[6]

Cranmer and his colleagues must cope with the uncomfortable reality that outside the court and the Council chamber, their chief support came from people who did not matter in politics: Cambridge dons, a minority of clergy and a swathe of people below the social level of the gentry, all concentrated in south-east England. The projected Edwardian Reformation could not expect enthusiastic support from the majority of lay people in positions of power, gentry and nobility. Likewise, few bishops would cooperate wholeheartedly with the dismantling of traditional religion; yet little could be done without them, and they had formidably aggressive spokesmen in Bishops Edmund Bonner of London and Stephen Gardiner of Winchester, third and fourth in the church's hierarchy. One of the conservative bishops' former colleagues, the doyen of evangelical preachers, Hugh Latimer, felt entitled to exploit his celebrity status by launching an open attack on them from the royal pulpit, with a plea for their forcible retirement: 'make them quondams, all the pack of them', he begged the king and Council in early 1549. However, the government could not afford such self-

22. *The Holy Roman Emperor Charles V, 1548, by Titian. Painted at the height of his triumph over German Protestants.*

indulgence. Its major preoccupation in the Somerset years was to conciliate the bishops, particularly Gardiner, in order to get grudging consent to a step-by-step reformation.[7] Intimidation or confrontation was only a last resort when consent was withheld.

Thus the regime felt the need to work around three hostile constituencies: the Emperor, the majority of the lay political nation and those bishops who were not part of the inner circle. Increasingly extrovert in general style, Somerset's government habitually gave out two contradictory or alternative messages in religious matters. It was not so much moderate as schizophrenic in its religious pronouncements, seeking simultaneously to please its own circumscribed constituency of sympathizers while seeking to divert everyone else who mattered. It urged on evangelicals to destructiveness, and everyone else to peace and unity.

We can see this dual pattern at the very beginning of the reign, for

23. *Stephen Gardiner, Bishop of Winchester: he was the most able and persistent opponent of religious change on the Edwardian episcopal bench.*

24. *A medal produced in gold and silver to commemorate the coronation of Edward VI. The inscriptions in Latin, Greek and Hebrew have identical texts, all stressing the royal supremacy; a similar medal had been struck for Henry VIII in 1545. The medal is curiously crudely inscribed 'Lambhith', but no definite connection can be made to Archbishop Cranmer's administration at Lambeth Palace.*

Edward VI came to the throne in the guise of two different boy-kings. In the address which Archbishop Cranmer is said to have given at his coronation, Edward was already Josiah, exhorted to see 'God truly worshipped, and idolatry destroyed'. The gold medal struck for the coronation made a point of stressing his supremacy, just like that of his father, or Josiah in his kingdom. Predictably, Edward as King Josiah enjoyed plays during the revels at his coronation which portrayed not merely the Pope with gilded pasteboard crown and cross but also priests in crimson and black caps: the old world of faith was mocked as superstitious and as sham as the Pope's pasteboard.[8] However, on the way from the Tower to Westminster the previous day, Edward VI had assumed the role of a very different young monarch: the fifteenth-century boy-king Henry VI. The London authorities chose to centre their pageants on those which had been used for the child king's return from France in

1432, the work of the poet William Lydgate. The minimal modifications of Lydgate's century-old verse and pageants were designed mainly to emphasize the royal supremacy which Henry VI had not realized he possessed.

Sydney Anglo, our leading authority on Tudor political ceremony, has considered this antiquarian revival to be a sign of panic-stricken haste: Anglo described Edward's royal entry to the city as perhaps the most tawdry on record. But there was no particular reason why the city authorities should have needed to hurry with their plans: the choice is likely to have been considered and deliberate.[9] It is worth noting the late Jennifer Loach's observation that at King Henry's funeral at the beginning of that month, the most significant innovation in the thoroughly traditional ceremony was the addition of a processional banner for Henry VI.[10] This sounds like more than coincidence, and one can see why reference to Henry would be a useful piece of symbolism to please conservatives. Today we remember Henry VI as one of the most disastrous of English monarchs: however, in 1547 he was still a royal saint, whose cult had been increasingly popular in early Tudor England. As the Duke of Somerset himself pointed out in a self-justificatory letter to his great enemy-in-exile Cardinal Pole in 1549, Henry's 'childhood was more honourable and victorious than was his man's estate'. It may be relevant, too, that the story of Henry's childhood prominently featured Humphrey Duke of Gloucester, who provided a useful precedent for a good duke chosen as Protector.[11]

It took some time to provide a legal framework to move away from Henry VI and towards Josiah. Throughout 1547, conservatives could exploit the fact that Henry VIII's exuberantly traditional Act of Six Articles of 1539 was still in force to regulate religion, and they used it to harass religious opponents for their eucharistic views. Some evangelicals imprisoned during the conservative clampdown of summer 1546 were still in gaol through King Edward's first spring; in Worcester, a young sacramentary called John Davis was sitting in irons in his cell until April 1547, while in York there were still victims of the Six Articles legislation in prison in May, needing Privy Council intervention to get

25. *Edward VI's coronation procession passes out of London into the Strand approaching Westminster: from a 1788 drawing of murals at Cowdray House, Sussex, destroyed soon afterwards by fire. Prominent in the picture is Charing Cross.*

them released.[12] There are several examples of new accusations being brought against evangelicals all through this year, while most remarkably of all, that April, the diocese of London received a new commission to inquire and make prosecutions under the Six Articles Act. It was headed not only by Bishop Bonner but by two of the more conservatively minded Privy Councillors, Lord St John and Lord Russell; perhaps Bonner had insisted on obtaining the commission in order to embarrass the regime, which could hardly have turned down such a request.[13] Quite what the London commission actually achieved is not now clear, but the Act itself could not be abolished until Parliament was summoned at the end of the year.

Accordingly, through the spring, a welter of confusing messages came from the government. Only a month after the Six Articles commissions were issued for London, in May, a royal visitation was announced, inhibiting the bishops' jurisdiction: the visitors were nearly all hand-picked for their evangelical enthusiasm. Yet there was almost immediate hesitation. Only a week later the Privy Council wrote in the most urgent terms to Archbishop Holgate of York telling him not to implement the inhibition as far as it affected preaching. They gave no reason, but it is likely that this particular problem resulted from delays to the proposed substitute for preaching, a book of twelve official homilies. The book was probably ready, but it had not been cleared with the conservative bishops, and it never would gain their wholehearted assent. During June Cranmer and Bishop Gardiner of Winchester started a lively and acrimonious correspondence about its contents, in which Gardiner frequently invoked the ghost of old King Henry: 'although his body liveth no longer among us, yet his memory should in such sort continue in honour and reverence, as your Grace should not impute to him now that was not told him in his life'.[14] When the Bishop of Winchester did eventually give a grudging public commendation to the homilies on 8 April 1548, he pointedly concentrated on the duty of obedience to the present king, rather than on the content of the book.[15]

By the end of May, the inhibitions laid on the bishops for the visitation were lifted completely, and no action on the visitation followed until the end of August. A proclamation of 24 May denounced rumour-mongering that the government was planning 'innovations and changes in religion and ceremonies of the Church', and it indignantly denied any such intention; Somerset took particular care to forward this to Bishop Gardiner with a courteous covering letter.[16] However, those in the Province of York soon discovered how hollow this claim was, for only two days later the Privy Council was ordering the Archbishop of York to stop parishes using the *Exoneratorium curatorum*. This was a widely distributed book of instruction for the laity, which had originally been drawn up especially for the northern province in the fourteenth century, but which had been put into print at least eight times up to 1530.[17] Perhaps the Council could justify this ban by reference to the order of 1545 enforcing universal use of Henry VIII's official Primer, but the functions of the *Exoneratorium* and the Primer were not identical. This was an effort to gag the teaching of traditional religion, even before there was any new official statement to put in its place. Yet in contradiction again, throughout June there was official discouragement of aggressive evangelical preaching, a restoration of the old fast days at Court, and liturgical performances of full traditional splendour in dirige and requiem to commemorate the death of King Francis of France.[18]

The government seemed to be marking time through much of the summer, and not just in religious matters: during May it had looked as if England was ready to launch a new military expedition into Scotland, but no action followed for three months.[19] There were good diplomatic reasons for hesitation. Negotiations for lasting peace with France were now wrecked by the French king's death. If relations with France were to worsen once more, it would force England to take more notice of the Emperor, just at the moment when he had shattered Protestant power in Germany in a decisive turn of the Schmalkaldic War. Charles V's victory over the Schmalkaldic League at Mühlberg at the end of April was greeted with widespread popular dismay in London, and the imperial ambassador saw it as directly affecting English religious policy.

It was not a good moment for England, now dangerously isolated as an evangelical kingdom, either to champion the Reformation or indulge in military adventures.[20]

Yet this period of prudence was noticeably brief: the evangelical establishment was impatient to push on with the revolution. Already by the end of July the regime's nerve was steadying, and it was picking up the threads of its programme. The homilies were finally published on the last day of the month, complete with their uncompromising assertions on the central importance of justification by faith alone. This was Martin Luther's doctrine of salvation, which Henry VIII had determinedly kept at bay, particularly in his official doctrinal statement of 1543, the King's Book: so here was a first step beyond what could be excused in terms of existing Henrician orders.[21] Nevertheless, it was only one step. There was a deafening silence in this tranche of homilies about a second vital subject, the nature of the eucharist. All that the book had to offer was a promise that the eucharist would be discussed in a proposed second batch of homilies, which in fact was not to appear until the reign of Elizabeth.

The main factor was undoubtedly the Act of Six Articles. By the opening months of Edward's reign, it is virtually certain that the key formers of official opinion, Cranmer, Latimer and Ridley, had abandoned belief in corporal presence in the eucharist, despite having maintained it in Lutheran fashion since the early 1530s. The reasons for the change are obscure, since those involved mostly had more sense than to express their opinions openly while the old king was alive: he was fiercely insistent on the corporal presence of Christ, and in his last year of life he had burnt some of those who openly disagreed with him on the subject. However, when Henry died, it became easier to rethink the question of eucharistic presence. We may consider such a shift unheroic or cowardly, but quite apart from our own safe distance from Henry VIII's court, we ought to remember not only the motive of fear but that of personal loyalty. Henry was Supreme Head of the Church, deliverer of England from the papal antichrist, and he ought not to be opposed openly. The sheer mesmerizing power of the old man – no mean debater of theology himself – must have inhibited his good servants in positions of responsibility from thinking new thoughts.[22]

From whatever combination of motives, Cranmer, Latimer and Ridley now moved in parallel with a steady tide of scepticism about Luther's eucharistic assertions, which characterized much of central European reformed opinion in the 1540s. Buoyed up in their shifting opinions through reassessing a number of pronouncements on the eucharist by theologians of the early Church, they came to regard the Lutheran view of eucharistic presence as verging on the trivial and blasphemous. It was a more fitting tribute to God's glory to see his presence as a spiritual fact about the service of eucharist, a revelation of his presence to true believers – not a transformation of bread and wine.[23] However, while the Six Articles Act was still in force, it would have been indecorous, embarrassing and indeed illegal for them to publish their new eucharistic convictions; any such statement would have been a gift to the watchful Stephen Gardiner. After all, Gardiner was already making hay out of the fact that the King's Book disagreed with the homilies on justification; but the Six Articles were a much greater menace than the King's Book. The Articles said nothing specific about justification; evangelicals knew to their cost how specific they were on the eucharist.

Consequently, at this stage, official evangelical strategy was to try to persuade the conservative leadership to live with the homilies' views on justification, exploiting genuine fears which both mainstream evangelicals and conservatives felt about more extreme radicalism – what contemporaries rather inexactly labelled Anabaptism. The radicals could be seen as overthrowing all consensus on the biblical sacraments, baptism and eucharist. As long as the bishops left the topic of eucharistic presence to one side, it would be possible to stress that all bishops were in broad agreement on theological basics in comparison with the radicals, and so the eucharist could act as a focus of unity rather than of division. Nicholas Ridley was sent as emissary from the Privy Council to Bishop Gardiner with this message, and according to his own account he said to Gardiner, 'You see many Anabaptists rise against the sacrament of the altar; I pray you, my lord, be diligent in confounding of them.' Ridley and Gardiner were, after all, both in commission investigating Kentish radicals at the time.

However, a conservative memory of the conversation was slightly more pointed: Ridley was heard to say, 'Tush, my lord, this matter of justification is but a trifle, let us not stick to condescend herein to them [that is, radicals]; but . . . stand stoutly in the verity of the sacrament: for I see they will assault that also.' However biased this account, there was an awkward ambiguity in Ridley's stance on eucharistic presence, which was also reflected in a Paul's Cross sermon he delivered on the subject later in 1547; his apparent endorsement of the reality of Christ's presence in the eucharistic bread and wine would long afford him embarrassment and fuel conservative attacks on him.[24] Yet the appeal to a common solidarity against the radicals was an important factor during the Somerset years in preventing complete schism and gaining enough consent for change among the bishops. Cranmer, after all, did make genuine and serious efforts to curb various varieties of theological radicalism. When the government issued a commission against heresy in spring 1549, the leading churchmen among the commissioners were a bipartisan group, traditionalist and evangelical, although significantly this was not the case in altered political circumstances two years later.[25]

In late August 1547, not only did the government launch its long-postponed invasion of Scotland but also the invasion of traditional religion, via the royal visitation of the Church. Bishops Bonner and Gardiner found that there were limits to conciliation when they protested both about the scope of the visitation and the content of the homilies; their bluff was now called, and they ended up in gaol. The injunctions provided for the visitors were announced proudly to the evangelical movement across Europe, for they were issued in condensed form in Latin translation, probably by an overseas publisher, alongside the English version used in the visitation itself; the demand for the Latin translation abroad was enough to produce two different editions.[26] The content of the injunctions amounted to a careful reworking of Henrician injunctions in the evangelical interest. As Eamon Duffy has recently demonstrated in detail, in certain respects they stepped out beyond Henry in

26. *Nicholas Ridley.*

ways which would inflict deep wounds on traditional devotion. For instance, processions were forbidden, striking a major blow against the dramatic use of movement in liturgy, and recitation of the rosary was comprehensively condemned. But even more importantly, there was a deliberate hidden agenda behind many injunctions. As Cranmer confided to his faithful secretary Ralph Morice, because of worries about public opinion, 'the council hath forborne especially to speak [of abuses], and of other things which gladly they would have reformed in this visitation, referring all those and such like matters unto the discretions of the visitors.'[27]

In other words, given the pronounced evangelical views of nearly all visitors and the use which they would make of their 'discretions', the real visitation programme exceeded what appeared on paper. For instance, in a clever extension of Henrician orders against 'feigned miracles, pilgrimage, idolatry and superstition', the visitation injunctions said that even images in stained-glass windows should be removed if they had been the object of devotion. Such devotion was highly unlikely, and went well beyond what continental connoisseurs of iconoclasm would have considered necessary, but it provided an excuse right at the beginning of the visitation for the wholesale destruction of stained glass in Westminster, a high-profile venue no doubt deliberately chosen to set fashions elsewhere.[28] Similarly, the injunctions forbade the burning of candles in front of the figure of the rood (the figure of the crucified Christ), flanked by figures of Mary and John standing above chancel screens: this had been one of the few exemptions for devotional lights which Henry VIII had allowed. Eamon Duffy points out that the ban on rood lights had the incidental advantage of attacking many devotional guilds which in Henry's reign had relocated their lights from other church images to the rood; however, it was also fatal for the rood itself, one of the most spectacular pieces of furniture in any traditional church, as it reared above the chancel screen, dominating the laity's view as they looked towards the altar or pulpit. Without official sanction for its lights, the rood became like any other church image, and equally vulnerable to the charge of being abused for devotion. The result in London was almost universal destruction of roods. Even the conservative stronghold of St Paul's Cathedral suffered, although there, to grim conservative satisfaction, the rood group figures fought back by collapsing and causing the death of one of the workmen involved in pulling them down.[29]

Throughout the kingdom, what must have been most memorable about the visitation was its gleeful destructiveness, utilizing public ridicule against traditional devotion on a scale not seen since Thomas Cromwell had orchestrated a similar campaign in 1538. During the autumn, just as in 1538, a setpiece London sermon at the open-air pulpit of Paul's Cross ridiculed image cults, using images with moving parts as comic visual aids; the preacher, Bishop William Barlow, was a prominent former client of Cromwell. Afterwards London boys smashed up the images, amid scenes of evangelical rejoicing. Early in the visitation there seem to have been some token official attempts to reprove

iconoclastic enthusiasm, but Barlow's aggressive Paul's Cross performance came after that, and showed that any restraint was no more than
temporary window-dressing to dampen conservative fears. Indeed
Barlow went out of his way to humiliate the conservative canons of
St Paul's Cathedral, whom he exposed in his sermon as having
concealed one of the images he displayed.[30]

All over the country, through the rest of the autumn, there are
glimpses of the visitors eagerly exceeding their instructions to remove
superstitiously abused images and end the last remains of the pilgrimage
industry. There was a bonfire of a local saint's bones at Much Wenlock
in Shropshire: a bonfire of parish church cult images in the market-
place at Shrewsbury, which we know to have happened during 1547, also

27. *After systematic destruction in the reigns of Edward VI and Elizabeth I,
not a single figure from rood groups over medieval chancel screens survives in
England. Uniquely, Cullompton parish church (Devon) retains parts of the massive
frame in which the three figures were socketed, carved as the hill of Golgotha,
littered with skulls.*

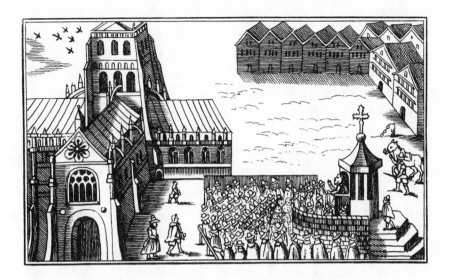

*28. Preaching at Paul's Cross at the north-east corner of the cathedral, at the beginning of the seventeenth century. The crowd, both men and women, stand to listen, with privileged spectators in the enclosure around the preacher.*

seems to have been part of the visitation holocaust. In Norwich, local enthusiasts took matters into their own hands in September, when 'divers curates and other idle persons' toured the city's rabbit warren of parish churches, tearing down and removing images. Notably, the Norwich city authorities did nothing more about these outrages than feebly requesting that the ringleaders (who included one leading parish priest of the city) to 'surcease of such unlawful doings'.[31]

The problem for the Norwich officers was indeed to decide just how unlawful such actions could be, when the king's representatives were indulging in equally dramatic behaviour. Far away to the north, the central parish church in Durham witnessed the remarkable spectacle of a royal commissioner jumping up and down on the city's giant Corpus Christi processional monstrance in order to smash it up more effectively. Since the royal injunctions had just abolished all processions, one can see the rationale, but the leaping royal commissioner was not merely serving a redundancy notice: he was dancing in triumph over the corpse of the old church. His action was a symbol of how the visitors used the 'discretion' which the Council had given them.[32] Precisely the same savagely symbolic overturning of the past was used in the following year in a literary context. A short pamphlet published a racily satirical dialogue on the eucharist, between the wily rustic John Bon and traditionalist Master Parson. It was prefaced by an illustration of a Corpus Christi procession bearing just such a monstrance as had been destroyed at Durham. However, the evangelical publisher was not using a new picture: he was economically (and perhaps with relish) cannibalizing old stock – the block came from a traditionalist devotional tract of 1516 where the context had been one of celebration and reverence.[33] What is remarkable throughout all this sudden renewal of the violent Cromwellian campaign of destruction is the lack of resistance, given that most of the population must have found what was happening bewildering and distasteful. The record seems barren of activist protest: the most harm which came to the iconoclasts appears to have been from the dumb images which collapsed on to the unfortunate workmen from the rood-loft in St Paul's Cathedral. The apparent paralysis of conservative reaction is a tribute to the policy of gradualism which Somerset's regime had adopted at the outset of the reign; it was a gradualism in the service of calculated destruction.

Across the Channel, the evangelicals of Strassburg, the Edwardian regime's closest friends in Europe, watched and applauded the atmosphere of festive mayhem. They had already been primed to anticipate a government programme of change to be pushed through Parliament and the Church's equivalent representative assembly for its southern province, the Convocation of Canterbury, which duly met in November 1547.[34] In these arenas, we can begin to gauge where evangelical political strengths and weaknesses lay. Opposition to the revolutionary

29. *Processional monstrance, carried in a Corpus Christi procession, from* John Bon and Mast' Person *(published late summer 1548; the illustration block dates from 1516).*

# ❡ John Bon and
## Mast person

❡ Alas poore fooles, so sore ye be lade
No maruel it is, thoughe your shoulders ake
For ye beare a great God, which ye yourselfes made
Make of it what ye wyl, it is a wafar cake
And betwen two Irons printed it is and bake
And Icke where Idolatrye is, Christe wyl not be there
Wherfore ley downe your burden, an Idole ye do beare
❡ Alasse poore
fooles.

programme was concentrated in Parliament among the lay nobility and the bishops, and in Convocation, among the Upper House of clergy. By contrast, elections for Convocation's Lower House had by whatever means produced a crop of middle-rank clergy ardent for change, who even rather embarrassed the evangelical leadership by stepping out on their own and demanding representation in Parliament along with the lay commons.[35] Equally the mood of cooperation in the Commons reflected the way in which Commons representation was biased towards the very area of the kingdom where evangelicals were most strongly represented: the urban communities of south-east England. It no doubt helped the general atmosphere of goodwill that the regime carefully avoided asking for any taxes in this session. The heresy laws were abolished, including the Act of Six Articles, so at last evangelicals could breathe easy in discussing the eucharist.

The French ambassador heard of fierce disputes on the eucharist in Parliament, but also of a clear majority wanting (as he saw it) to abolish the sacrament of the altar.[36] The resulting legislation was naturally rather more nuanced than this observation of a scandalized French Catholic might suggest, and it was a classic instance of the double-message strategy in Somerset's religious policy. Two bills on the sacrament of the altar started out, but they were eventually combined into one, which went forward to receive the royal assent. One bill embodied the gambit used by Bishop Ridley in dealing with Bishop Gardiner in summer 1547: it stressed the threat to all mainstream religion from radicals who reviled the eucharist, and it sought to curb such insolence. The other enacted a key evangelical requirement, communion in both kinds. When these were combined, the passage of the bill lost the evangelicals nothing and gained them a major step forward. Their opponents were divided, perhaps because they were deprived of Gardiner's incisive leadership, for the government had made sure that he was still languishing in prison after his September protest against the royal visitation. Five conservative bishops voted against the sacrament bill, unimpressed by its fierce penalties for profanation of the eucharist, but five more conservatives, including the veteran champion of the old faith, Bishop

Cuthbert Tunstall of Durham, were seduced into voting for it. Did they know that riding on the back of this legislation, though not announced in it, was a further incremental step of change? The restoration to the laity of communion in both kinds was made the excuse for the Council to publish a vernacular Order of Communion to be inserted into the Latin mass, and to be used throughout the realm from March. Josiah was purifying by stealth.[37]

There was a clear difference in atmosphere between Lords and Commons. The Commons were perfectly prepared to forward the progress of legislation abolishing compulsory clerical celibacy, which had also just been given an overwhelming endorsement in the Lower House of Convocation. The bill went on to die in the Lords, and clerical marriage was not properly legalized by Parliament until 1549, after bills had been delayed by continuing strenuous opposition in the Lords.[38] Despite this, Cranmer clearly felt that the degree of endorsement which clerical marriage had received from clergy and legislators was enough for the Church to behave as if it was fully legal; he himself was already living openly as a married man in 1547, and within a year, routine official documents emanating from Lambeth Palace began mentioning clerical wives.[39] In fact, in the Commons, government religious legislation only seriously faltered over the future of chantry lands once the chantries were dissolved. On this matter, many knights and burgesses were angry at the prospect of losing community assets for no obvious gain, and the obstruction had to be dealt with by some direct deals with certain particularly noisy borough representatives. This was the only time in Edward's reign when any official measure of religious change ran into trouble in the Commons, and even though the chantry dissolution Act preamble contained an aggressive attack on purgatory, opposition to it does not seem to have been on religious grounds. In any case, as the imperial ambassador sourly observed, protest ran in parallel with eager anticipation of another shareout of church lands among those able to afford it.[40]

While this Parliament continued, the final ingredient was added to the Edwardian Reformation with the arrival of distinguished refugees from

30. *Archbishop Cranmer, bearded, after the death of Henry VIII. This break with the customary clean-shaven appearance of early Tudor clerics coincided with Cranmer's open admission of his marriage. It became the standard Reformation image of Cranmer (taken here from the influential published collection of portraits by Boissard, first published in 1560); the image, for instance, is to be seen in Oxford's Bodleian Library, in the Upper Reading Room's early-seventeenth-century painted frieze of great theologians and reformers. Only in the more decorous Anglicanism of the later seventeenth century did an earlier clean-shaven portrait become the normative picture of the Archbishop.*

abroad. The first prominent men were two renegade former leaders of the Italian monastic revival, Bernardino Ochino and Pietro Martire Vermigli, known in England as Peter Martyr. They were given red-carpet treatment; their travel expenses from Strassburg were refunded to Archbishop Cranmer by the Privy Council, the huge sum of £126.[41] Within a month Ochino had been authorized to set up an independent congregation in London catering mainly for Italians, but also for any other 'strangers' (that is, resident aliens) who might choose to attend. It was never large, but it has the distinction of being the first officially recognized foreign Protestant congregation in England, anticipating by three years the much better known Stranger Church led by the Polish evangelical Jan Łaski. Clearly the regime was not sufficiently worried by the Emperor's wrath to avoid openly harbouring refugee reformers. Perhaps Charles V might overlook the reception given to Ochino and Martyr, since they were not his subjects, but even before that, it had not escaped the notice of imperial officials that Cranmer was giving employment to Low-Countries-born Pierre Alexandre, a former chaplain to the Emperor's sister, Mary of Hungary.[42] Later arrivals, particularly prominent Strassburg reformers like Martin Bucer or the Spanish biblical translator Francis Dryander (Francisco Enzinas), were also very much the Emperor's concern: yet they were still treated as heroes in England. This demonstrates the priorities of Edwardian government. If there is any one respect in which the Edwardian Reformation was different in flavour from the later Church of England, it was in the fervent Protestant internationalism which it displayed: there was little sense of any distinctive English ecclesiastical identity, and there was a longing for England to stand at the centre of a renewed universal Church at a time of particular military and political crisis for the reformed movement.

The inauguration of Ochino's congregation in the City in January 1548 was an extraordinary affair, for Cranmer sadistically insisted on the close involvement of Bishop Bonner, as ordinary of the diocese of London. Bonner was badgered into finding a place for Ochino to preach; Cranmer thanked him warmly for his efforts, but then told him to make sure that there were enough forms for the Italians to sit on, 'because

BERNHARD. OCHINUS[39]
*Prediger bey St. Moritzen in Augspurg. A:1541.*

31. *Bernardino Ochino, the first leader of a refugee congregation in England, pictured soon after his flight from Italy to Augsburg in 1541.*

their manner is not long to stand'. At the same time, he invited Bonner to come with him to hear Ochino's inaugural sermon, and to show that this was a request expecting the answer yes, he arranged for the bishop to entertain the preacher to dinner. Unfortunately, said Cranmer, with infuriating courtesy, he himself would be prevented from joining them by a prior engagement with Protector Somerset. All this was part of a letter which must have given Cranmer particular pleasure to write, because it was a personalized version for Bonner's benefit of a general circular ordering the bishops on Somerset's authority to forbid candles at the imminent feast of Candlemas, together with prohibitions on ashes on Ash Wednesday or palms on Palm Sunday. Bonner would have to send this out to his fellow-bishops in the Province of Canterbury, since he was *ex officio* registrar of the province. The letter was written exactly twelve months after King Henry had drifted into his final coma.[43] One could hardly find a more emphatic witness to the rapid success of evangelicalism and the policy of a step-by-step revolution.

So at the end of this first year Somerset and his colleagues had gained everything they needed for further progress towards purifying the Church. They had eliminated any serious opposition within the Privy Council. They had enshrined the doctrine of justification by faith in the Church's official statements, elbowing aside the statements on justification in the King's Book. They had robbed the Church's traditional liturgy of the drama, movement and visual impact which gave it much of its power, dealing a fatal blow to the use of sacred objects in devotion – not just images, but the symbols used in the ceremonies of Candlemas, Ash Wednesday and Palm Sunday. They had persuaded Parliament to pull down the defences of traditional religion provided by the heresy legislation, and to deliver the *coup de grâce* to the moribund purgatory industry. They had secured a *de facto* acceptance of clerical marriage, opened up new possibilities in the celebration of the eucharist, and begun recruiting star overseas theologians to link the English Church to the international reform movement.

The pattern of this first twelve months could be demonstrated over the next two years: constant repetition of the themes of unity and peace, and careful, incremental wearing down of opposition, at each stage accompanied by ostentatious and empty gestures of reassurance to Charles V and to conservatives at home. Naturally the government exploited the English habit of deference to the monarchy, in a country where it was customary to doff one's cap when mentioning the king or reading royal letters. One wonders which spin-doctor had the brainwave of nicknaming the new English Prayer Book of 1549 'the King's Book', to blot out memories of Henry VIII's embarrassingly conservative doctrinal book of 1543, which had gone under the same name.[44] The Chapel Royal, the king's personal religious establishment, which followed him from palace to palace, was an obvious model for other churches to follow. Even while the committee preparing the Prayer

Book was still at work in September 1548, Protector Somerset wrote to Cambridge University, almost certainly circularizing Oxford and other major churches at the same time: in the cause of uniformity they should follow Chapel Royal liturgical practice, which by that stage clearly included draft versions of the new vernacular eucharist, mattins and evensong.[45] The specialist royal chapel community of St George's Chapel, Windsor, was one of the first major churches to silence its organs: its organists were being given other duties as early as autumn 1550, and the instruments themselves may already have been destroyed by then.[46]

The government paid a great deal of attention to other places which could act as showcases for liturgical change and propaganda. For instance, among certain key churches in the provinces where the leadership was sympathetic was Worcester Cathedral, placed in a centre of trade for the west Midlands and the Welsh border. Not only would an edition of the 1549 Prayer Book be printed at Worcester to supply the western market, but the drastic and precocious Edwardian changes in the cathedral are recorded for us in a detailed chronicle kept by a dismayed local conservative observer. Worcester Cathedral under Dean John Barlow, brother of William, one of the leading evangelical bishops, meticulously and immediately observed the government's timetable of liturgical change, and the dean was even inclined to go faster and further than official orders prescribed. So he removed the reserved sacrament from his church in October 1548, well before many leading English churches and without any specific government instruction, and he introduced the new English Prayer Book on Easter Tuesday 1549, more than six weeks in advance of the Whitsun deadline ordered in Parliament's enactment.[47]

Above all, the regime was conscious of the importance of the capital. Nicholas Ridley observed as its bishop in 1551 that from London 'goeth example ... into all the rest of the king's majesty's whole realm'.[48] The city was a large and complex community to manage, and to begin with, both the cathedral staff and the bishop (Edmund Bonner) provided centres of resistance to change, rather than cooperation. It was therefore

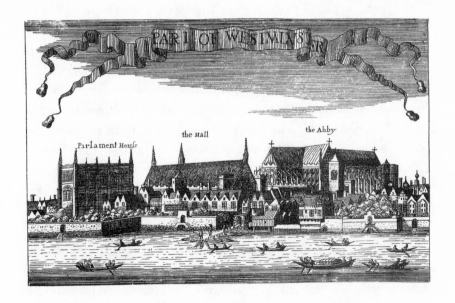

*32. Wenceslaus Hollar's view of Westminster from the river, 1641.*
*Hollar gives a good sense of the intimate relationship between Edwardian*
*Westminster's Cathedral and the Palace of Westminster, seat of Parliament, of*
*royal administration and of the lawcourts in Westminster Hall. Behind the*
*prominent royal bell-tower at the right is the smaller tower of one of*
*Westminster's two parish churches, St Margaret. Whitehall Palace*
*is at the extreme right.*

important for London to be given its own showcase, more closely under
the government's control: the adjoining community of Westminster,
with its complex of royal palaces, its meeting place for Parliament and
the former royal abbey church, which between 1540 and 1550 briefly
became the cathedral of a new diocese. Great care was taken to turn
Westminster into a miniature version of the reformed city-states of the
Continent. The royal injunctions for Westminster diocese in September
1547 specified that Sunday service was to end in the churches of the
community by nine o'clock, so that priests and laity could resort to the
sermon in Westminster Cathedral, unless the churches themselves had
a sermon. All Westminster clergy were to turn up to every divinity

lecture in St Stephen's College.[49] The college's suppression in 1548 along with all England's remaining chantries put paid to this last idea, but help was at hand. Bishop Hugh Latimer was given lodgings in the cathedral precincts with the Dean of Westminster, William Benson, to act as a resident celebrity preacher for this model community; the palace of Whitehall could still boast its own up-market version of London's pulpit at Paul's Cross with Henry VIII's recently built open-air preaching place in the Privy Garden. This became the setting for some of Latimer's most celebrated sermons.[50]

Given the progress made in 1547, during 1548 the evangelical establishment could afford to indulge its friends and gag its opponents. It let loose propaganda by tolerating evangelical preaching and making little effort to control printing; around three quarters of all books published in Somerset's time were on religious themes, virtually none defending traditional religion. This year represented a peak in the numbers of book and pamphlet titles published in English, which would not be exceeded until after 1570. The Protestant chronicler Bishop Thomas Cooper later looked back on 1548 as the time when 'by reason of continual preaching and teaching of divers that were to that office [i.e. duty] appointed: the people in many places declared themself very forward and ready to forsake their old religion'.[51] Simultaneously the regime hamstrung the opposition by heavily restricting preaching, a paradoxical step for an evangelical church to take, and one which rather puts into perspective Somerset's supposed spirit of liberal tolerance.[52]

Henry VIII, or rather Thomas Cromwell, had obliged parish clergy to preach quarterly in their own churches, but now Cromwell's heirs overturned the measure: from April 1548, only a very restricted list of clergy with a royal licence had the right to preach at all, and inevitably most of them were card-carrying evangelicals.[53] In the West Country, by contrast, the alarmingly talented conservative preacher Roger Edgeworth found himself banned from preaching in his numerous benefices and multiple cathedral offices for virtually the entire reign.[54] The rhetoric employed in these preaching prohibitions was the Henrician theme of suppressing seditious and contentious preachers, but it

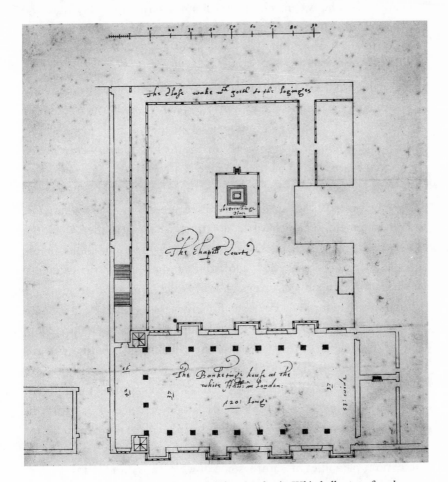

33. *Plan of the preaching place and Privy Garden in Whitehall, 1609, after the building of James I's Banqueting Hall.*

was clear that apart from the inevitable Anabaptists, sedition and contention were labels for traditionalists, particularly if they tried to expound eucharistic theology. The government line was that the eucharist should not be discussed, because an official decision was soon to be made about it in order to preserve national unity: again, a standard Henrician refrain now put to frankly partisan use. Thus it was on these grounds that Bishop Gardiner was told to avoid the subject of the eucharist when he was made to preach a test sermon in May 1548, and his ostentatious disobedience to this instruction was one of the chief pretexts for his immediate arrest and permanent removal from active Edwardian politics.[55]

The same reason – that a major decision on liturgy was imminent – was used again when preaching was forbidden altogether in September 1548, by which time a committee was indeed putting the finishing touches to a uniform prayer book for the realm. There were enough conservatives on this committee to give it a respectable appearance of consensus, yet as soon as the group had done its work, the government moved the goalposts again. The committee appears to have prepared an agreed statement on eucharistic doctrine, which was then doctored before Parliament was scheduled to debate it. The omissions in the revised document concerned adoration of the eucharistic elements, which had been a subject of evangelical attack through that autumn.[56] Adoration was naturally a key issue for anyone who believed in the corporal presence of Christ in the eucharist, and it was linked to the custom of reserving eucharistic bread in the pyx. Far from avoiding contention, a number of strategically high-profile churches like Worcester Cathedral and York Minster abandoned reservation during the autumn.

Indeed, throughout autumn 1548, in blatant defiance of its own supposed total ban on preaching, the Privy Council condoned prominent pulpit attacks on traditional eucharistic theology; this was backed up by contentious pamphlet literature, some of which was directly inspired by the court or by Lambeth Palace. John King's survey of Edwardian Protestant printing identified no fewer than thirty-one tracts published during the year supporting something like the new official line on the mass.[57] Not all of this literature exactly conformed to the government's agenda: on occasion it was critical of official hesitancy in attacking traditional views of what the eucharist meant. Thus the dialogue between *John Bon and Mast' Person* subversively portrayed pompous and conservative Master Parson as commending Cranmer's official catechism issued in summer 1548; that unfortunate and hastily produced translation from a German Lutheran text had inadvertently left too much room in its exposition of the eucharist for a real-presence interpretation of the bread and wine. However, the embarrassed authorities were swift first to amend the text of the catechism on eucharistic matters and then to forget the book altogether; so the author of *John Bon* had successfully made his point.[58]

For the moment the thrust of official policy was negative rather than positive. It is not always realized just how long Edwardian England lacked anything resembling an officially defined doctrinal statement on the eucharist: no statement of any sort appeared until 1550, well after the first Prayer Book was issued, and the process of definition was not complete until 1553. Clearly this would be one of the most fraught issues in any Reformation. Traditionalists would be most likely to rally to resist change in the mass, as became only too obvious in the 1549 western rebellion, and evangelicals might split along the fault lines which had already destroyed their unity in Europe. There was an extra international dimension to the problem, quite apart from the Edwardian establishment's usual preoccupations with Charles V: the evangelicals of central Europe, principally Bullinger and John Calvin, were seeking an understanding on the eucharist, which eventually resulted in the Zürich Agreement or *Consensus Tigurinus* in May 1549. In 1548–9 it would have been fatal for England, the most important surviving evangelical power in Europe, to make any official pronouncement on the eucharist while delicate efforts were being made abroad to heal the twenty-year-old wounds of the eucharistic quarrel between Luther and Zwingli, and to counteract the disaster for evangelicals represented by Charles V's Interim. The implications of the *Consensus* for the afterlife of the Edwardian Reformation will concern us in Chapter 4 (below, pp. 167–70); what is important to note now is that only after mid-1549 was it possible to create an official doctrinal or confessional statement for England which would not unduly divide evangelicals at home, or complicate international relationships.

Therefore, in 1548, definitive statements lay in the future. In December of that year, the government staged a four-day debate on the eucharist in the House of Lords, a gathering of Councillors, peers and

34. *Peter Martyr Vermigli: a seventeenth-century version of a contemporary painting, now at Christ Church, Oxford. His briefing paper for Somerset in the 1548 eucharistic disputation was a new departure for the refugees in the English Reformation.*

bishops of which we have an abbreviated though still eloquent record. Somerset entered the debate newly briefed on the eucharist by an English translation of a short tract by Peter Martyr, the first recorded occasion on which the refugees had made an active contribution to England's religious politics.[59] The whole occasion may have been an example of the Protector's readiness to try out new ideas; there was nothing else like it in the whole of England's Reformation, and it was the nearest English equivalent to the set-piece disputations which launched the Swiss Reformation in the city of Zürich in the 1520s. Yet unlike the Zürich disputations, it led nowhere, in the sense that it produced no policy statement or legislation: all that the debate did was to expose the doctrinal divisions among the bishops, and the doctrinal solidarity between leading evangelical churchmen and laypeople, before Parliament went on to forward the legislation authorizing the Book of Common Prayer for the royal assent.[60] The event thus showed that for all the tactical gains which the reformers had made, as yet the balance of political forces had hardly shifted between traditionalists and evangelicals. This meant that the regime must persevere in its religious policy with the double-message strategy which so far had proved such a success.

The eucharistic stance of the 1549 Prayer Book itself was an example of speaking with two voices. On the one hand, in constructing the service of eucharist and giving it a distinctive dynamic, Thomas Cranmer so manipulated the liturgical material at his disposal that his rite expressed the personal convictions which he had reached in the previous three years, and which he had spelled out in the December Lords debate – that is, that there is no corporal presence of Christ in bread and wine, and that the self-offering of Christ on the cross has nothing to do with the congregation's offering of thanksgiving in each individual eucharist. In this respect, as I have argued at length elsewhere, the eucharistic theology of the first Prayer Book was no different from that of the second, and it had parted company with Luther, let alone with Henry VIII.[61] However, this was not the whole story. Notoriously, there was enough scope for traditionalist ceremony in the book to scandalize foreign reformers not in Cranmer's confidence, and to enable its eucharist to be dressed up as something very like the old mass by those who wanted to. The book ostentatiously avoided committing itself to any one view of eucharistic doctrine in its catch-all title at the beginning of its eucharistic service: 'The supper of the Lord and the holy communion, commonly called the mass'.

That word 'mass', hated by evangelicals, including the king himself, had been generally absent from official statements during 1548, but its ungracious return now was probably the pilot which guided the liturgy past the shoals of conservative hostility in Parliament. The evangelicals could afford to put up with its presence, because the Prayer Book still did not constitute an official doctrinal statement on what the Church of

# THE SVPPER

### of the Lorde,and the holy Com-
### munion, commonly cal-
### led the Masse.

S O many as intende to bee partakers of the holy
Communion, shall sygnifie their names to the Curate,ouer night:or els in the morning, afore the beginning of Matins, or immediatly after.

And if any of those be an open and notorious e-
uill liuer,so that the congregacion by hym is offended, or haue
doen any wrong to his neighbours , by worde,or dede: The
Curate shall call hym,& aduertise hym,in any wise not to presume
to the lordes table, vntill he haue openly declared hymselfe,to haue
truly repented,and amended his former naughtie life:that the congregacion maie thereby be satisfied, whiche afore were offended:
and that he haue recompensed the parties,whom he hath dooen
wrong vnto, or at the least bee in full purpose so to doo , as sone
as he conueniently maie.

Thesame ordre shall the Curate vse , with those betwixt whom
he perceiueth malice,and hatred to reigne, not suffering them to
bee partakers of the Lordes table,vntill he knowe them to bee
reconciled.And yf one of the parties so at variance,be content
to forgeue from the botome of his harte,all that the other hath
trespaced against hym,and to make amendes for that he hymself
hath offended:and the other partie will not bee perswaded to a
godly vnitie,but remaigne still in his frowardnes and malice:
The Minister in that case,ought to admit the penitent persone to
the holy Communion,and not hym that is obstinate.

Vpon the daie,and at the tyme appointed for the ministracion
of the holy Communion,the Priest that shal execute the holy ministery , shall put vpon hym the vesture appoincted for that
ministracion , that is to saye: a white Albe plain , with a veste-
ment or Cope. And where there be many Priestes, or Decons,
there so many shalbe ready to helpe the Priest, in the ministracion,as shalbee requisite: And shall haue vpon theim lykewise,
the vestures appointed for their ministery , that is to saye , Al-
bes,with tunacles . Then shall the Clerkes syng in Englishe for
the office , or Introite,( as they call it) a Psalme appointed for
that daie.

F.j.          The

England believed about the eucharist. Liturgical practice was not based on a single theological statement: *lex credendi* (a rule for belief) was not in this case implied by *lex orandi* (a rule for worship). Even the catechism which the book contained failed to discuss the sacraments at all, uniquely among official catechisms of the period.[62] There can be no greater proof of the stopgap nature of the 1549 Prayer Book than this. Practising Anglicans who lived through the 1960s and 1970s may recall the proliferation of little floppy books which contained experimental services before the arrival of the *Alternative Service Book*: it is in this light that we might regard the Prayer Book of 1549. In Ireland it was allowed to endure throughout Edward's reign, but the Irish agents of Edwardian government were very cautious in their introduction of change, showing a greater sensitivity to the Irish situation than would be the case in later reigns: the compromises of the 1549 book proved well suited to the complexities of the Edwardian Irish Church.[63]

The absence of any officially defined eucharistic theology within the 1549 Prayer Book was spelled out in public by Richard Cox, Dean of Christ Church, Oxford, when he summed up four days of formal debate on the eucharist in Oxford University's Divinity School on 1 June 1549 – in other words, nearly three months after the Prayer Book was published. The Oxford debate was one of a pair held in the two universities in the presence of the royal visitors who had been sent to bring the universities into line on religion. Of the paired debates, that in Oxford was the more important, for conservatives were much stronger in Oxford than in Cambridge, and the evangelical case was led by the international star theologian Peter Martyr. The king himself annotated his copy of the officially published Latin account of the Oxford proceedings, picking out

*35. The first page of the communion service in the 1549 Book of Common Prayer, with its threefold title, reflecting three different theologies of the eucharist. In this copy, a Protestant user of the book has on this page angrily replaced the word 'mass' in the title with the word 'sacrament', and has gone through the whole service altering it for use in the shape of the 1552 rite. The opening instructions (rubrics) order the choir to sing a psalm in English, and they sidestep the use of the traditional eucharistic vestments by ordering the celebrant to wear a cope.*

rival arguments with partisan enthusiasm; the book sold well, not only in England, but also in Germany and Switzerland, leading to a second Zürich edition in 1552.[64] Cox, presiding at the debate, extravagantly praised Martyr's presentation of the case, emphasizing that he had 'singularly well answered the expectation of the great magistrates, yea, and of the king's majesty'. However, Cox also announced that he was not going to deliver a formal judgement about victory between champions of the government line and the conservative opposition, on the grounds that the time was not ripe: 'but it will then be decided when it seems good to the king's majesty, and to the leaders of the Church of England'.[65]

For the moment we will postpone consideration of whom Cox might have meant by the 'leaders of the Church', and note the steps which created England's official eucharistic theology. The first stage was the publication in summer 1550 of Archbishop Cranmer's *Defence of the true and Catholic doctrine of the sacrament of the body and blood of our saviour Christ.* Now there was no question of double messages. Cranmer had been drafting this book already in the contentious autumn of 1548, so Cox was disingenuous in talking of a future decision: the decision was there, only waiting a suitable time for announcement.[66] Cranmer's work emphasized on its title-page that it was written by the 'Primate of all England and Metropolitan', and it did no harm to the cause of evangelical consensus on the eucharist when the following year Cranmer was forced to amplify the message of the *Defence*, writing an *Answer* to a published attack by his imprisoned arch-rival Stephen Gardiner. The essence of Cranmer's exposition was to affirm a spiritual eucharistic presence granted by grace only to the elect believer, not to all who received bread and wine. Cranmer's modes of expressing this doctrine were closer to Bullinger's than to Calvin's interpretation of their agreement in the 1549 *Consensus Tigurinus.*[67] The next step was the creation of a liturgy which was a more obvious fit than the 1549 book for the theology of the *Defence* and the *Answer*. This was done by 1552, when Parliament passed the second Act of Uniformity, to which a new Prayer Book was annexed, and which declared the revision to be the only permissible liturgy in the

36. *The sumptuous fifteenth-century interior of the Divinity School of Oxford University, scene of the eucharistic debate in May and June 1549.*

realm. The third and final stage was the eucharistic discussion in the long-delayed doctrinal statement of the Edwardian Church, the Forty-Two Articles, published only a few weeks before the king's death.

Thus the process of defining what the regime believed about the eucharist stretches seamlessly from 1548 to 1553. It is evidence that neither the popular commotions of 1549 nor the transfer of power from the Duke of Somerset to John Dudley Earl of Warwick made a material difference to aims and objectives, only to strategy. Conservative noblemen joined the coup of October 1549 against Somerset, led by Wriothesley, the Lord

A. DEFENCE
OF THE TRVE AND CA-
tholike doctrine of the sacrament of the body and bloud
of our sauiour CHRIST, with
a confutation of sundry errors
concernyng thesame, groun-
ded and stablished vpon God-
des holy woorde, & approued
by ý consent of the moste auncient doctors of the Churche.
Made by the moste Reuerende
father in GOD
THOMAS ARCHEBYSHOP
of Canterbury, Primate of all
ENGLANDE
and Metropolitane.

Yt ys the spirite that giueth lyfe, the
fleshe profiteth nothinge. Ioannis.6.

Chancellor who had been ousted in 1547. However, the reality of the coup was that the evangelical establishment under Warwick's leadership had spearheaded Somerset's overthrow. The conservatives found themselves quickly outmanoeuvred and their concerns were given the most cursory consideration, whereas, within a few days of Somerset's surrender, the King's Privy Chamber was being reinforced with evangelical gentlemen and the Privy Council were making overtures to the reformed strongholds of Zürich and Berne for a General Council – in effect, an evangelical international. By the end of October a proclamation emphasized not only that none of Somerset's religious changes would be abrogated, but that the government would 'further do in all things, as time and opportunity may serve, whatsoever may lend to the glory of God and the advancement of his holy word'.[68]

The Spanish refugee Francis Dryander, always an acute observer who seems to have charmed people into giving him confidential information, was able to look back on what he had observed in England over that autumn of 1549 and tell Bullinger in Zürich that he had 'not only seen the outward and deplorable appearance of the change, but the purposes of the leading actors are well known to me ... religion is now in a better condition than it was before the imprisonment of the Protector'.[69] He was writing at the beginning of December, on the eve of a second and very differently led coup attempt which, in its failure, was one of the most decisive moments of the reign. The conservative grouping around Wriothesley now tried to isolate Warwick and associate him with Somerset in a treason charge; their defeat sidelined them from power and brought to an end any need to conciliate traditionalist opinion. On Christmas Day 1549 a royal circular to the bishops made this shift of power to the evangelicals brutally clear: it reinforced the

37. *The title-page of Cranmer's* Defence of the true and Catholic doctrine of the sacrament of the body and blood of our saviour Christ, *1550. Cranmer at last spelled out his mature eucharistic views. This copy has many sympathetic theological notes in both Latin and English, in a contemporary italic hand.*

message of the earlier proclamation by ordering the destruction of all Latin service books.[70] Bonfires of books followed all over England, reviving the set-piece public feasts of destruction seen in the royal visitation of 1547; and this time it was the bishops who willy-nilly were forced to act as masters of ceremonies. At last the revolution was secure.

During 1550, moreover, the episcopal bench itself witnessed a decisive shift in the balance of forces which had hobbled the pace of religious change throughout the Somerset years. Through confrontations with the newly aggressive government, plus one death and two forced retirements, conservatives lost no fewer than seven sees out of a total of twenty-seven. Bonner and Gardiner were already in gaol; by the end of 1550, Rugg of Norwich, Tunstall of Durham, Wakeman of Gloucester, and Day of Chichester had gone from their sees. Veysey of Exeter was negotiating the terms of his retirement, completed in 1551. All but one of these dioceses eventually went to evangelicals, and the one exception among the new bishops, Thomas Thirlby, was sent to Norwich as a way of removing him from the showcase city of Westminster, which was reunited with the diocese of London under the safe leadership of Nicholas Ridley.[71] Furthermore, Thirlby was an absentee diplomat not disposed to cause trouble, and he arrived at Norwich to find an evangelical *fait accompli*. Archbishop Cranmer had exploited his powers of visitation in a vacant see (*sede vacante*) to maintain the momentum set by the book-burning order: Norwich diocese became a guinea-pig for more general changes. In February 1550, Cranmer imposed as visitors on the unwilling and still very conservative clergy of the Norwich diocesan establishment his trusted household servants Rowland Taylor and William Wakefield.[72] One notes the significant contrast with Cranmer's action in a previous vacancy-in-see on 6 December 1549, that is, just before the failed conservative attempt at a second coup: when Gloucester diocese had fallen vacant on Bishop Wakeman's death, the Archbishop had granted the custody of spirituals to John Williams, a clergyman of the diocese who showed no signs of sympathy with the evangelical cause.[73]

Unlike Williams in Gloucester, Taylor and Wakefield seized the opportunity offered to them, and went to work in Norwich with zeal. They worked to visitation articles and injunctions which were a development of Cranmer's diocesan visitation articles of 1548; in turn their instructions formed the basis of subsequent visitation inquiries elsewhere. The Norwich articles and injunctions had certain novel features: they were notably alert for symptoms of Anabaptist belief in East Anglia, which presumably reflected official fears about the aftermath of the 1549 stirs. However, they also intensified the attack which Cranmer had made on traditionalism in the Canterbury diocese two years before. For instance they pitilessly specified a range of traditionalist ceremonial which could no longer be used to dress up the eucharistic rite of the 1549 Prayer Book as if it were 'the old popish mass': an abuse which was already infuriating reformers a few months after the book's publication.[74] Moreover, in typically Edwardian fashion, their actions outstripped their instructions on paper. Their articles still talked of altars, and even at one point mentioned 'the high altar', implying that there might be other altars within the church building. Yet in their relatively brief time in visitation, the visitors masterminded the destruction of stone altars throughout East Anglia, a pilot scheme which would be extended to the rest of the kingdom by the end of the year.

At the same time, now that the diocese of London was vacant through the deprivation of Edmund Bonner, Cranmer began formally exercising *sede vacante* jurisdiction there. This only gave legal sanction to existing reality; he had already been acting as *de facto* bishop of London in Bonner's place since the previous summer. So now, with the dioceses of Canterbury, London and Norwich at Cranmer's disposal, the capital and the entire English seaboard from the Wash to the Weald was under his direct control. He may have felt that London diocese demanded more high-powered action than Norwich, because a royal visitation of London was announced in February. Although no further proceedings can definitely be traced to this royal visitation, an unattributed set of articles very like those for Norwich may relate to it, and a month later the articles also seem to have been circulated throughout the kingdom in Edward's name. In any case, Nicholas Ridley drew on both this set

ARTICLES.

dynge of the Homilies oz scripture.

XXVII.   Item, whether you knowe any executours oz
administratours of dead mens goodes, whiche
doo not duely bestowe suche of the sayd goodes,
as were geuen and bequeathed, oz appoynted to
be distributed amonge the pooze people, repay-
ryng of high waies, fyndyng of pooze scholers,
oz marying of pooze maydens, oz such other lyke
charitable dedes.

XXVIII.   Item, whether you knowe any that speaketh
agaynst the baptisme of chyldzen, oz agaynst the
holy communion.

XXIX   Item, whether ye knowe any that say, that the
wickednes of the mynister doothe take away the
effecte of Chzist is sacramentes.

XXX.   Item, whether ye know any that say, that chzi-
sten men can neuer be allowed to repentaunce, yf
they synne voluntaryly after baptysme.

XXXI.   Item, whether ye knowe any that affirme all
thinges to be common, oz that there ought to be
no magistrates, gentlemen, oz riche menne, in
chzistian realmes.

XXXII.   Item, whether you knowe any that saye, that
chzistian men may not swere, oz take an othe be-
foze a iudge, oz go to lawe one with an other: oz
XXXIII   maye sweare contrary to the trewthe.

Item, whether ye know any that say, that pzi-
uate personnes may make insurrections, vpzozs
oz sedition: oz compell men by fozse oz feare, to
gyue them anye of theire goodes.

XXXIIII   Item, whether you knowe any that holdeth,
that

38. *Part of the visitation articles for Norwich diocese issued by Cranmer's visitors during the vacancy of the see, winter 1550. This page, dealing mainly with inquiries about radical and Anabaptist belief, has manuscript additions presumably made by the visitors in the course of their work, and intensifying their concerns about absence from church.*

and the Norwich articles and injunctions when he held his own visitation as Bishop of London later in the year.[75] By 1552 even Bishop Bulkeley's remote Welsh diocese of Bangor was facing a developed version of the articles which Cranmer's henchmen had devised for Norwich and London back in winter 1550.[76]

After the pace set by Cranmer that winter, Edwardian religious policy hardly needs description. Even while the young king was dying, its destructive consequences were still unfolding, as the nation's churches were robbed of their traditional ornaments, bells and plate. However, two factors slowed down further positive change. One was the question of priorities between national and international reformation. Cranmer's dearest wish was to create a general council of reformers which would outshine the false Council of Trent, and to draw up unifying doctrinal statements for the reformed universal Church. I have argued elsewhere that it was only when the major continental reformers showed themselves lukewarm to any immediate meeting that England was compelled to issue its own doctrinal statement, the Forty-Two Articles, long-postponed but finally issued in 1553.[77] The lack of concerted international action was a disappointment for Cranmer, but there was a second and far more damaging problem: the gulf which opened up between Cranmer's clerical circle and John Dudley, Duke of Northumberland. In autumn 1549 Cranmer had played an equivocal role in the events which had led to Somerset's fall and Dudley's arrival in power: the Archbishop had done what the Primate of All England should in the circumstances, reassuring his godson the king that all was well, and acting to lower the political temperature. Thereafter, through that tense time, he had been Dudley's firm ally in his struggle to keep the conservatives at bay. Similarly, Cranmer probably saw the inevitability of the Duke of Somerset's second removal from the Council in autumn 1551, after Somerset's political behaviour became more erratic and dangerous for the evangelical cause.[78]

During winter 1552, however, Somerset was not merely disgraced but executed. This ruthless excess was only one of a whole range of issues which provoked a breach between the religious and secular leaders of

LORDS SUPPER

39. *This illustration to a catechism for the Church of England, published in 1674,*
*still assumes the arrangements for celebrating the eucharist pioneered in the reign of*
*Edward VI: no altar at the east end, but a table set lengthways in the chancel*
*for the communion service.*

the evangelical establishment. The split was never complete, mainly thanks to the vital role played by the royal servant William Cecil in maintaining communications between the two sides, but it was serious enough.[79] Three basic elements in structuring the Edwardian religious revolution all suffered delay: doctrinal statement, revised liturgy and the new scheme of canon law. If the Forty-Two Articles were held up mainly because of the Archbishop's hopes for some greater international action, no such idealism can be detected in the case of the other two projects. The Prayer Book, revised to remove the embarrassing traditionalist survivals in the 1549 book, was accepted by Parliament and stood complete in spring 1552, but, unlike its predecessor, it was not given an immediate release to the public, but was kept under wraps until the autumn.

One might argue that the postponement in issuing the Prayer Book was in order to avoid the sort of trouble which the 1549 book had caused in some parts of the country, but in 1552 there was no especial security scare to justify the long delay. That summer was the first in which the regime permitted itself some measure of relaxation, and the king set out on his first major cross-country progress through southern England. So, rather than any security worries, the delay is likely to indicate the troubled state of relations within the regime itself. This was certainly the case when the publication of the book was further obstructed at the last moment, by a row over kneeling at communion provoked by Northumberland's imported Scots protégé John Knox. In this contest, Cranmer only defeated Knox by some passionately confrontational politicking with the Privy Council, and by the addition to the Prayer Book text of the so-called 'black rubric', making it clear that kneeling at communion did not imply any adoration of the eucharistic elements – a rubric only 'black' because it was a last-minute insertion, and therefore had to be printed at first in black, rather than in the red of the book's other instructions and explanations.[80] A more permanent disaster was the ignominious fate of the revision of canon law, Cranmer's pet project for two decades. It marked time for most of 1552 and in the end Northumberland himself spitefully vetoed the completed draft in the spring Parliament of 1553, for reasons to be examined in Chapter 3.[81] Only in the last few months did the dire prospect of losing all the gains of six years, backed up by the intervention of the dying king, reunite the evangelical leadership behind the gamble to alter the succession away from the Lady Mary and in favour of Lady Jane Grey. This gamble would have worked, if English politics had been confined to the council chamber. Alas for the revolution, the provinces had other ideas, and decisively humbled central government in an action which had no close parallel in the Tudor age.

If we review this sketch of Edwardian religious policy, we observe a driving, unrelenting energy behind it. Sir Richard Morison, an ex-Cromwellian who was one of the lesser members of the Edwardian evangelical establishment, looked back from his Marian exile with pride on the speed of it all: 'The greater change was never wrought in so short space in any country sith the world was.'[82] The continuity for this programme across the apparent political disruption of 1549 was provided by one man: Thomas Cranmer. By 1547 Cranmer was one of the longest serving figures in politics, with a nationwide clerical clientage mostly sharing his Cambridge background, and with a network of overseas contacts which still remains shadowy in its extent. Throughout the 1530s he had been able to leave secular politics to the ruthless skills of Henry's minister Thomas Cromwell, but any evangelical politician who managed to survive the Henrician court after Cromwell's destruction had received a formidable political training. Cranmer weathered the so-called 'Prebendaries' Plot' of 1543, in which some of the most formidable conservatives in the land combined in an effort to bring him down; he also survived the dangerous summer of 1546, when many of those he knew were arrested or even burned. He and his staff had learned much about tactics and strategy.

If anyone could have kept a sense of coherence among the evangelicals in the Privy Council as they grew steadily more alarmed at Somerset's populist antics, it was Cranmer. He was the one Edwardian bishop to live in the style of the other noblemen on the Council, maintaining his four palaces and his military resources as the equal of any

40. *Edward VI presiding at the opening of the last parliament of his reign,*
*spring 1553; this had to take place in Whitehall rather than in Westminster because*
*of the state of his health. The Chancellor and Lord Treasurer stand flanking the*
*throne; the bishops (on the left) are still shown wearing mitres, which, if an accurate*
*representation, would have infuriated some of them. Soon Edward would be too*
*ill to appear in public, and the formal harmony of this scene was belied*
*by the contention in this parliament.*

other magnate.[83] No doubt we ought to look elsewhere for the detailed orchestration of policy: principally to the 'master of practices', William Paget, ally to Cranmer and Seymour from Henry VIII's last years into Edward's reign.[84] Yet Cranmer is always to be found at the centre of government action until the chill descended in his relations with Northumberland in 1552: he was equally involved in the two-voice policy of the Somerset years and then in the newly unleashed religious aggression perceptible from December 1549.

John Knox, reproaching Queen Mary's persecutions in his *First Blast of the Trumpet against the Monstrous Regiment of Women*, called Cranmer 'the mild man of God': a judgement both inaccurate and generous, considering that in the 1552 row over kneeling at communion, the Scots reformer had experienced at first hand the streak of ruthlessness which lay beneath the surface in the Archbishop's character.[85] An examination of Cranmer's career reveals how repeatedly ends justified means for him, so that he could cut legal corners to get the result he wanted, and even turn the prose of his enemies inside out in his liturgical work, to redeploy it in the service of the revolution.[86] His instinct for self-preservation has often been mocked, but the story of supple adaptation in his public career had more to it than that: Cranmer displayed that inflexible determination to further the evangelical goal by fair means or foul which I have identified as the keynote of Edwardian policy. If anyone ensured that King Edward could play the role of King Josiah successfully and comprehensively, it was his godfather, the Primate of All England. Alcibiades Cranmer was not, but in the drama of the Edwardian Reformation, neither was he Polonius.

# 3

# King Solomon: Building
# the Temple

So far this study has concentrated on the less inspiring aspects of the official Edwardian Reformation: its politicking and its destruction of traditional religion. A negative image of Edwardian religion has prevailed since the early nineteenth century, the result of disapproval from both Roman Catholics and (within the Church of England itself) Anglo-Catholics. The distinguished Anglo-Catholic church historian Bishop Walter Frere would speak for many when in 1910 he contemplated the six years after 1547 and dismissed them as 'the lowest depth to which the English Church has ever sunk'.[1] In recent decades, 'revisionist' historiography of the English Reformation and some historians of the late medieval parish have echoed that dismissal of one Edwardian age by another. Eamon Duffy has written a moving study of the Devon parish of Morebath, in which the Reformation of Edward VI appears as an unmitigated disaster imposed by alien forces, wrecking not just the beauty of the parish church but also the intricate and orderly structure of village life and the financial system which sustained it. Bishop Frere would have recognized a kindred spirit in Christopher Trychay, parish priest of Morebath for half a century, for whom in the 'time of King Edward the VI, the church ever decayed'; and it was small wonder that the parishioners of Morebath paid for their young men to join the Western rebels in 1549.[2] Here, King Josiah brought vandalism and parochial bankruptcy; and many studies of churchwardens' accounts have told a similar story.[3]

But not everyone felt the same way as the villagers of Morebath. To

write the history of the Edwardian Reformation from churchwardens'
accounts and parish records is positively to invite a negative view of
what happened, as the comfortable formulae of a settled system broke
down under the strain of sudden change. Unless an archival accident
hits on a parish of evangelical zealots, the theme of the wardens' payments will be the decline from a rich devotional life to its steady im-
poverishment and dismantling: there will be the added indignity for
the parish of frequent payments to government representatives for the
privilege of telling it what should be dismantled. It is also a curious
phenomenon that parish accounts have survived particularly well in the
south-west of England, which was undoubtedly one of the most conservative parts of the kingdom, and this may exaggerate the negative
verdict in the records.[4] Revolutions are in any case not best glimpsed
in account books, but in contemporary subjective judgments and stray
remarks, frail traces of past moods and emotions. Such a task is fraught
with danger of misrepresentation and wishful thinking, but it may be the
best way of seeing what was positive in the Edwardian Reformations: to
whom they appealed, and why.

Let us first put side by side some contrasting pictures of consumer
reaction. Negative material is easy to find. Many people voted with
their feet against the new services, judging from repeated official efforts
to get them back. Absenteeism from church may not have been new, but
now it represented a statement of opinion on government policy. The
second Edwardian Act of Uniformity (which authorized and enforced
the use of the second Prayer Book of 1552) openly acknowledged that 'a
great number of people, in divers parts of this realm' were refusing to
come to their parish churches. Surviving inquiry articles for bishops'
visitations are also alert for the missing churchgoers. Already in 1548
Archbishop Cranmer was worried about people ostentatiously leaving
church during sermons or the English parts of the service, or abandoning their parish churches altogether for nearby churches with a more
congenial atmosphere. Similarly, Bishop Hooper in Gloucester diocese
in 1551 was aware not only of absentees but also of those who shopped
around to find the Prayer Book performed in a traditionalist fashion: he

demanded to know whether the laity of the diocese 'refuse their own parish, and frequent and haunt other, where as the communion is more like a mass than in his own: or whether he take the communion where as he knoweth his faith shall not be examined'.[5]

Both episcopal inquiries and leading evangelical preachers commented on deliberate disruption of the new services and expressions of boredom at homilies and sermons. 'Surely it is an ill misorder that folk shall be walking up and down in the sermon-time, as I have seen in the place this Lent: and there shall be such huzzing and buzzing in the preacher's ear, that it maketh him oftentimes to forget his matter': this was the complaint of England's star evangelical preacher, Hugh Latimer, about the most fashionable preaching-place of the realm, the king's pulpit in the Whitehall Privy Garden.[6] Moreover, the Edwardian Church failed as badly as John Calvin in Geneva in its effort to establish the eucharist as the community's chief weekly service. The royal letter to the bishops on Christmas Day 1549 already complained about this, and admitted that one of the main problems was widespread resentment at the requirement that householders should provide bread and wine for the whole parish on a rota basis.[7] Bishop Ridley seems already to have acknowledged defeat in London diocese in summer 1550: he urged frequent communion, but he sought merely to enforce the medieval requirement of once-a-year communion which many reformers deplored.[8]

However, we need to remember that Queen Mary's government after 1553 also had a problem getting people to church. One Spanish courtier, travelling from Portsmouth to London for the royal wedding of Mary to Philip of Spain in spring 1554, noted poor and grudging attendance at mass when there was no official scrutiny. A Venetian diplomat, in a careful report home the following summer, hinted at a noticeable degree of absenteeism, and thought that a majority of the population was dissatisfied with Mary's religious policy.[9] The London stationer and Marian propagandist Miles Huggarde, writing about London two years later in Mary's reign, produced a diatribe which could have come from the mouth of an Edwardian evangelical preacher: 'nothing is less used than morning and evening prayer, more unreverence in the church never more frequented ... repairing to the churches, is counted a thing of no importance'.[10] One interpretation of this absenteeism from the services of both Edward and Mary might be that it was the manifestation of a superficial Christianization within England and Europe generally: the consequence of a religion which had been skin-deep before the Reformation upheavals was that it became still more thinly spread in the confused conditions of the mid sixteenth century. However, the whole trend of recent detailed research on late medieval England – the work of historians like Eamon Duffy, Ronald Hutton, Beat Kümin or John Craig – suggests a broadly based medieval Western church which had intimately engaged the population in a complex and rich life of devotional practice. If that is so, it was not so much indifference as trauma which emptied the pews in the early Reformation: a polarization of religious attitudes, not an abandonment of religion. The background to the fresh crop of Marian absentees was an Edwardian success story which had bred real hostility to Queen Mary's reversal of religion.

From the outset of Edward's reign, the imperial ambassador Van der Delft and his secretary had been gloomily impressed with the impact of the Protestant Reformation on ordinary people below the level of the gentry: they repeatedly reported how the 'common people', encouraged by dramatic preaching, had turned against traditional religion.[11] This is confirmed by Marian complaints about what the Edwardian clergy had achieved. The zealous Catholic churchman Nicholas Harpsfield, who as Cardinal Pole's Archdeacon of Canterbury had first-hand knowledge of one of the most Protestant areas of England, bewailed the fact that Cranmer, Ridley and Latimer had corrupted the minds of the common people (*plebis animos*) in their snares of evil opinions.[12] The same impression is gained from the writings of Miles Huggarde and Dean John Christopherson: both Marian propagandists made a particular point of reformist religion's appeal to London apprentices. Huggarde sketches a portrait of sulky street-corner teenagers which is alarmingly recognizable – however, worse still, these were rebels with a cause and with a Bible: 'no regard they have at all to repair to the church upon the holy days, but flock in clusters upon stalls, either scorning the passers-by, or with their testaments utter some wise stuff of their own device'. Christopherson complained that such servants and apprentices 'count themselves witty, if they can make a merry mock at the Mass, and at the ceremonies thereof, and jest at priests, God's ministers, and prate and babble against the holy sacraments of the church, and the divine service done therein'.[13]

One obvious feature of these anecdotal contrasts is the concentration of evangelical enthusiasm in the capital and the south-east. Foreign diplomats inevitably had a metropolitan perspective, which led the imperial ambassador's secretary to talk of 'the north' when he meant Norfolk. On one occasion Van der Delft said specifically that he was describing the religious atmosphere in the London area.[14] This geography can readily be confirmed in more detail from the biographical listing of pre-1558 evangelicals compiled over the last few decades by John Fines.[15] Fines was able to assign a principal place of adult residence to 2,443 of his individuals, excluding twenty-six living in Wales. Rather more than half of these can be given a social ranking; they range across the whole social spectrum, from gentry and clergy down to husbandmen and labourers, but the largest single group, about a third of the whole, consists of skilled craftsmen or tradesmen. What we are looking at in Fines's figures is a sample only, and no expanded version of it will ever tell us the actual extent of evangelical strength in early Tudor England. Nevertheless, the sample is reasonable enough in size to give an idea of the regional distribution of those who favoured the Edwardian changes.

In Fines's statistics, London is in the lead with 17 per cent of the total. Clearly success bred success: London provided perfect conditions for the conversion of migrants, cut off from the religious practice of their home communities, and the city would attract existing enthusiasts from all over England and Wales anxious to escape the restrictive atmosphere at home. It offered a sympathetic community and security even during the uncertain Henrician years. After Henry's 1543 restriction on Bible-reading, one evangelical commented that London was the only

41. *The scale of London made it utterly different from any other English town. The density of its population can be gauged from the multitude of parishes, each here marked with a church steeple on the skyline of what is only a section of Visscher's early-seventeenth-century panoramic view of the city. Even London Bridge, seen here from Southwark, was covered in housing.*

place in England where the Bible placed in parish churches was still being widely read and the royal injunctions promulgated in Thomas Cromwell's time still properly observed. A further remark of his, while pitched for pessimistic effect, also highlights the contrast between the capital and the benighted provinces: 'the tenth man in London neither the hundredth man in the whole realm knoweth the gospel'.[16] In Fines's figures, the counties nearest the capital provide the greatest proportion of evangelicals after London itself, led by Essex at 14 per cent of the total and Kent at 12 per cent; Suffolk and Norfolk between them score 15 per cent, with the majority in Suffolk. So overall, the capital and the south-eastern seaboard counties make up nearly three fifths of the total. Next are the Thames and Severn river-systems as far west as Bristol. Beyond that, to the south as well as the north and the west, the proportions are uniformly low. The lowest proportions of all come from the four counties of the south-west, Somerset, Dorset, Devon, Cornwall, where the combined total is no more than 2.5 per cent.

Now this distribution of known evangelical individuals represents an imperfect fit to the official forces either promoting or resisting reformation from the 1530s. The geography of the Fines statistics mirrors something other than a reformation from above: it is a set of independent movements which had begun as dissent from official orthodoxy. In London, official and unofficial reformations most readily coincided. Naturally a state as centralized as Tudor England concentrated resources on the capital, and the religious practice of Edward's court must have been influential within its quite restricted orbit around London in the Thames Valley from Greenwich to Windsor. There were plenty of parishes in the capital ready to mount extrovert displays of reformed worship in imitation, and we have already noted the way in which Westminster became a showcase for Edwardian official policy.[17] However, London must not be oversimplified as a predominantly evangelical city. It defies crude categorization as radical or conservative: it was a city different in scale from any other in the British Isles, a place of extremes, where lay and secular hierarchies conflicted in complex ways and where there was a good deal of freedom to make up one's own mind.[18]

A similarly ambiguous conclusion can be drawn from John Fines's figures for evangelical Oxford and Cambridge graduates. The numbers differ between the two universities less than one might expect from the common stereotype of Cambridge in the vanguard of evangelical reform and Oxford as the home of a lost traditionalist cause: there are 207 from Cambridge and 189 from Oxford. Cambridge's very modest lead should be slightly accentuated since it was probably a little smaller than mid-Tudor Oxford, but it is interesting that the undoubted bias towards conservatism among Oxford's leadership and teaching staff does not seem to have produced a more marked bias among the student population. Students made up their own minds, with all the intellectual resources and opportunities of the universities at their disposal and, then as now, the opinions of their tutors were not necessarily the strongest influence on them.[19]

If we leave the capital and the universities, and try to assess the interplay between official and unofficial reformations, Kent's prominent place in Fines's figures is not surprising, because of Archbishop Cranmer's consistent drive to promote his evangelical cause since his coming to Canterbury in 1533. However, Suffolk and Norfolk developed evangelical strength in defiance of the robustly conservative clerical hierarchy of Norwich diocese.[20] Similarly, the tally of reforming sympathizers in the two great river systems in southern England down to Bristol cannot simply be accounted for by sporadic influence from various evangelical bishops in the region – Shaxton, Latimer and Hooper. Most higher clergy in those areas continued unsympathetic through King Henry's time. In these regions and in East Anglia we are observing the independent effect of Lollardy, that movement of dissent against the official church which had sprung in the late fourteenth century from the ideas of John Wyclif. Persecuted out of the universities and of polite society by fifteenth-century church and state authorities, the Lollards had persisted in a certain strength in well-defined areas of lowland England: their identifiable distribution at the beginning of the Tudor age foreshadowed the regions where mid-Tudor evangelicals came to be concentrated. In Kent, Lollards could welcome Cranmer's coming and adapt themselves to his forward policies; in Norwich and by the Severn and by Thamesside, they waited for better times than Henry VIII afforded them. By contrast, in southern counties with little Lollard prehistory, evangelicals were fewer in numbers, and in such areas conservative clerical leadership helped to maintain traditional religion in forms more often associated with distant parts of the kingdom.

Winchester diocese, that is, the counties of Hampshire and Surrey, provides an instructive comparison with Norwich. Here, in a similar lowland setting, a conservative governing élite managed to set the local agenda. Evangelical polemicist, playwright and clergyman John Bale was briefly beneficed in Edwardian Hampshire, and for once he had good cause to indulge his lifelong state of righteous indignation. He has

42. *The jumble of buildings which made up Lambeth Palace seen from the
east, with the parish church of St Mary to the left, and over the river to the right the
vill of Westminster; by the eighteenth century, the towers of Westminster Abbey had
been completed. Cranmer's archiepiscopal administration, though based here on the
Thames near the heart of government, effectively encouraged the precocious
development of evangelical religion in Kent.*

left us a series of vivid vignettes of the harassment which he endured
from powerful local conservatives in his *Expostulation or complaynte
agaynste the blasphemyes of a franticke papyst of Hamshyre*. He reveals that
the combination of Bishop Gardiner and his entourage, plus clergy of
the cathedral and Winchester College and like-minded lay magnates,
had spectacularly prolonged older religious habits into Edward's reign.
A continuing group of nuns was still able to maintain their communal
life in the city of Winchester, alarming even Gardiner's traditionalist
diocesan officials by insisting on wearing their habits in public, 'and
utterly contemning the preachings that are now'.[21] This formidable

female defiance of King Henry's monastic dissolutions surely ended with the arrival of Bishop Ponet in 1551. Certainly about that time in another part of Winchester diocese, the newly ordained John Foxe began his public career by suppressing one of the last shrines in England. This was a Marian cult sited near Reigate, showing that only ten miles or so from Archbishop Cranmer's favourite palace at Croydon, the devout people of Surrey could behave as if they lived in the remoteness of Wales or Ireland.[22] Religious conservatism persisted among the gentry of Winchester diocese in Elizabeth's reign, to form the basis of an unusually strong Roman Catholic recusancy.[23]

The presence or absence of Lollardy was thus one fundamental element in the regional shape of popular reformation. Within its south-eastern base, evangelical religion had a history, a tradition of reformation by self-help. Dissent spread outwards through England's internal trade routes, creating other lesser nuclei of evangelical enthusiasm in manufacturing or market towns. A different impulse to reformation came newly imported from abroad through a chain of seaports. The great historian of the English Reformation, Geoffrey Dickens, has pointed out that every port of any significance around the coast between Hull and Exeter offers early reformers in the Fines biographies. Up to 1558 those ports included the last remnant of the medieval English dominions in France, Calais: a vital window on Europe for England, and a garrison town which recruited soldiers from the remotest parts of the realm and exposed them to the newest ideas. Calais has an importance in the English Reformation which remains to be assessed.[24] For another great port, Bristol, the conservative West Country preacher Roger Edgeworth rather less sympathetically prefigured Dickens's observation, from his own experience of ministry there in the mid-1540s. He ranked the arrival of evangelical religion on the dockside along with *haute couture* and venereal disease: 'where little concourse of strangers is, there is plain manner of living ... but in port towns they be of another sort. The Germans and Saxons bring in their opinions. The Frenchmen their new fashions. Other countries given to lechery, run to the open bars or stews.'[25]

England's own coastal shipping then redistributed these various commodities, creating further bridgeheads for reformism in more remote ports, even beyond the boundaries of the kingdom into the rest of the archipelago. English trade with western Scotland may account for the presence around the port of Ayr of the only traceable Scots Lollards, well before the Luther explosion; an early Reformation persisted around Ayr, showing strong English links into Elizabeth's reign. Further down the Scottish coast at Dumfries, the inhabitants felt positively enough about the English invaders of 1548 to ask them for a Great Bible and a preacher, and it is remarkable that pro-English feeling in the western Highlands seems to have survived throughout the 1540s despite the brutal ineptitude of English official policy towards Scotland.[26] One also wonders about the Scots east-coast pirates who preyed on the ships of the Holy Roman Emperor's subjects in 1550, using the East Anglian evangelical stronghold of Ipswich as their base; was this an entirely unholy alliance between Suffolk and Scotland?[27]

Looking at this geography of religious opinion, it is clear that evangelicals remained a minority of the population, albeit a minority placed in the wealthiest and most influential part of the country. Even in their heartlands, they would have been outnumbered in the 1540s by those who viewed the Edwardian Reformation in the fashion of the parish priest of Morebath. Eamon Duffy has drawn our attention not only to Morebath in the West Country, but also across the country to the traditionalist devotional life of East Anglia. This was manifested in community generosity still visible in the region's late medieval church furnishings: the provision of furniture, especially rood screens, was still running its course in the 1530s in full strength.[28] Yet the significant fact about East Anglia is that there was a spectacular transformation within forty years of Edward's death. As a Jesuit missioner commented in the early 1590s, outside a network of Catholic gentry families, this was now a region of 'most fierce Protestants'.[29] The new mood in East Anglia did not so much represent the disappearance of white-hot devotion as a radical turn-around in its direction. The intensely devout became convinced that the Church had played a confidence trick on them

by diverting their devotion to the performance of ritual and charitable works. Edwardian preachers told them not so much that the old
system did not work, but that it had no right to work; so the devout
desperately needed to find a structured alternative, and the preachers
had it to hand. The impact was greatest in the south-east because that
is where provision for evangelical preaching first achieved effective
coverage.

The difficulty for the leaders of conservative opinion in resisting the
evangelical message was to present a coherent and exciting alternative.
The prime problem amid Edwardian gradualism was deciding at what
point change should be resisted: some conservatives seem genuinely to
have been trying to honour the government's frequent calls for unity.
What does one make, for instance, of a tract produced in 1549 by John
Proctor, a conservative Kentish schoolmaster? In this *Fal of the late Arrian*,
Proctor (who would write once more in Mary's reign, to describe and to
condemn the Protestant-inspired rebellion of 1554 led by Sir Thomas
Wyatt) denounced and refuted in detail the confession of faith of an
unnamed intellectual who had been examined by the Privy Council and
by Archbishop Cranmer for his Arian denial of the full divinity of Jesus
Christ. Proctor dedicated his work to the Lady Mary, whom he likened
to Mary the Mother of God, 'your Grace's celestial pattern'; his reader-
ship would certainly have known of the princess's conservative religious
views. He also unfashionably prefaced his text with woodcuts of the
Annunciation and the Holy Family; yet he quoted the Athanasian Creed
in the newly published version in the Book of Common Prayer, and
he extravagantly praised Henry VIII ('That heavenly Josias I say') for
expelling the Pope and authorizing the Bible, 'that comfortable light, that
pleasant food of souls'.[30] Was this meant to be a helpful gesture for the
official Reformation, or was it a subtle denunciation of it, aligning evangelicals with unacceptable radicals and implying that Cranmer was soft
on heresy? Proctor certainly managed to smuggle into his text a good
many critical sneers at mainstream evangelicals: 'within England I say,
where every man, every woman pretendeth to be a gospeller, every
boy, each girl trained and exercised in reading the holy Scripture of

*43. John Proctor's* The fal of the late Arrian *of 1549 was illustrated with a woodcut of the Annunciation (emphasizing the divine origins of the Christ-child) immediately opposite its dedication to Princess Mary: a highly traditionalist form for an attack on Arianism, which had the potential to embarrass or annoy evangelicals.*

Jesus Christ'. Was this gratuitous abuse, or constructive schoolmasterly criticism?

Proctor's intention is thus difficult to read; he may be genuinely try-ing to establish a conservative version of the middle ground as a defence against religious radicalism, just as the evangelical Bishop Ridley had set out to do with Bishop Gardiner back in summer 1547 (above, Chapter 2, p. 68). Similarly, when evangelicals such as John Hooper angrily denounced performances of the 1549 eucharistic rite dressed up with the panoply of traditional ceremony 'like a mass', they may have

assumed duplicity where there was a genuine attempt to be concilia-
tory, in the same fashion as many evangelicals in the last years of Henry
VIII. Conservatives, faced with an unsympathetic regime, had to decide
what they now made of Henry VIII's ambiguous theological legacy. One
could resist change as the Lady Mary did, by insisting that her traditionalism was only obedience to Henry VIII's laws, but the strategy of
relying on the eccentric opinions of the old king brought its own embarrassments.[31] For instance, when Richard Smith defended the efficacy
of masses for the dead, he felt constrained to respect Henry's dislike of
the name purgatory, and conservative reluctance to name or defend
purgatory persisted into the Edwardian period. In 1552 the veteran
champions of traditional religion in the diocese of Worcester, Canons
Henry Joliffe and Robert Johnson, vigorously debated matters of belief
with their bishop, John Hooper, in what became a no-holds-barred literary contest. On purgatory, however, they trod very warily: 'the name
purgatory is none of our business'. In another area of contention, Robert
Crowley teased the newly conservative Nicholas Shaxton in 1548: how
could Henrician conservatives defend vows of clerical celibacy, since
they had apparently been happy to see monks, friars and nuns forced to
break their vows when they discarded their habits in Henry's monastic
dissolutions? It was an effective thrust, even though technically it was
inaccurate, since Henry had sought to maintain celibacy for the ex-
religious. The wider point was that most conservatives had accepted the
monastic dissolutions with apparent equanimity.[32]

The biggest problem was, of course, the Pope. The Venetian envoy in
1551 noted that no one either of the old or the new religion could bear to
hear his name; and yet a coherent defence of the Catholic faith was very
difficult without reference to the papacy.[33] On this matter, once more
Canons Henry Joliffe and Robert Johnson found themselves treading an
increasingly fragile Henrician line against their uncongenial father-in-
God John Hooper in 1552: they refused to assent to Hooper's assertion
that the Roman Church had erred in matters of faith, but they were prepared rather grudgingly to quote St Bernard's twelfth-century criticisms
of papal excesses in jurisdiction. Bishop Gardiner, writing a few months

later from his prison cell in the Tower of London to defend Joliffe and Johnson against Hooper's triumphant riposte, also scented the problem: he sidestepped altogether the question of the Pope.[34] Peter Martyr had exploited the same conservative weakness when he presented the evangelical case at the great 1549 Oxford disputation about the eucharist: for instance, how could the doyen of Oxford conservative dons, Dr William Chedzey, defend the doctrine of eucharistic transubstantiation by reference to the Lateran Council of 1215, without bringing in papal authority? The council, after all, had been called by the Pope, and had been convened in his Lateran Palace in Rome.[35]

Most troublesome of all was the fact (also gleefully exploited by Martyr in the same 1549 debate with Chedzey) that the most effective modern champion of traditional orthodoxy was John Fisher, late Bishop of Rochester, Henry VIII's *bête noire* and an attainted traitor, executed in 1535 – an execution then defended by Bishop Gardiner with a literary skill which subsequently became an embarrassment to that prelate. In reply to Martyr's teasing citation of Fisher's work, the best riposte that Chedzey could make was the rather lame and sulky 'But I am not now embarking on a defence of the bishop of Rochester.' Conservative theologians could use Fisher's work, but they were reluctant to name him. Bishop George Day, who had once been Fisher's chaplain, showed a rare courage when he cited the martyred Bishop of Rochester openly in the Lords eucharistic debate of 1548: Day pointedly did so in order to correct citations from the Church Fathers by the present Bishop of Rochester, Nicholas Ridley.[36]

Despite such ideological difficulties, in 1549 many thousands of English parishioners did decide that enough was enough in Edward's religious proceedings, and took to arms against the new English Prayer Book. Yet the commotions which followed in that spring and summer revealed stark regional polarities in attitudes to the Reformation. Devon and Cornwall's rage in their 'Prayer Book rebellion' about religious changes imposed from outside was enough to outweigh the long-lived tensions between the two counties; the historian of the rebellion, Joyce Youings, has drawn attention to the leadership role played by Robert

44. *Bishop John Fisher: a drawing by Hans Holbein the Younger, c. 1532, on the eve of Fisher's political disgrace. The image was much copied, testifying to the reverence in which the bishop's memory was held, but theologically he was a non-person during Edward's reign.*

Welsh, a priest who had been born in Cornwall but who had a parish in the suburbs of Exeter.[37] Oxfordshire commotions in July also prominently figured conservative clergy, parish priests from the north of the county, four of whom the government promptly executed once it had regained control of the situation. In August there were belated attempts at rebellion in Yorkshire and Hampshire, both involving traditionalist religious rhetoric: the Hampshire rebels commissioned a banner with the symbols of chalice and five wounds: the same combination which had led the Pilgrimage of Grace back in 1536 against Henry VIII's Reformation.[38] However, by contrast, the heartland of the other set of rebellions in spring and summer 1549 – what contemporaries called the 'camping time' – was the region which we have already found identified in John Fines's statistics as containing the greatest concentrations of evangelicals: the south-east and East Anglia. In these areas, the thousands of protestors who gathered in camps displayed very different religious sympathies: they looked for further reformation of the Church, they were happy to use the new Prayer Book, and they used the religious buzzwords familiar to Somerset's governing circle.

We have always had a considerable body of evidence about the religious sympathies of the 1549 south-eastern commotions. Their reformist character was widely noted at the time, and it was even obliquely acknowledged in the Elizabethan homily against rebellion, which made no attempt to include them among its list of risings fomented by the Pope.[39] Now we can add as witnesses the nine official letters preserved

*45. A silk badge survives from the Pilgrimage of Grace of 1536, showing the traditionalist symbolism revived on a Hampshire banner in 1549: the five wounds of Christ on the cross, the fifth of which is represented by a bleeding heart-shaped eucharistic host over the chalice.*

by Robert Beale and rediscovered by Ethan Shagan: the letters sent to various camps in July 1549. These reveal Somerset praising 'the seditious persons in Essex' because 'by the allegation of sundry texts of scripture ... ye do acknowledge the Gospel which ye say ye greatly hunger [for]'. So the Essex leaders had been enthusiastically marshalling biblical texts when they addressed the Privy Council. Somerset used this as a springboard to shame them, by pointing out that they ought to take seriously the Bible's message of obedience, 'the principal lesson of Scripture to subjects'.[40] Two paired letters in the name of Edward VI plugged the same theme to the Norfolk and Suffolk commons respectively, on the same basis as the Essex folk, that they were 'professing Christ's doctrine in words'. Here were evangelicals arguing with each other in evangelical terms.[41] Even in conservative Hampshire, there were two varieties of rebellion during the summer of 1549: this was a borderland county where the two contrasting worlds of west and east met. For whereas in August one set of Hampshire men was prepared to revive the symbolism of the Pilgrimage of Grace on their banner, a month before that, another group had been among the insurgents who had submitted to the Privy Council, declared themselves for its religious policy, and said that they were ready to fight under the government's commander, John Lord Russell, against the Western rebels.[42]

Coupled with evangelical rhetoric and practice in the eastern stirs was their stress on the rhetoric of commonwealth, with all its associated ideas of remedy and redress of grievances. This potent word of the Tudor political vocabulary was so important to them that in Kent those taking part were known as 'commonwealths', and the stirs were known later as 'the Rebellion of Commonwealth'. The Kentish leader Latimer (who has often been confused with Bishop Hugh Latimer simply on the basis of the coincidence of their surnames) was called 'the Commonwealth of Kent', or simply as 'Captain Commonwealth' when his operations extended to Surrey and Sussex.[43] Here the commons showed that their combination of ideas was very similar to those set out in the writings of the evangelical government servant John Hales; and this was not just a temporary marriage of convenience.[44] An anonymous manuscript treatise now in the British Library pushes the combination of evangelical enthusiasm and radical commonwealth ideas back into the last years of Henry VIII.[45] Addressed to Henry himself, it is dateable to 1544 or 1545. Its main concern, larded with much praise for Henry VIII's achievements as a reformer, is to analyse and provide radical remedy for the failings of the church, schools and universities, but it also ends with a list of proposed statutes for social reform. Many of the evils to be remedied are the same as those singled out by East Anglian insurgents in 1549, both in the articles sent to the Council in July and later from Mousehold Heath: the overall similarities are such as to be beyond coincidence. Some remedies demanded are matters of church reform, like an end to clergy holding more than one benefice or the dismissal of clergy who cannot preach. Other shared grievances are economic, such as agricultural enclosures, abuse of rights in common land, engrossing of multiple leaseholds into one, people following more than one trade, or gentlemen directly farming beyond the immediate needs of their household.[46] But these are all part of a single integrated programme of change in church and commonwealth.

Nor did this populist commonwealth enthusiasm end in 1549 with Kett's defeat at Dussindale. Soon after Queen Mary fought her way to the throne in 1553, a group of yeomen got together, describing themselves as the 'poor commonalty ... of ... Norfolk', in a petition to the queen, recently rediscovered by Professor Richard Hoyle. The Norfolk commonalty wanted parliamentary redress of a long series of agricultural grievances, which once more are strikingly reminiscent of the Mousehold articles. They showed the same hostility to greedy local gentry that had fired Kett's rebellion, though this time they could exploit the more recent events of summer 1553, drawing Mary's attention to the way in which their social superiors had backed Queen Jane when they themselves had not: 'the said gentlemen had not us your said subjects and commonalty at their commandments in their proceedings against your most honourable grace'. Considering that they were trying to charm a Catholic queen and her administrators into listening to them, their silence on the matter of religion is eloquent. Even when they

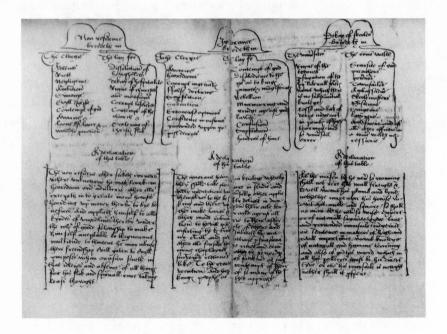

*46. Extract from an evangelical commonwealth treatise addressed to Henry VIII, dateable to 1544 or 1545 and still in the Royal Library. The author is fond of drawing up systematic tables of ideas, in this case illustrating the damage done to the commonwealth by clerical non-residence, ignorance and decay of schools.*

talked about the dissolution of the monasteries, in contrast to Robert Aske back in the Pilgrimage of Grace, they showed no nostalgia for the purely religious benefits of the monasteries, merely recalling the monks' economic and social utility in providing hospitality and pasture for the poor, and asking the queen as the heir of Henry VIII to discipline the greedy gentry purchasers of monastic lands. These were no Catholic zealots; there is little doubt that their religious outlook remained that of the Edwardian Church.[47]

To make all these connections between the cause of the Reformation and the cause of wider social reform is not to reinvent the common-wealth party which the late Sir Geoffrey Elton satirized so mercilessly in his writings on mid-Tudor England, but it is to reaffirm the existence of a widespread Edwardian commonwealth ethos and programme.[48] The term 'commonwealth' was, admittedly, an old cliché in English political discourse: it was not the invention nor the exclusive property of evangelicals. Thus the great northern rising of 1536 to defend traditional religion was known as 'the Pilgrimage of Grace for the Commonwealth': those last three words are often overlooked in discussions of the Pilgrimage.[49] However, clichés have a habit of lighting up and taking on a life of their own at a particular moment: this is what happened to 'commonwealth' in the late 1540s. And its associations were now with evangelical religion.

From the 1530s on, there was a sense of a new world of possibilities. The mood had been encouraged by Henry's greatest minister, Thomas Cromwell, who had set bright young men to producing blueprints for the future in a number of areas: finance, law reform, building prosperity in farming and industry. Not many of these schemes came to anything, but the excitement remained, and there was a continuing link with the universities, particularly with Cambridge. In the middle of most of Cromwell's projects had been the word 'commonwealth'. Characteristically and repeatedly, the projectors had seen what they were doing in terms of the whole community's good.[50] The evangelical dimension was provided by the fundamental Reformation critique of works theology: the medieval church had allowed ritual works to divert and waste people's instinct to do good. As Archbishop Cranmer put it in his 1548 visitation articles: people should 'that bestow upon the poor chest, which they were wont to bestow upon pardons, pilgrimages, trentals, masses satisfactory, decking of images, offering of candles, giving to friars, and upon other like blind devotions'.[51] The social activism of the Cromwellian reformers represented the same refocusing of energy.

The programme of projects and proposals for change and innovation in all areas of society continued after Cromwell's fall. The first fruit, depressingly, but predictably, was in armaments: a new impetus to the Wealden iron industry in Sussex, an initiative on which Henry VIII embarked very successfully in the 1540s, and which was designed to provide a secure source of weapons for his new round of military campaigns. But even amid the cynical realities of government, a genuine idealism remained. One evangelical Cambridge don, Sir Thomas Smith, became a leading administrator under Edward VI, and in the middle of the 1549 crisis he drafted a treatise with the significant title *The Discourse of the Common Weal*. Its scope was ambitious: suggestions for new industries and crops which would diversify England's economy and limit reliance on imports, as well as proposals for reforms in English government and law. Smith was a notably innovative thinker, but he was writing in a context where such ideas had already escaped from their original government setting. They fuelled an optimistic mood which in the first three years of the reign united a large section of the king's subjects with the concerns of the Lord Protector and with the clerical group seeking Reformation.

Now we are close to uncovering the appeal of the evangelical Reformation under Edward VI. It was a movement of hope and moral fervour, capable of generating a mood of intense excitement, so intense that by 1549 thousands of people over hundreds of square miles in southeast England were prepared to gather in 'the camping time'. Their aim was not to bring down government, but to help it correct the faults of local magistrates and identify the ways in which England could be reformed: hence their gatherings in camps, fiestas of justice and the remedy of grievances. Somerset evidently expected the 'camp men' to be enthusiastically in favour when he made King Edward boast to them of 'the multitude of things reformed in the short time of our reign'.[52] This was a time of apparently infinite possibilities, when ordinary people believed that they could themselves influence the future, and when the government appeared to agree. Two years before 1549, it had even looked as if dynastic union with Scotland would create one realm of Great Britain, and that project was an evangelical cause too: a wave of propaganda led but not entirely orchestrated by Somerset's government made 1547 into what the historian Arthur Williamson has called 'the Edwardian moment' of unionist hope.[53] That moment passed, killed by the betrothal of Mary Queen of Scots to the French Dauphin in 1548, but the general atmosphere of youth and renewal persisted into the commotions.

The king himself was a symbol of youth – as Somerset warmly agreed with the Essex insurgents, 'by [God's] grace so abundantly adorned with the gifts of faith, meekness and godliness, as yourselves write, as the like hath scantly been seen before our days in kings of much elder years'.[54] Edward headed a young evangelical élite, a generation of notably clever aristocrats and gentry receiving the same sort of de luxe education as himself: the Lady Elizabeth, Lady Jane Grey, Henry Brandon Duke of Suffolk and his brother, Somerset's three daughters, the formidably bright daughters of Sir Anthony Cooke, two of whom married the cultured Edwardian bureaucrats William Cecil and Nicholas Bacon.[55] Beyond this world of privileged youth, Susan Brigden's research has pursued the theme of Reformation's appeal to the energy and irreverence of the young, which, as we have already seen, became the subject of gloomy comment by supporters of Queen Mary's regime. And the young formed the majority of the population in Tudor England.[56]

Symbolic of this excitement, but also of the dangers attached to it, was the idea of liberty. Liberty was a word particularly fraught in usage in the sixteenth century. John Calvin discussed the right use of the word at length in his *Institutes*, but notoriously he was also able to play on it in Geneva to establish his authority against those he called Libertines, a word which nervous members of England's evangelical establishment were also beginning to use during Edward's reign to demonize radical opponents.[57] Yet one hardly needs Calvin to point out that the positive aspect of evangelical liberty, Martin Luther's *Freedom of a Christian*, was a primary theme of the whole European Reformation; it was one which English opponents of the Reformation singled out as a foreign import – one which they particularly feared and detested, precisely because it was so successful. 'O devilish liberty,' cried Miles Huggarde bitterly in 1556, 'I would to God Germany might have kept thee still: so England had never been troubled with thee. I would to God thou haddest had all our English beer to drink drunk with Hans and Yacob in Strassburg, upon condition London had never retained thee. I would to God thou

47. *The two sons of Charles Brandon, first Duke of Suffolk, by Hans Holbein the Younger, 1541: Henry (above) and Charles (right). Highly educated, charming and talented, they died in the sweating sickness epidemic of 1551, and their loss is said to have been a terrible blow to their contemporary the king.*

haddest remained in Swicherland a conqueror, so that thou haddest never had conquest in England.'[58]

Huggarde sneered at the evangelical pulpit message of liberty from the demands of the law, but we can hear its drama simply by detaching it from the hostile matrix of his text: 'Hope in the blood of Christ, trust in his redemption, he is our satisfaction, his death only can justify us.' Huggarde sarcastically mimicked the enthusiasm of Edwardian sermon-gadders at hearing such preaching: 'Oh this man hath made a goodly piece o' work, this man is verily a prophet.'[59] Such angry mockery is a better tribute to the impact of evangelical sermons, and the excitement of their message of liberty, than any self-advertisement from the reformist corner. Roger Edgeworth, himself no mean preacher in the traditionalist cause, similarly recalled the impact of his opponents on

the city of Bristol: 'there came among you a great multitude of pleasant preachers, preaching liberty, and so pleasures following of such lewd liberty'.[60]

The sexual overtones of this last phrase were not accidental: one of the excitements of the Edwardian Reformation was that it spoke to the most basic of human instincts, offering a reassessment of the institution of marriage for clergy and laity alike. The clergy were offered the abolition of compulsory celibacy. It was a gift taken up by a substantial proportion of clergy in south-east England, but also less predictably by significant numbers in Wales, where the old Church's rules on celibacy had never won universal assent.[61] Equally, the laity were faced with the interesting implications of the Reformation denial that marriage was a scriptural sacrament. If it was not a sacrament, then it was not indissoluble, and the institution of divorce became a possibility; indeed divorce did become available in every other Protestant country in Europe. The 1547 homily against adultery admitted with alarm that private divorces had already become common, and when a proclamation of April 1548 denounced people who were advocating divorce and bigamy, it quoted them saying in good evangelical fashion 'that these things be prohibited not by God's law, but by the Bishop of Rome's law'.[62]

The evangelical establishment could hardly summon up very convincing outrage about this, since the same line was currently being taken by one of their number, William Parr, Marquis of Northampton, brother of King Henry's last wife, Queen Catherine Parr. Northampton spent most of Edward's reign struggling with his colleagues and with Parliament in order to establish his divorce from his detested first wife Elizabeth Bourchier, eventually overcoming great opposition by his dogged persistence. In January 1548 he truculently told his embarrassed colleagues around the Council table that his second marriage to Elizabeth Cobham 'stood with the word of God, his first wife being proved an adulteress'. Some earnest souls might have dismissed Northampton as a 'carnal gospeller', an example of a nobleman who found reformist jargon a convenient cloak for rearranging his private life; however, the same could not be said of one of the greatest contemporary heroines of Edwardian martyrology, Anne Ayscough or Askew, tortured and burnt at the stake in 1546. Ayscough had made the same choice as the Marquis, for she had walked out of a marriage with an unsatisfactory and religiously incompatible husband, and her actions were canonized by evangelicals from John Bale onwards, who never referred to her by her married name of Kyme. It was not surprising that Mary's propagandist, John Christopherson, was able to claim that evangelical preachers used the pulpit to announce 'that there were two sorts of fornication, for which men or women might be divorced, one carnal, and another spiritual. Carnal, as when the wife had committed adultery with another man, or the husband with another woman. Spiritual, when the woman, or man was a papist, and an enemy to God's word, as they called it.' That was precisely Anne Ayscough's justification for abandoning her marriage.[63]

For some, the debate on marriage was no doubt deeply alarming; for others, it was exciting and full of possibilities. The intense nationwide interest in the question is shown by the way in which the English translation of Heinrich Bullinger's German textbook on marriage ran to

48. *William Parr, 1st Marquis of Northampton, a drawing by Hans Holbein the Younger, 1541–2, made during his first marriage.*

twelve editions before 1553; it is an eminently sane and sensible work in Tudor terms, but notably it advocates the introduction of divorce. Notably, also, many of its editions proclaimed its authorship by the Swiss reformer on the title-page: the English reading public were clearly not hostile to the idea of taking advice on the most intimate aspect of their lives from a distinguished foreigner. Wedding-goers would also note that the new 1549 marriage service produced by England's first married archbishop, for the first time in a liturgical

49. *The burning of Anne Ayscough and other evangelicals, summer 1546,*
*with as a backdrop the church of St Bartholomew the Great, Smithfield, and with*
*members of the Privy Council getting a grandstand view. Bishop Nicholas Shaxton,*
*an evangelical leader whose nerve had broken, is preaching his recantation to the*
*martyrs from the pulpit within the arena. Note the scenes of drunken debauchery in*
*the detail of the foreground; conservatives might retort that Ayscough had shown*
*equal immorality in walking out of her marriage. John Foxe took this picture*
*from Robert Crowley's attack on Bishop Shaxton and reused it in his*
Acts and Monuments.

context affirmed that marriage was a relationship for human beings to
enjoy, that it had been designed among other things 'for the mutual
help, society and comfort, that the one ought to have of the other, both
in prosperity and adversity'.[64]

Miles Huggarde singled out a passage from the first epistle to
Timothy as being a favourite evangelical theme: this is an attack on liars
who forbid marriage and enjoin abstinence from certain foods, and it

affirms the goodness of all things created by God. Huggarde said that the passage became a proof-text against compulsory clerical celibacy and fasting rules including Lent, and that it was one of the texts characteristically painted on church walls in Edwardian England.[65] So to preach liberty in the Edwardian Church was very specifically to announce the triumph of carnival over Lent. Dean Christopherson also picked up the carnival theme of inversion in deploring what he termed 'the Lutherans libertie' in Edwardian England: 'vice ruled virtue, and foolishness ruled wisdom, lightness ruled gravity, and youth ruled age'.[66] This is the cry of outraged authority throughout the ages; but many more would enjoy the carnival.

The Edwardian age began as one of glasnost, with the abolition of the heresy laws and the lapse of censorship, and it remained a period where there was an extraordinary degree of theological discussion, both formal and informal. The evangelical establishment constrained conservative voices, but protests were not suppressed altogether even after the shift in power to evangelicals in 1549. Moreover, it is not making a cheap point to note that the consequences for conservatives taking part in Edwardian public debate were a good deal less dire than they were for Protestants in Mary's reign. The evangelical leadership retained something of the reasonableness of Erasmian humanism when it argued with its opponents. It was not entirely an empty or boastful piety when Dr Richard Cox announced to the conservatives in his audience in the Oxford Divinity School after the summer 1549 eucharistic debate: 'we have the power to give orders to you by authority, and threaten deserved punishment to the stubborn, but we prefer to entreat and exhort, in consideration of our high esteem for you'.[67]

It is also notable that much of the discussion encouraged in Edwardian England involved laity as well as clergy. One might expect Oxford and Cambridge to host disputations like those of 1549, particularly given the presence of internationally renowned theologians like Martyr and Bucer, but the House of Lords debate on the eucharist in December 1548 had less precedent in England, including as it did both lay and clerical political leaders. The heresy commissions issued by the

Edwardian government included besides the predictable leading clergy some prominent informed laity like Sir Thomas Smith, Sir William Petre and William Cecil, and one of the functions of these commissions was to argue heretics out of their errors: the lay people would be part of the discussion. Analogous to these debates with radicals, and as remarkable as the 1548 Lords debate in character, was the pair of disputes on the eucharist held in late 1551 at the London homes of William Cecil and Richard Morison, where, before an invited audience of notables, a mixed team of clerical and lay evangelicals disputed against leading conservative clergy. John Feckenham, one of the conservatives involved in the Cecil/Morison disputations, had been given temporary release from the Tower of London to take part, and he went on to tour Worcester diocese in a remarkable variety of theological roadshow with local support from conservative canons of Worcester, publicly engaging such prominent local opponents as John Jewel and Bishop John Hooper.[68]

To set up the gospel theme of liberty as the one standard of salvation was to deny the authority of custom, throwing off the accretion of church tradition to which the old Western Church attributed an authority beyond the text of scripture: 'unwritten verities', a favourite target of evangelical attack.[69] In turn, that rejection enabled evangelicals to discard the burden of history as it had been presented by the Western Church for centuries, a history which justified the place of unwritten verities as part of the authority of the church. This is an essential dimension of Edwardian iconoclasm: to destroy images and objects associated with this deceiving history was a positive assertion that all things from the past had lost their imprisoning power over the English people. Only thus can we explain how the distinguished scholars in charge of the Royal Library could preside over the ruthless weeding-out of its medieval devotional books, or how one of the same scholars, Oxford's most senior academic, Richard Cox, the Dean of Christ Church, was probably responsible for the Edwardian bonfires which appear to have consumed nearly every book in Oxford university library.[70] Only thus can we fathom the psychology which made people

*50. This picture of the interior of Duke Humfrey's Library, the medieval university library of Oxford, was taken during major restoration work in the 1960s. However, it is poignantly reminiscent of the probable appearance of the library at the end of Edward VI's reign. The library was emptied of its books, probably in 1550, and soon after, the medieval desks and book-stalls were sold off to Christ Church. The stalls are represented by the dark upright shadows on the masonry, revealed here when the seventeenth-century library fittings were removed.*

cheerfully reuse the metal from monumental brasses to commemorate their own loved ones, even when the original brasses were memorials to people who had been dead for only a few years.[71]

To see all this destruction merely in terms of cynical greed is to miss an important point: there were elements both of carnival and of altruistic fervour. Some evangelical crusaders even took the risk of touring their iconoclasm abroad, so that Edwardian travellers may have been in danger of acquiring something of the reputation of modern English

*51. A monumental brass from Cobham, Surrey, reused for a new monument in Edward's reign; about 1550, an armoured figure has been engraved on the reverse of the effigy of a priest, engraved only about forty years before. Such brasses are termed palimpsests.*

football supporters. English visitors to France were accused of image-smashing in France in 1551. One young English enthusiast, Oxford-educated William Gardiner, who desecrated the host during mass in the Portuguese Chapel Royal in 1552, was only saved from lynching by the appalled congregation in order to be burnt alive by the Portuguese authorities.[72]

Liberation from papal history led some scholars into explorations of the past to reveal a new version to the evangelical public. So Archbishop

*52. William Gardiner being burned in chains for his sacrilege in Portugal, as depicted in Foxe's* Book of Martyrs. *His sacrilegious hands have been cut off. This was a rare chance for Foxe's publisher to portray a martyr during Edward's reign.*

Cranmer took a precocious and benevolent interest in the Anglo-Saxon church, which he pointed out in his 1540 preface to the official Bible, had translated scripture into the people's language, 'whereof there remaineth yet divers copies found lately in old abbeys'. For Cranmer, the Anglo-Saxons had been relatively innocent of Romish taint, for he saw most of the doctrines which he hated most as being twelfth- or thirteenth-century imports: 'ceremonies, pilgrimage, purgatory, saints, images, works and such like, as hath these three hundred or four hundred years been corruptly taught'. The Archbishop may have influenced his friend Martin Bucer into praising Anglo-Saxon heroes of the Church of England in a 1547 tract printed in Strassburg but intended to flatter an English audience: Bede, Alcuin, Scotus Eriugena, Boniface – heroes who would no doubt have been baffled and angered to see themselves enrolled in an anti-papal cause.[73]

More directly relevant as heroes battling with Antichrist were the Lollards, who could claim that their survival into Edwardian England provided a real and continuous century and a half of precedent for the religious revolution. John Bale built on the pioneering work of Bible translator William Tyndale in telling their stories, with the added refinement that he used sources captured from the enemy, books written by the official medieval Church, in order to illuminate the past in a new way.[74] Edwardian England enjoyed a vogue for literature from the glory days of the Lollards at the turn of the fourteenth and fifteenth century. William Langland's poem *Piers Plowman* was regarded as Lollard fellow-travelling literature: not only did it go through three editions in 1550, but it inspired a crop of medieval pastiches.[75] By contrast, there was a notable lack of interest in the gritty theological and philosophical writings of Wyclif himself: his concerns did not always match those of contemporary reformers. Only two works bearing his name were put into print, and neither of them was actually by Wyclif. One was the justificatory preface of the Lollard Bible, which two separate publishers put on the market, using different manuscripts, one of which was lodged as a precious relic in the King's own Privy Chamber. The other was the tract called *Wyclif's Wicket*, a late-fifteenth-century work which had been a

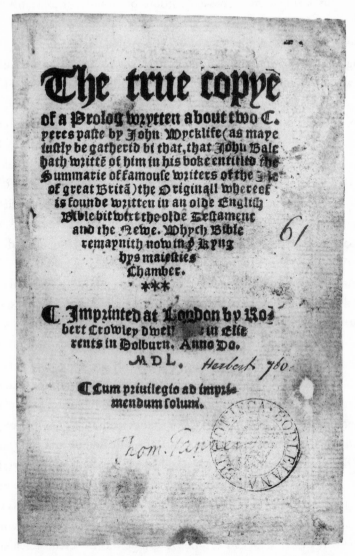

53. *Title-page of* The true copy of a Prolog wrytten about two
C. yeres paste by John Wycklife *(London, Robert Crowley, 1550). The text
tried to preserve something of the archaic spelling of the original: a humanist
exercise in historical scholarship applied to contemporary propaganda. Its proud
reference to the royal ownership of the Bible is an early example of using
royalty to sell publications.*

Lollard favourite: there were four editions of this after 1546, testifying to a buoyant continuing Lollard market in Edwardian England.[76]

However, to rewrite history like this revealed a basic dilemma of the gospel of liberty which was common to all the Reformations of Europe, and which posed a fatal question for the regimes of Edward VI. If history refocused the spotlight on a faithful and dissenting remnant, the Lollards, what did this say about the authority of the church structures which had persecuted them and which still remained in place in England? Many people would make the choice to continue building religious systems for themselves without the Church's help. Part of the popular excitement of the Edwardian Reformations was the variety of independent thought which they generated. This was the time when Anabaptists publicly challenged preachers like John Hooper to debate; when Unitarianism briefly dared to speak its name; when the Free-willers emerged as an identifiable group, proclaiming the possibility of salvation for all humankind and reminding humankind of its responsibility to seek salvation – rejecting the predestinarian emphasis which increasingly characterized the evangelical establishment.

These phenomena, the inevitable result of an ethos of open religious debate, terrified the mainstream reformers: Cranmer felt that such people were worse than papists, for they betrayed the cause and stopped conservatives seeing the light.[77] We have seen that the regime was already trying to repress religious radicalism during its first summer. At first repressive measures had the subsidiary agenda of preserving a degree of cooperation with traditionalist religious leaders; yet the bipartisan approach fell away with the new mood of evangelical aggression in winter 1550, and thereafter the campaign against radicalism became an exclusively evangelical cause. The government connected radicals with the camping time of summer 1549, after abandoning fairly unconvincing efforts to blame the 1549 stirs on papist agitators.[78] In fact the lack of surviving radical rhetoric from the camping time is striking; its leaders were substantial men with much experience of minor administration who were anxious to cooperate with the government and who left behind them a reputation for paying decent money for supplies for their camps.[79] What is less certain is how this leadership interacted with rank and file radicalism, which was after all based in precisely the same evangelical heartland as the camping commotions. Cranmer and Ridley were closer to the events than us, and in the wake of 1549, their 1550 inquiries in Norwich and London dioceses were alert for a range of radical beliefs, among which they were looking for those who affirmed 'that private persons may make insurrections, uproars or sedition: or compel men by force or fear, to give them any of their goods'.

Undoubtedly the trauma of 1549 stimulated a general emphasis on discipline among leading evangelicals. In 1551, censorship of the press was restored. After the brief triumph of carnival, Lent was returning.[80] Notoriously the regime moved from inquiries, disputations and moral pressure to staging two burnings for heresy in 1550 and 1551: Joan Bocher the alarmingly self-possessed and articulate Kentish radical, and the emigré George van Parris. When the Church of England came to draw up its doctrinal statement, the Forty-Two Articles, many of the questions previously asked in episcopal visitations were turned into articles combating radical belief. The London Stranger Church of Jan Łaski was given a remarkably privileged status by the Edwardian government, including valuable Crown real estate in the city of London, despite the implicit criticism of English church structures which its congregational church polity represented. As far as the government was concerned, this was a necessary investment in security: the Stranger Church was there to control the immigrant population which was the chief source of religious radicalism. The Stranger Church leadership under Łaski was happy to cooperate. Without them, van Parris would not have ended up burnt at the stake. When Łaski devised a baptismal rite for his congregation, he stretched liturgy rather unhappily in the direction of polemic, for his text made the minister read out an argument in favour of infant baptism.[81] A parallel concern affected the English liturgy: the revised Prayer Book of 1552 more than doubled the number of occasions in the year that congregations were required to recite the Athanasian Creed, in order to confront unitarians at least once a month with its merciless trinitarian detail.[82]

54. Interior of the Austin Friars Church (the 'Dutch Church'), London,
before its destruction in the 1940 blitz. This sumptuous building, formerly full of the
monuments of London city worthies, was given to the Stranger Church in 1550
by the Edwardian government.

The radical interpretation of liberty therefore increasingly strait-jack-
eted official evangelical reform. This caused considerable problems for
the self-image of Edwardian reformers. Catharine Davies has brilliantly
analysed how difficult they found it to abandon the self-image of a persecuted little flock, which was implicit in the Lollard heritage, even while
they were taking over an established national church and persecuting
other little flocks.[83] One way of squaring the circle might have been to
face the problem directly: to gather the godly together more closely,
as Puritans would do in Elizabeth's reign, or as the Pietist movement
was later to do in Germany. The precedent was there in Martin Bucer's

*Euening prayer.*

which two laste Collectes shalbe daiely said at Euening praier without alteration.

The second Collecte at Eueuyng prayer.

GOD, from whom al holp desyres, al good counsaples, and all iuste woorkes dooe procede: geue vnto thy seruauntes that peace, whiche the worlde cannot geue: that both our heartes may bee set to obeye thy commaundementes, and also that by thee, we beyng defended from the feare of oure enemies, may passe our time in rest and quietnes, throughe the merites of Iesus Chrpste our Sauiour. Amen.

The thirde Collecte, for aybe agaynst al perisses.

Jghten our darkenes we besethe thee, O lord, and by thy great mercy, defende vs from all perylles, and daungers of thys nyghte, for the loue of thy onely Sonne oure Sauyoure Iesus Chrypst. Amen.

In the feastes of Chrisstmas, the Epiphanie, sainte Mathie, Easter, Thassencion, Pentecost, Saint John Baptist, Saint James, Saint Bartholomew, Saint Mathewe, Saint Symon and Jude, Saint Andrewe, and Trinitie Sundaye: shalbe song, or sayd immediatly after *Benedictus* this confession of our Christen fayth.

Hosoeuer wyll be saued : beefore all *Quicũ* thinges it is necessary that he holde *que vult:* the catholike fayth.

whith faith except euery one dooe kepe holy and vndefyled : wythoute doubt he shal perishe euerlastyngly. And the catholyke fayth is this : that we worship one God in Trinitie, and Trinitie in vnitie. CC.ii. Neyther

55. *The opening of the Athanasian Creed, as printed in the 1552 Book of Common Prayer, with detailed specifications of the occasions when it must be recited. This aggressively uncompromising confession of faith, probably originating in fifth-century Gaul, deals at length with the doctrines of the Trinity and the Incarnation of Christ, and no unitarian radical could have recited it with a good conscience.*

ministry in Strassburg. Here Bucer had put much effort into establishing a voluntary core-church movement in the years just before his departure; his specific aim had been to steal Anabaptist thunder by lending fervour and tight discipline to the official church. The sad reality, however, was that Bucer's scheme had been a flop. It was noticeable that when in 1550 he presented King Edward with his book *De Regno Christi*, a blueprint for turning England into a bigger and better Strassburg, the text contained a deafening silence on the subject of core churches.[84] Bucer's scheme met with no Edwardian imitators. Both Lollards and the early evangelical dissidents had called themselves brethren and sisters to identify and strengthen themselves in gathered groups, but under Edward, the custom was abandoned to the radicals; mainstream evangelicals called it divisive, just as conservative commentators had done earlier. So the Kentish schoolmaster Thomas Cole (himself a convert from Freewiller radicalism to religious respectability) sneered at his former fellow-radicals of Edwardian Kent that 'Anabaptists and such sects wheresoever they be, as in Christian religion [i.e. monasticism] call themselves Brothers and Sisters, and divide themselves from other Christian people'.[85] It took Mary's persecution to send mainstream evangelicals willy-nilly back to the conventicle model, dividing themselves once more from the corruptions of the established church.

Far from using fraternal language, the Edwardian Church remained an institution at war with itself. We have seen how most bishops were the enemies of government policy in 1547, and it was a commonplace of evangelical pamphleteering and preaching throughout the reign that most of the Church's serving clergy should be regarded as untrustworthy or contemptible.[86] Traditionalist clergy were thus publicly treated with suspicion and ridicule: they were accused of ignorance, selfishness, seduction of women in the confessional, and notably of twisted sexuality. What could be a more obvious sign of the corruption of the old religion than sexual perversion? One evangelical pamphleteer, for instance, recommended to Henry VIII in his last years that the king ban all spiritual persons from being schoolmasters to the rich, for 'thus shall the nobility of this realm be preserved from papistry and buggery'.[87] John Bale's obsession in his writings with the homosexuality of traditionalist clergy is notorious, and was no doubt fuelled by some unhappy personal experience in early life. Another evangelical propagandist clergyman, John Olde, could equal Bale in the savage relish of his prose, relentlessly alliterating his attack from Marian exile on former clerical colleagues in England as 'hollow-hearted whoremongers, most saucy shameless sodomites, the manciples of mischief'. Taking up another aspect of sexual perversion, John Foxe was to make a good deal out of accusations of gratuitous sadism against Bishop Bonner's persecutory activities in the reign of Mary, including the index entry in *Acts and Monuments* that 'he delighted much in beating men's breeches with rods and whips' – a graphic illustration of which is one of the more startling pictures in the Book of Martyrs.[88]

On the other side, traditionalists attacked reformers for their greed for gold, but also for their supposedly gross sexual appetites following the abolition of clerical celibacy. The logic of their rhetoric made them emphasize heterosexuality rather than homosexuality, although they still considered clerical libidos as disordered and promiscuous. Miles Huggarde painted a lurid picture of wife-swapping parties in the parsonage which was rather a long way from Bullinger's decorous discussion of evangelical wedded bliss:

the said women ... being led with divers lusts, using their bodies with other men as well as with their supposed husbands: yea and one of them [i.e. the husbands] with another's woman, taking it (as it is thought) for a brotherly love, one to help another, after the doctrine of Friar Luther, the first author of their marriage.[89]

The minimal basis for this canard had been provided in Edwardian England when (to the gloomy relish of conservative observers) some of the most prominent of the new clerical marriages went spectacularly wrong, including those of Archbishop Holgate of York and Bishop Ponet of Rochester; it was the reforming bishops' excessive love of women to which Huggarde was referring when more than once he sneered at 'bishops effeminate'.[90] But what is so striking amid all this

*56. Bishop Bonner exercises in his palace garden at Fulham by scourging
a Protestant: one of the more openly pornographic images in Foxe's* Book of
Martyrs. *Bonner is stripped to secular working dress, with his tonsure the
incongruous reminder of his clerical status. The bearded standing figure is
another Protestant dragooned into helping the torture; he shields his
gaze from the disgusting spectacle.*

shower of abuse and tabloid prose is that under Edward VI these mutually despised and reviled clergy were nearly all still in office in the same
Church. Apart from a few high-flyers like Bishop Latimer under Henry
VIII or half a dozen bishops in Edward's reign, there were few expul-
sions from the active ministry on either side until Queen Mary came to
power, and so the wave of ridicule and abuse was quite consciously
being directed both ways against existing authority figures within every
English parish. It is hardly surprising that the discipline of the church
courts broke down very seriously in mid-century: after all, the courts
had been one of the first institutions of church authority to be attacked

by Henry VIII in the late 1520s. Many people started ignoring the penalties imposed by church courts, and absentee rates in court cases soared.[91]

But the problem of authority spread more widely than the Church. A common theme of evangelical preaching was that commitment to right religion and godly life was more important than noble lineage or even gender. An evangelical society which had set up stringent new standards of morality for the Church and found it wanting would soon look at other authority structures with the same morality in mind – but the resulting tensions might be extreme. 'It is justice, mercy, liberality, kindness, gentleness, hospitality for the poor, and such other godly gifts of the mind, and not the multitude of riches, that declare who is a gentleman and who a churl, who is noble, who unnoble,' Thomas Becon asserted in 1550. Only a year after the Earl of Warwick's defeat of Kett's Norfolk rebellion, Becon may have been over-confident that such sentiments would not annoy his dedicatee, a Norfolk knight whose daughter had just married Warwick's son Robert Dudley.[92] Likewise, one of the very few major textual variants in the 1547 Homilies was the omission of a whole paragraph from the *Exhortation to Obedience*. This was an admonition not to contend for worldly dominion and a warning to princes to rule according to law; its scriptural references directed attention to unsatisfactory stewards and to the Johannine command not to labour for the food which perishes. After appearing in one edition from the press of Richard Grafton in 1547, the paragraph must have been considered too pointed a modification of obedience; Grafton immediately withdrew it, while Edward Whitchurch, the other printer of the homilies, suppressed the offending material from the first edition which he printed, leaving an untidy hiatus in his text, and the passage was never seen again.[93] The same dilemma was encapsulated by the nervous intimacy of Protector Somerset's correspondence with the insurgents of the camping time in 1549. His effort to assert that the central biblical message for subjects was obedience sat uneasily with his admission that the commons had real grievances about the sins of their social superiors. Yet this social critique had been the premise of the enclosure commission which he himself had launched in the previous year.[94]

## Of obedience.

For truly the scripture of god, alloweth no such é vsurped power, ful of enormities, abusions and blasphemyes. But the trewe meanyng of these, and suche places, be to extoll and set furth gods trewe ordinaunce, and the authoritie of gods anoynted kynges, & of theyr officers appoynted vnder them. And concerning the vsurped power of the Byshop of Rome, whiche he most wrongfully chalengeth, as the successoure of Christe, and Peter, we maye easely perceyue, howe false, seyned, and forged it is, not onely in that it hath no sufficient grounde in holy scripture, but also by the fruites and doctrine therof. For our saviour Christe and Sainte Peter, teache moste earneslye, and agreably, obedience to kynges: as to the chyefe, and supreame Rulers in thys worlde, nexte vnder God. But the Byshop of Rome teacheth immunities, priuileges, exempcions, and disobedience, most clearely agaynste Christes doctrine, and sainte Peter. He ought therefore rather to be called Antichriste, and the successour of the Scribes and Pharisies, than Christes vicare, or saynte Peters successour, seyng that, not onely in thys poynte, but also in other weyghtye matters of Christen religion, in matters of remission of sinnes, and of saluacion, he teacheth so directly, agaynste both sainte Peter, and agaynst our saviour Christe.\ Who not onely taught obedience to kynges, but also practised obedience, in their conuersacion & lyuyng. For we rede that they both payed tribute to the

*Math.xvii.*

## Of obedience.

to the kyng. And also we reade that the holy virgin Mary, mother to our saviour Christe, and Joseph, who was taken for his father, at the emperours commaundement, wente to the Citie of Dauid, named Bethleem, to be taxed amoung other, and to declare their obedience to the Magistrates, for gods ordinaunces sake. And here let vs not forget the blessed virgin Maries obedience: For although she was highly in Gods fauour, and Christes natural mother, and was also great with chylde that same tyme, and so nigh her trauayle, that she was deliuered in her iourney: Yet she gladly without any excuse or grudging (for conscience sake) did take that colde and fowle winter iourney, beyng in the meane season so poore, that she laye in the stable, and there she was deliuered of Christ. And accordyng to the same: Loe, howe s.Peter agreeth, writyng by expresse woordes, in thys fyrst Epistle: Submytte youre selues, (sayeth he) vnto kynges, as vnto the chyefe heades, or vnto Rulers, as vnto them that are sente of hym, for the punyshment of euil doers, and for laude of them, that do well, for so is the wyll of god. I nede not to expounde these woordes, they be so playne of themselfes. Sainct Peter doth not saye: Submit your selues vnto me, as supreme head of the Churche, neyther he saith, submit your selues from time to time to my successours in Rome: But he sayth submit your selues vnto your king, youre supreme head, & to those that he apointeth in authoritie vnder hym. For.

*Luke.ii.*

*I.Pe.cctc.ii.*

## Of obedience.

Rome. For truly the scripture of God alloweth no such vsurped power, ful of enormities, abusions & blasphemies. But the true meanynge of these, & suche places, be to extoll and set furth, Gods true ordinaunce, & the authoritie of Gods anointed kynges, and of their officers appointed vnder them.

AND concernynge the vsurped power of the Bisshop of Rome, whiche he moste wrongfully chalengethe, as the successor of Christe, and Peter: We maye easely perceaue, how false, seyned, and forged it is, not onely in that, it hath no sufficient grounde in holy scripture, but also by the fruites and doctrine therof. For our saviour Christe and sainte Peter, teache moste earnestly and agreably obedience to kynges, as to the chiefe and supreame Rulers in thys worlde, next vnder God. But the Bisshop of Rome teacheth immunities, priuileges, exempcions, and disobedience, moste clearely agaynste Christes doctrine, and sainct Peters. He ought therfore rather to be called Antichriste, and the successor of the Scribes and Pharisies, then Christes vicare, or sainte Peters successor, seyng y, not onely in this poynt, but also in other weightye matters of Christen religion, in matters of remission of synnes, and of saluacion, he teacheth so directlye agaynste, both sainte Peter, and agaynste our saviour Christe. Who not onely taught obedience to kynges, but also

## Of obedience.

also practised obedience, in their conuersacion & liuing. For we rede that they both paied tribute to the kynge. And also we reade, that the holy virgyn Mary, mother to our saviour Christ, and Joseph, who was taken for his father, at y Emperours commaundemet, wente to the citie of Dauid, named Bethleem, to be taxed emong other, and to declare their obedience, to the Magistrates, for Gods ordinaunces sake. And here let vs not forget the blessed virgyn Maries obediece: For although, she was highly in Gods fauour, and Christes naturall mother, & was also great with chylde that same tyme, and so nyghe her trauayle, that she was deliuered in her iourney: Yet, she gladly without any excuse or grudging (for conscience sake) did take that colde & foule wynter iourney, beynge in the meane season so poore, that she lay in y stable, and there she was deliuered of Christ.

Our saviour Christ refused the office of a worldly Judge, & so he dyd the office of a worldly kyng: Commaudyng his disciples, and al that beleue in him, that they should not contede for superioritie, nether for worldly dominió in this worlde. For ambition and pryde is detestable in al christian persones of euery degre. And the Apostles in that place, do not represent the persones of Bisshoppes, and Priestes onely, but also (as auncient authores do wryte) they represent the persones of kynges & Princes: Whose worldly rule

*Matt.xvii.*

*Luce.ii.*

*Luce.xii.*

*Iohan.vi.*

*Mat.xviii.*

The coup against Somerset in October 1549 represented his colleagues' verdict that he had failed to ride this tiger. The Privy Council
thereafter settled for a more conventional strategy in government, led
by the Earl of Warwick, who had crushed Robert Kett's Norfolk protestors for commonwealth. Some of the demands of the camping time were
met in the next few years, such as the manumission of villeins which had
been sought by the Mousehold camp in their articles addressed to the
government, but this redress of grievances came without an elaborate
display of public consultation as in the Somerset years.[95] The Norfolk
gentry who had been the subject of commonwealth protest showed their
gratitude to Warwick by displaying his emblem of bear and ragged staff
outside their houses. Among the commons of East Anglia, there was corresponding anger and a sense of betrayal. Even twenty years later, a
Suffolk protestor making a renewed attempt at raising the region could
bitterly recall in his rousing speech that 'then we were promised enough
and more than enough – but the more was an halter': a fair summary of
the abrupt turn-around from Somerset's promises to the aftermath of
Warwick's Norwich massacre at Dussindale.[96]

The year 1549 also represented a deep disappointment and trauma for
the evangelical clergy who had promoted commonwealth rhetoric as
part of reformation, and who clearly felt that popular activism had
besmirched the cause. It was noticeable how after 1549, moralist commentators like Thomas Lever and Thomas Becon came regularly to
deploy the phrase 'carnal liberty', a usage which had been invented by

57. *Government censorship embarrassed the printers of the Homilies in 1547.
Richard Grafton issued one complete edition of the Homilies, and was then told to
remove a paragraph, beginning after 'she was delyvered of Christ'. Edward
Whitchurch (below) had begun printing his edition, which had identical
pagination and layout of text to that of Grafton (above), up to this spread of pages.
Thereafter, his pagination diverged from Grafton's previous edition, and his text
shows an awkward break after 'she was delyvered of Christ'. Evidently Whitchurch
reacted in mid-production to an order to remove the paragraph from his text, but
with little time to hide the omission.*

58. *On this piece of tournament armour made* c. *1575 for John Dudley's son, Robert Earl of Leicester, to protect his horse's head in jousts, the Dudley family's bear and ragged staff emblem is the central motif of the decoration, and ragged staffs proliferate in the rest of the design.*

their conservative opponents to describe all evangelicals. Now Lever and Becon emphasized it in order to reproach evangelicals among the commons who had betrayed their cause by joining the commotions.[97] They felt that popular disobedience threatened God's plan for the kingdom. Thomas Lever in 1550 likened the Edwardian Reformation to a version of the miracle of feeding the five thousand where the end of the story had gone wrong: 'Meat was provided for the Commons of England, and ready to have been delivered: but when they were bidden to sit down in quietness, they rose up by rebellion, and have lost all the cheer of that feast.'[98]

But it was not enough to castigate the common people for ingratitude. Like Somerset, the clergy recognized genuine popular grievances which had not been solved by the massacre at Mousehold; and they also saw the danger to further reformation if the gulf widened between the government and the commons. The strategy in this crisis was to give a new prominence to another rhetorical cliché-word: covetousness. This was not a new theme in 1549. A concern with covetousness was a response to the peculiar economic conditions of Henry VIII's last decade, when the dissolution of the monasteries and chantries produced a volatile land market and rich pickings for those with money, and when the government made its own irresponsible contribution to mayhem in the national economy with successive debasements of the coinage. It was not surprising that making money became more than usually an English obsession, or that preachers frequently pointed this out and deplored the fact. The theme that landowners were covetous lay behind most of the commonwealth demands of the later 1540s, as seen especially in the articles of the camping time.

However, the theme of covetousness was now given a wider application. The agenda was set by Archbishop Cranmer in a meticulously prepared sermon in St Paul's Cathedral; he preached it on 21 July 1549, as the centrepiece of the government's propaganda offensive against the protestors in the camps. Cranmer consciously assumed the mantle of a prophet, invoking the Holy Spirit to draw an explanation from Scripture for the disaster which England now faced. He began with the particular fault of the magistrates, which was lack of severity in administration, but having made that grim point, he ingeniously pointed an accusation of covetousness in two directions, to rulers and ruled. He admitted the wrongs done by greedy gentlemen, but also singled out the insurgents who had coveted the power which rightly belonged to the king. 'Let both parties lay away this so furious and excessive desire of vain and worldly things', as otherwise an equal damnation waited for them both. This was a message of unity to a divided nation menaced by foreign invasion and popish plots.[99]

Curiously, this is the only surviving text of any sermon by Cranmer, so we have no way of knowing whether he continued to pursue the theme of a twofold covetousness. However, for others, the covetousness theme became one of the mainstays of evangelical discourse in the second half of the reign, often with the same Janus-like reference as in the Archbishop's sermon.[100] Parallel was the increasingly common use of the phrase 'carnal gospeller', a term which had a rather wider social reference than 'carnal liberty': this evangelical fifth columnist was a new enemy within the reformation, who might emerge in the shape of seditious rebel, greedy gentleman or even self-interested clergyman.[101] The advantage of this discourse was its apparently unifying evenhandedness: its castigation of high and low, its attempt to restore a single purpose to the revolution. For this reason, to single out the Edwardian preachers' criticism of the rich, in order to emphasize their social radicalism, is a bad distortion of their intentions. In the spirit of Cranmer's 1549 sermon, they were prophets trying to recall a whole nation to godliness. They could express continuing popular anger at landlord exploitation and encroachment on common rights; they could express government horror at popular disobedience and religious radicalism. They could, as did Lever and others, equate covetousness with idolatry, on the basis that greed made an idol of money: this was a useful spur to moral earnestness in a society which hated images, particularly since by the end of 1550 the official campaign to destroy real physical images and altars had run its course, and there was iconophobic energy to spare.[102]

Nevertheless the covetousness theme provoked its own tensions.

Some of these became apparent when covetousness was made the centrepiece of a government-sponsored preaching campaign in July 1551. The country was gripped by a mysterious and terrifying new epidemic, the sweat, and the Privy Council ordered the bishops to stir people to prayer, 'to refrain their greedy appetites from that insatiable serpent of covetousness, wherewith most men are so infected, that it seemeth each one would devour another without charity or any godly respect to the poor, to their neighbours, or to the commonwealth'. It is noticeable that this essay by the Council in 'commonwealth' rhetoric was headed with the Duke of Somerset's signature, and that it was not signed by the Earl of Warwick. However, the commonwealth message also came with an anticlerical spin from these lay magnates of the Council. It made forthright remarks about the clergy's incompetence and previous neglect of such exhortation: 'as well the chief as the particular ministers of the church have been both so dull and so feeble in discharging of their duties, that it is no marvel that their flocks wander'.[103] Five days later, Bishop Ridley of London was heatedly sarcastic about this insult in a private letter to the king's tutor, Sir John Cheke; in this he listed at length some instances of Council-sponsored covetousness at the Church's expense. 'Sir, what preachers shall I get to open and set forth such matters, and so as the king's majesty and the council do command them to be set forth, if either ungodly men, or unreasonable beasts, be suffered to pull away and devour the good and godly learned preachers' livings?'

Naturally Ridley did not repeat this outburst in public when on the same day he sent out a circular to his own clergy conveying the Council's order on prayer against covetousness – but neither did he pass on the Council's criticism of the Church.[104] What happened next was an intense but also short-lived religious revival, remembered vividly if cynically by contemporary observers. There were direct responses to the moralism of the Council order, as 'some abated their unreasonable rents, and many sought for the poor and needy in prisons, and elsewhere, to relieve them'; the clergy suddenly found themselves greatly in demand. But when the lessening of the epidemic brought a rapid lowering of the emotional temperature, public selfishness was restored to normal levels. Then in the autumn, as we have seen (p. 99 above), came the very open falling-out in the Privy Council, which destroyed Somerset and opened up serious division between Council and leading clergy.[105]

These tensions were expressed in another exploitation by clergy of the covetousness theme. This was the open expression of their own clerical grievances. In contrast to Bishop Ridley, who restricted himself to private grumbling, the ordained ministry began expressing its growing fury and frustration at the misuse of confiscated church revenues. Indeed, the radical writer Anthony Gilby later said that Edwardian preachers had rather overdone the poverty of the Church, with selfish considerations in mind, when there had been plenty of other things to worry about – but Gilby, one of John Knox's greatest admirers, was looking back from Marian exile with the advantage of hindsight, and with old scores to settle against the Edwardian evangelical establishment.[106] Certainly for Thomas Lever, a Cambridge don with a keen sense of the missed opportunity for strengthening education, the theme became well-nigh obsessional in a series of sermons during 1550. In the same Lenten sermon before the king in which he had criticized popular ingratitude, Lever saw the diversion of church revenues as a scandal which discredited England's Reformation: 'England having occasion, by the abolishing of Papistry, to embrace sincere Christianity, turned that occasion, to take the spoil of Papistry, which is the cause that many neglect, and slander sincere Christianity.'[107]

After a peak of such pulpit agitation in 1550, such criticism seems to have subsided in intensity, until in 1552 the government tried to solve its disastrous financial situation with a fresh wave of chantry land sales and confiscations of church goods. In the last winter of the reign, a concerted campaign of preaching focused the covetousness theme squarely on the secular leaders of government, much to the fury of the lay Privy Councillors. The consequences were disastrous for reform: in an act of malicious sabotage, the Duke of Northumberland intervened in the 1553 Parliament to derail the scheme for reforming canon law. An incidental

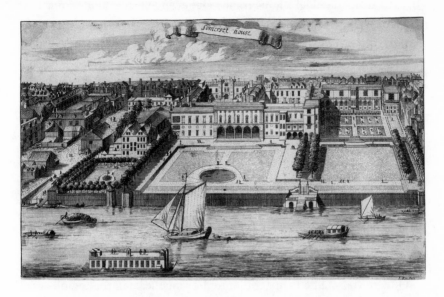

*59. The river façade of the modishly classical Somerset House between the*
*Strand and the Thames, before its demolition in the eighteenth century. Churchmen*
*were well aware that even the most ostentatious of their evangelical allies among the*
*nobility were plunderers of church property. Somerset House, the Duke of Somerset's*
*London home, was built on the site of three demolished London homes of bishops,*
*and it cannibalized stone from two London parish churches and from the*
*precincts of St Paul's Cathedral.*

casualty of this disaster was the prospect of introducing a comprehensive divorce law, leaving England the only Protestant country in Europe
not to provide for divorce, and thus dealing another blow to the
prospects of change which had been one of the excitements of the
Somerset years.[108]

The culmination of Edward's reign, therefore, hardly suggests a very
positive result for King Solomon the builder of the Temple. There is
much within the story so far which can only be regarded as depressing,
as much for enthusiasts for the Reformation as for its opponents. So
many early hopes appeared to have been disappointed. Despite all the
constant official rhetoric about avoiding contention, England was left

divided in its ideological geography. Its evangelical regions from East Anglia to Dover and the Bristol Channel moved in different rhythms to the rest of England, while the evangelical society which the Edwardian reformations had begun to build was now itself divided between mutually distrustful magistrates, commons and clergy. It is not accidental that commotions and threats of commotions, which disturbed England every year after 1549 well into Mary's reign, went on focusing on the evangelical heartland, the south-east and the Midlands; by contrast, the conservative north and west ceased to be troublesome to Edwardian government after the crushing of the western rebels in 1549. Nor is it surprising that it proved impossible to turn the accession of Queen Jane in 1553 into a popular crusade for the evangelical cause. Instead, the commons of Norfolk, who still treasured a commonwealth programme, scorned their social superiors' support for Jane and turned to Queen Mary. The many committed evangelicals in the region acted against what one might have assumed would have been their natural partisan inclinations. Throughout south-east England – even in Queen Jane's naval squadron off the Suffolk coast – ordinary people did the same, confounding the expectations of the governing class. Jane's Privy Council, forgetful of any commonwealth rhetoric and remote from Somerset's appeals to populism, blustered that Mary had 'only the concurrence of a few lewd, base people' in her challenge; but it was this popular 'concurrence' which gave momentum to Mary's crusade against Jane and destroyed the prospects of continued Protestant government.[109] We witnessed the rise of a revolution: bliss was it in that dawn of 1547 to be alive. Have we now witnessed the revolution's collapse in shame and failure? To find an answer, we have to consider how the Edwardian Reformation survived the death of its king.

# 4

# The Afterlife of the Edwardian Reformation

We have already viewed one perspective on the afterlife of the Edwardian Reformation: the forthright High Church disgust expressed by Bishop Walter Frere, as he finished the uncongenial task of editing the articles and injunctions of King Edward's Church. However, in the manner of the dog that failed to bark in the night during one of Sherlock Holmes's assignments, silence can be as eloquent as an angry voice. In 1957 another prominent Anglo-Catholic, Fr. Humphrey Whistler (like Frere, a monk of the Community of the Resurrection) produced an engaging little pamphlet on the Reformation which was intended as an exercise in ecumenism between Roman Catholics and Anglicans, picking up the pieces of misunderstandings from the sixteenth century. He was writing in a decade when the Catholic movement in the Church of England seemed at last to be achieving the dominance for which it had struggled since the 1830s. Increasing numbers of Anglican bishops came from the Catholic tradition; the modest but unmistakable surge in church attendance after the Second World War made for a mood of quiet Anglican self-confidence; as yet, there was no indication how the Church of Rome would move the theological goalposts in the Second Vatican Council by disturbing old confessional certainties. Inevitably, when Whistler looked back at the English Reformation, he operated within the same Anglo-Catholic perspective on English church history as Bishop Frere, and in his pamphlet, he provided an instructive proclamation of this position: 'We believe, in common with many Roman Catholics, that the task of the Church of England is to be true to itself, as

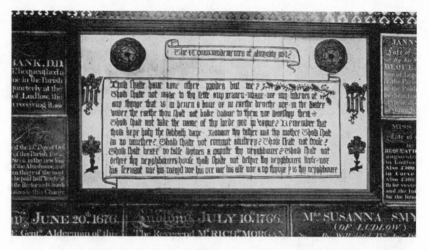

60. *The painted board in Ludlow parish church (Shropshire) setting
forth the Ten Commandments. This set, early Elizabethan since it can be dated
by the churchwardens' accounts to 1561, bridges the old world and the new, because
the text is flanked by the Sacred Monogram of Christ's name and by the
lily of the Blessed Virgin Mary. Edwardian leaders would not have
approved of such symbols.*

interpreted by Hooker, Andrewes, Laud, and the great Carolines: by
Ken and the Non-jurors, and the "Catholic underground" in the eighteenth century; and by the Tractarians of the nineteenth century who
rebuilt on their interpretation the Catholic revival."[1]

In this we hear one solution to the problem of the Edwardian Reformation: simply to deny it any part in the Church of England story. In
listing his sequence of Anglican heroes from the 1580s to the 1700s and
beyond, Fr. Whistler was completely silent on the first half-century of
the English Reformation, a silence which embraces the whole subject of
this book. Evidently to be Edwardian, or even mainstream Elizabethan,
was not to be true to the Church of England. What was particularly
offensive to such commentators about the Edwardian adventure was
that it was a religious revolution, demolishing the traditional church in
order to rebuild another. The revolution involved rewriting history and

eliminating objects which evoked that history – the very history and objects which Frere and Whistler treasured.

The extent of the change would have been obvious to anyone walking into a fully reformed English church building in 1553. The greatest visual impact came from words: words in painted plaster, boards or on printed posters stared down from the whitewashed walls, turning the church interior into the pages of a giant scrapbook of scripture.[2] Three new pieces of church furniture stood out amid the hastily adapted and purged remains of the old. A wooden table, moveable into the body of

61. *Even now, Hailes church (Gloucestershire) offers a glimpse of how a church interior looked after Edward's religious changes. This nineteenth-century photograph, taken before Victorian liturgical censorship, shows a central communion table, its long axis east–west. Two ranks of benches for communicants cover the altar's former site (note the medieval piscina at south–east). The Victorian text 'This do in remembrance of me' on the east wall consciously emphasizes the eucharist as primarily a memorial – echoing Cranmer's words for administering communion in his 1552 Prayer Book.*

the church for communion services, symbolized the overthrow of the old mass, with all its associated theology of a sacrificing, celibate priesthood; to emphasize this rejection, the table was placed at right angles to the alignment of the old altars. A poor box to collect alms, which the Edwardian government ordered to be placed in every church, was an official reminder that people's charity was to be directed not to masses or graven images, but to needy people made in God's image.[3] A pulpit reinforced the message of the walls that God was to be approached most directly through his biblical word: even where the pulpit was inherited from the old pre-Reformation days, it was now used exclusively for preaching, not for leading the recital of the rosary or the medieval extended vernacular prayers known as the bidding of the bedes.[4] The pulpit would remain the central visual emphasis of most English parish

62. *Hailes chancel, looking west: the medieval rood screen, the rood figures and loft removed, survives as a useful partition from the nave (the preaching-room, with its prominent pulpit). The communicant benches return right round the chancel.*

63. *This cheerful representative of the poor has been soliciting donations above the almsbox of Watton parish church, Norfolk, since 1639.*

churches down to the nineteenth century, when the Oxford Movement, in a remarkably successful piece of theological alchemy, restored the primacy of the altar.

Our visitor of 1553 would note one other new acquisition of furniture in the church, the only picture not to attract official disapproval: this was a set of the royal arms of the king, normally placed where once the rood group of Christ crucified, Mary and John had stood, above the chancel screen. Only one authentically Edwardian set seems now to survive, thanks to Queen Mary's attempt to eliminate these offensive symbols of the royal supremacy, but Elizabeth and her successors brought the royal

64. *The stone pulpit of Wells Cathedral was financed by a bequest in the will of Bishop William Knight, who died in 1547. Knight was a religious conservative, and it is likely that the evangelical Edwardian cathedral authorities, rather than the deceased bishop, chose the visual message of his bequest: austerely Renaissance, devoid of imagery and with the inscription from Coverdale's Bible 'Preache thou the worde be fervent in season and out of season. Improve, rebuke, exhorte with all longe sufferyng in doctrine. 2 Timothy.'*

*65. Royal arms of Edward VI at Westerham parish church, Kent. Most sets of royal arms with initials 'ER' are clearly Elizabethan, but this is marked as the arms of a Tudor king by its inscription 'Vivat Rex curat lex', and is the only definitely surviving set from Edward's reign. The Sacred Monogram above is likely to be a Victorian addition.*

arms back to parish churches, and they remain a characteristic feature of English church interiors. The display of royal arms announced an essential feature of the Edwardian Reformation: it was a revolution directed from above by the monarch, his council and the Parliament at Westminster. Those who ruled the realm took it upon themselves to decide the form in which the European Reformation would be presented to the people of England.

A prime example of this is the way in which Edwardian theology about the eucharist was defined. When Dr Richard Cox announced, in his summing-up of debate in the Oxford Divinity School in June 1549, that the Church of England as yet believed nothing definite about the eucharist, he said that the decision would be taken when it seemed good to Edward VI and 'to the leaders of the Church of England', '*ecclesiae Anglicanae proceribus*'.[5] This was a conveniently vague phrase. Who were these leaders of the church? We have seen in Chapter 2 that in the first place, and unsurprisingly, they consisted of Archbishop Cranmer, writing his *Defence of the sacrament* (above, p. 92). After that, the 'leaders of the church' metamorphosed into Parliament, which passed the Act of Uniformity to which the 1552 Prayer Book was annexed. Then at last came the doctrinal statement of 1553, the Forty-Two Articles, whose authorization was as untidy as so much else in the feverish weeks before Edward's death, and which tells us a good deal about how decisions were made in the Church of Edward VI.

These Articles were published along with a new catechism which was straightforwardly 'set forth by the King's Majesty's authority'. However, the Articles as appended to the catechism were styled on the same title-page as 'agreed upon by the bishops and other learned and godly men in the last Convocation at London ... likewise published by the King's Majesty's authority'. This description was in fact a sleight of hand; the agreement of bishops and godly men had not amounted to a formal agreement in the Convocation of Canterbury, even though Convocation had indeed been meeting at the same time as Parliament. The 'bishops and learned and godly men' were simply a set of leading clergy who would do what the evangelical establishment wanted. Archbishop Cranmer, who had not been told of the title-page, was furious at what it said, both because of its inaccuracy and because of the hostage to fortune which it offered conservatives out to cause trouble for the religious revolution.[6] This messy affair underlines the fact that at no stage were the Convocations of Canterbury and York given any formal decision-making power in creating Edward's Reformation. The regime did not trust them. Even in 1547, when the Lower House of the Convocation of Canterbury was making the right evangelical noises, its opinions on clerical celibacy and the Act of Six Articles were secondary to

Parliament's role in legislation. This is not to say that the Convocation of Canterbury (which represented most of the kingdom's population and land area, and was far more important than that of York) had no role at all in the detailed discussions which created Edwardian legislation. Its part has been obscured because its archive has disappeared, so that commentators have wrongly supposed that it did not meet during some parliamentary sessions. Only once, in 1550, can we glimpse its debates on reforming the 1549 Prayer Book.[7] But whatever contribution Convocation made, formal decisions were made elsewhere; preference even went to groups with no formal legal standing, like the consortium of clergy who drafted the Forty-Two Articles and market-tested them in the dioceses – in other words, 'bishops and other learned and godly men'.[8]

So action came either directly in the name of Edward as supreme head, most notably in the 1547 royal visitation, or, during most of the reign, from the Crown exercising the supremacy in collaboration with Parliament. Twice Archbishop Cranmer won battles with more impatient evangelical colleagues by recalling the Privy Council to the erastian principle that a parliamentary decision on religion could not be overturned just because some individual divine had a good idea for reform. The first time, in 1551, John Hooper was forced to wear the prescribed episcopal garments of white rochet and black chimere at his consecration as a bishop, and, in autumn 1552, John Knox failed in his bid to make the Prayer Book require communicants to sit to receive communion. Both these represented victories for Cranmer.[9]

However, many thoughtful members of the Church of England in later generations would find Cranmer's principle wrong-headed. From the later seventeenth century, High Churchmen sought to establish the claims of the English Church to govern itself, particularly through the two convocations, and the Edwardian Reformation seemed increasingly tainted by the role which the royal supremacy had played in it. One of the most extreme statements of such disapproval came from a late-seventeenth-century lawyer-turned-clergyman called Edward Stephens, who, in the course of a varied literary career, managed to

66. *In 1863, evangelical Anglicans erected a statue of Bishop Hooper on the site of his martyrdom at Gloucester. Although the monument was in part a gesture of defiance against the emerging power of the Oxford Movement, its designer could not face the full implications of Hooper's radicalism, and so depicted him in the bishop's garments of rochet and chimere, against which he had protested so vigorously.*

despise erastianism, Roman Catholicism, the Quakers and Cranmer's second Prayer Book with impartial ferocity. In 1702, despite his pronounced and unusual enthusiasm for the churches of the Greek East, with their long tradition of close association between church and state, Stephens termed the setting up of royal arms in parish churches 'an Insolent, profane and impious thing', and he said that the flying dragon on the steeple of St Mary-le-Bow in London was a suitable emblem of the royal supremacy. At the time, Stephens still sounded like an eccentric, and even most Anglican Non-jurors – High Churchmen who had parted company with the Church over its acquiescence in the 1688 Glorious Revolution – would have found this dangerous talk. However, in the nineteenth century, many Anglo-Catholics would come to agree with him.[10]

As we explore the afterlife of the Edwardian Reformations, there is one final dimension to re-emphasize: the internationalism of what happened. Thanks to Henry VIII and the religious uncertainties of his last years, several significant English reformers were given extended involuntary sabbaticals in other European churches during the 1540s, and it is worth remembering that a number of major players in the Edwardian drama had wives from overseas: Thomas Cranmer, John Hooper, Miles Coverdale. In one particularly important respect, the future of the English Reformation was decided in Switzerland in 1549, when the church leaders of Zürich and Geneva found a way of producing a joint statement on the eucharist, the Zürich agreement or *Consensus Tigurinus*. This was an effort to heal the rift which had so damaged the Reformation over the previous twenty years about how evangelicals should understand the presence of Christ in the eucharistic drama. In Zürich, Heinrich Bullinger was doing his best to be loyal to the memory of his mentor and pioneer of the city's Reformation, Huldrych Zwingli. He was faced by a loose coalition of theologians who wanted to find some way through the bitterness which Zürich and the Lutherans of Wittenberg had sustained on the eucharist after the quarrel between Zwingli and Martin Luther. The leader of this coalition had once been Martin Bucer in Strassburg; however, by 1548 Strassburg was in deep

MARTINUS BUCERUS THEOLOGUS

Anne ideo Bucere alio petis arbe Britannos,
Ut cinis & cineris gloria tanta fores.

67. *Martin Bucer. The writing-tablet notes the burning of his*
*bones by Queen Mary and his posthumous Elizabethan rehabilitation*
*at Cambridge University.*

political and religious disarray after Charles V's victory in the
Schmalkaldic War, and Bucer was looking for a secure refuge elsewhere, so leadership passed to John Calvin in Geneva.

As a result, Bullinger and the Genevans circled round each other
during 1548–9 in negotiations about the eucharist. At this delicate
moment, the evangelical leaders in England were marked out as partisan, not because they were especially close to Calvin, but because they
were intimately bound to Bucer, thanks to his long-standing relationship with Archbishop Cranmer. For many of Bullinger's less subtle
admirers, Bucer was no better than a Lutheran, simply because he disagreed with Bullinger; and this meant that Cranmer and his circle were
tarred with the same brush. If Zürich and Geneva had failed to agree at
this moment, it would permanently have damaged relations between

*68. Heinrich Bullinger, the leader of the Zürich Reformation after the death of Zwingli. The engagingly realistic snails are probably a hermetic symbol for the perfection of cosmic eternity.*

Zürich and Canterbury. It was thus of major importance for England when, in one of the few statesmanlike moments in the sixteenth-century Reformation, Bullinger and Calvin brokered the *Consensus Tigurinus*, creating a formula comprehensive enough to avoid the appearance of victory for either side.[11] Moreover, further negative developments in the 1550s cemented the unity of Zürich and Geneva, through the hostility which they experienced from hard-line Lutheranism: ultra-loyal Lutherans captained by Joachim Westphal of Hamburg routed any attempt to extend agreement further to heal the eucharistic rift.[12] After that, the *Consensus* became one of the symbols of an evangelical group identity which was non-Lutheran, even anti-Lutheran: the grouping would soon be labelled Reformed.

The consolidation of this Reformed identity came just at the time when (as we have seen) Thomas Cranmer and the English evangelical leadership had also consciously moved out of step with Lutheranism in their eucharistic thought. Admittedly, Canterbury and Wittenberg were by no means totally estranged during Edward's reign. One of the great might-have-beens of Reformation history was the invitation by Edward VI's government to Philipp Melanchthon to fill the gap left by the death of Martin Bucer as Regius Professor of Divinity at Cambridge University. Melanchthon had always shown himself ready to explore ways of healing the Reformation's wounds, and English theologians of the 1540s and 1550s were much more likely to have his books on their shelves than those of Luther.[13] Astonishingly, it looks as if in 1553 Melanchthon was ready to accept the Cambridge invitation, overcoming his lifelong superstition about seafaring, in order to travel to England. Only Edward's death stopped him coming, although there is a curious silence about what happened to the very handsome travel expenses which he was granted by the beleaguered Edwardian government.[14] So Melanchthon stayed at Wittenberg. The English invitation had been the last chance for him to step out from under Luther's shadow. Within four years Westphal and his fellow-ayatollahs forced Melanchthon to play the role of Lutheran patriarch: he signed up to a swingeing condemnation of Zwingli's eucharistic doctrine at Worms in 1557, and all prospect of his playing an ecumenical role was at an end.[15] From 1558, the heirs of the Edwardian Reformation steered the English Church into an increasingly confessionalized Protestant Europe as part of the Reformed camp.

Without the achievement of the *Consensus Tigurinus*, therefore, it would not have been nearly so easy for the Swiss Reformation to develop its future creative relationship with the English Church. Yet we need to be discriminating when we describe the relationship. Two adjectives have often been hurled at Edwardian religious thought, 'Zwinglian' and 'Calvinist'. Both are primarily used as terms of abuse, and in fact they originated in early Roman Catholic accounts of Edward's reign, such as those of the Jesuit Robert Parsons. In his *Third part of a treatise* of 1604, Parsons launched a major attack on *Acts and*

*69. Philipp Melanchthon: Boissard's version of an engraving by Albrecht Dürer, c. 1526.*

*Monuments*, John Foxe's magisterial celebration of English Protestantism, and his assault repeatedly used the Zwinglian label to characterize the later Henrician and Marian Protestant martyrs commemorated by Foxe. When Parsons totted up his anti-hagiographies, he made the vast majority (268) of them 'Zwinglians and Calvinists', with a minority (59) of 'Anabaptists, Puritans, and doubtful of what sect'. The clear implication was that pure English Tudor and Catholic theology had been polluted from abroad by these foreign notions.[16]

The usages developed by Parsons and his fellow-propagandists were soon borrowed from Roman Catholic commentators by Laudian Anglicans in the early seventeenth century, in order to explain the features of the English Church which Laudians did not like, and they have been a feature of less sophisticated High Church Anglican accounts of English church history virtually down to the present day.

The main target was the eucharistic theology of the second Edwardian Prayer Book of 1552. Once more, the Revd Edward Stephens can be relied on to put it more brutally than earlier Laudians or later Anglo-Catholics would dare: he said that the godly order of 1549 had been 'corrupted and disordered by the counsels and assistance of foreigners, and by the practice and contrivance of Cranmer', so that, ever since, the 1552 book had been 'hugged like a bastard child by a silly abused husband' – the husband, of course, being the Church of England.[17]

As seventeenth-century documentary research discovered a great deal of correspondence about Edwardian England in Zürich, there seemed to be confirmation of a Zwinglian development during the reign. It became apparent that many Zürich sympathizers began by displaying an extraordinarily bitter suspicion of Archbishop Cranmer's eucharistic beliefs. This was at its greatest during 1548–9, but after that, abuse of the Archbishop faded away into general praise. These changing attitudes have often been misread as telling us what Cranmer actually believed: that somehow at this time he had come to a 'Zwinglian' understanding of the eucharist, to which Zürich partisans could now give their seal of approval. The chronology of this move was always rather tricky for High Churchmen, if one was not going to get Cranmer arriving at Zwinglianism too early, in time for his first Prayer Book rather than his second: hence some rather tediously complex efforts to analyse Cranmer's eucharistic development, which culminated in 1926 with a brilliant but misleading monograph by Charles Smyth.[18]

A more accurate account would suggest that Cranmer came to firm conclusions on the eucharist rather earlier, between 1546 and 1547. He did then develop a eucharistic theology which resembled the mature theology of Bullinger in Zürich, but as Brian Gerrish has usefully pointed out for us in his discussions of Reformation eucharistic thought, it would be crass to label even Bullinger a Zwinglian, let alone Cranmer.[19] What in fact the Zürich letters reveal is partly the reluctance of Cranmer to display his beliefs openly in the delicate opening years of Edward's reign, but more especially the acute tensions in the run-up to the 1549 *Consensus Tigurinus*. Cranmer, as we have observed, was associated in the minds of Zürich partisans with Bucer and therefore with Calvin. Once the agreement was achieved, tensions relaxed. Bucer, never one to take the easy way out, continued to tread his self-consciously individual middle path between Luther and the Swiss, but the Swiss came to recognize that Cranmer was no blind follower of Bucer. That is why abuse of the Archbishop began to fade from Zürich correspondence, not because his views on the eucharist changed in any noticeable way during 1548–9.

The Edwardian Reformation has also often been characterized as Calvinist, particularly in its doctrinal statement of 1553, the Forty-Two Articles. This is a venerable misrepresentation, pioneered in the 1580s by the Roman Catholic controversialist Nicholas Sander; Sander's scatter-gun use of the term 'Calvinist' even included applying it to Joan Bocher the 1550 Kentish martyr for the Unitarian cause, which would certainly not have amused John Calvin. Like the use of 'Zwinglian', the Calvinist label was taken up with enthusiasm from Sander and Parsons by anti-Calvinists in the seventeenth-century Church of England. Thus the advanced Laudian clergy John Cosin and Augustine Lindsell were not only accused in 1630 of anticipating Dr Samuel Johnson by calling the Reformation 'a Deformation' (characteristically, a phrase also earlier invented by papists), but they were also said to have called the great Edwardian Reformers 'ignorant and unlearned Calvinistical bishops'.[20]

Calvin did indeed take a keen interest in Edwardian England, but he was not well-informed about what was going on. The most spectacular symptom of this was that right up to the summer of 1551, he still regarded Somerset as the most important figure in English politics.[21] In fact, after Somerset's execution, Calvin had to be told fairly firmly by his exile friends in England that it would not be helpful to write to English politicians lamenting the duke's death.[22] The reality is that in the time of Edward VI Calvin was not the towering international figure which he later became. For Elizabethan England, he was indeed the Reformation theologian par excellence; but when Edwardian evangelicals thought of Switzerland, it was primarily of Zürich and its presiding churchman

Bullinger, or of the university city of Basel, where around a hundred Englishmen studied between 1532 and 1600.[23]

Prominent Edwardians could afford to take a generously wide view of what a Reformed identity might mean. For instance, the king's tutor Sir John Cheke was a great admirer of the biblical scholarship of Sebastian Castellio, one of Calvin's most effective critics, who in 1545 had left Geneva for Basel rather than join the Calvinist fan-club.[24] The great Polish exiled reformer Jan Łaski, who likewise was not a soulmate of Calvin, even encouraged the English authorities in 1551 to recruit Castellio from Basel to fill the Regius Chair at Cambridge left vacant by Bucer's death: although Łaski did not succeed in his advocacy, the English government's eventual decision in favour of an invitation to Philipp Melanchthon showed that the England of Edward VI was disinclined to blacklist those of whom Calvin disapproved.[25] Even before Castellio had heard of Bucer's loss, he had reciprocated the admiration of London-based evangelicals by dedicating his 1551 Latin biblical translation to Edward VI, with politely oblique praise of Cheke, and his Bible dedication explicitly presented his work as a revival of an abortive attempt at an improved version of the biblical text sponsored by Archbishop Cranmer in 1549. Calvin would have been particularly annoyed by the dedication's vigorous defence of freedom of worship, and also by a restatement of the doctrine of human free will which was contained in Castellio's annotations on the Epistle to the Romans. To rub salt in the wound, Castellio reproduced a large proportion of his Edward VI dedication in his *De Haereticis an sint persequendi* ('Whether heretics ought to be persecuted') of 1554. This tract was a ringing proclamation of religious toleration in the wake of Geneva's burning of the Unitarian theologian Michael Servetus, and it caused horror and fury in Geneva.[26]

Calvin's unique international standing began to develop after 1553. Notoriously, the event establishing Geneva as the major reference point in Protestant theology was precisely the decision to burn Servetus, which Castellio so deplored, and the burning happened a few months after Queen Mary's *coup d'état* against Queen Jane. But after this, one of

70. *An unusual perspective on John Calvin: sketches of him made while he was teaching, by one of his students, Jacques Bourgoin of Nevers.*

the first marks of Calvin's new status in the Reformation world was a pair of interventions in the troubled affairs of the English-speaking and French-speaking exile communities of Protestants who had left Mary's England to settle in Frankfurt. At the centre of the English dispute was the Scots reformer and Calvin's admirer, now exiled both from his native land and from England, John Knox. Most of the events in the English church (though not the French) are well-known to historians of the Church of England and of Puritanism, thanks to a printed tract of 1574 which gathered up documents and narrative about them: the Puritan-sympathizing compiler of this dossier found his material predictive of the Elizabethan church disputes which were then gathering momentum.[27] It is still worth pointing out that Calvin's involvement in the disputes of the English at Frankfurt was very tentative: his intervention was confined to a couple of reproachful letters to the winners in 1555, and to the provision of a refuge to John Knox's defeated friends when they left Frankfurt for Geneva. By contrast, in the contemporary rows in the French Church at Frankfurt, Calvin travelled up there in person, and he played a decisive part in overturning the Church's existing leadership.[28] Even so, Knox's associates in the Frankfurt troubles were laying down markers for the future, first by unsuccessfully seeking a new status for Calvin as the ultimate referee in their struggle, and then by installing themselves in a Genevan Cave of Adullam. They fashioned an image of Calvin despite himself, as a living reproach to Edwardian imperfections. This is a far cry from the idea that the Edwardian Reformation had a Calvinist identity.

The troubles at Frankfurt carried a powerful symbolism even without Calvin. The English Church was riven by separate disagreements about the future shape of the liturgy and church government, but, if one lays aside the Elizabethan preoccupations of the pamphleteer about presbyterianism versus episcopacy, it was the liturgical issue which was of the greater significance during the Marian exile, and which had the most lasting implications. To argue about liturgy was to argue about the pace of change interrupted back home in 1553. The Geneva party maintained that the 1552 Prayer Book was as much a temporary production as its

1549 predecessor, and that Cranmer and his colleagues would have 'drawn up a Book of Prayer a hundred times more perfect than this that we now have', given more time.[29] The claim is plausible enough: however, the radical step which Knox and his allies then proposed was not to modify the book as Cranmer might be presumed to have intended, but to replace it altogether by the English translation of the Geneva liturgy published in London in 1550. No other English exile community was prepared to do this: no one else was even prepared to accept the compromise pick-and-mix of Geneva and the Prayer Book which Frankfurt then offered. It was at this point that Dr Richard Cox, the former Chancellor of Oxford who had been involved in Prayer Book revision since 1548, plunged zestfully into the Frankfurt troubles. He

71. *The authorities of Frankfurt-am-Main granted the exiled French and English congregations the use of a former nunnery church, the White Ladies (Weissen Frauen Kloster), in a quiet south-west corner of the city. This bird's-eye view of 1628 by Merian shows the buildings little changed from the exiles' troubled years of worship in the church from 1554 to 1559.*

*72. The statue of John Knox in St Giles High Kirk, Edinburgh, is the ultimate icon
of the man who came to personify the Scottish Reformation. However, up to his
defeat at Frankfurt in 1555, Knox's sights were fixed on the Reformation in England.*

defended his old handiwork by making his famous demand 'that they
would do as they had done in England; and that they would have the
face of an English Church'.[30]

What was at stake in this 1555 confrontation was a verdict on the faults
of the Edwardian Reformation. Should one take the line of Sir Richard
Morison (above, p. 102) and be grateful for the speed of change over six
glorious years, or should one emphasize the disappointments of high
hopes, the things left undone which ought to have been done? The same
day as Cox's outburst, John Knox spelled out that second option to a
restless and deeply divided congregation. He provided his own checklist
of three fatal faults in Edwardian England: want of discipline, John

Hooper's defeat over clerical dress in 1550–51 and pluralist clergy. This indictment from the pulpit was in addition to a witheringly caricatured written account of the 1552 Prayer Book which he and his friends had already sent off to Geneva for the delectation of John Calvin. It was alas only some time after the encounter with Dr Cox (as is always the way of such exchanges) that Knox thought of the perfect put-down for Cox and his wish for an English Church: 'The Lord grant it to have the face of Christ's Church.'[31]

Meanwhile, back home in England, Mary's regime was lending a powerful hand to save the Edwardian Reformation from itself by burning a wide range of evangelicals as heretics. Edward had burnt two Unitarians, but the scale of Mary's burnings was, in Andrew Pettegree's words, 'now both intense and somewhat anachronistic', not simply by English but by European standards; it looked back to the holocausts in the Low Countries in the 1520s and 1530s, or in France in the 1540s.[32] The English fires neutralized the evangelical squabbles of Edward's last eighteen months; they helped to erase humiliating memories of the abortive Jane Grey adventure. Moreover, those who died included distinguished church leaders alongside more humble victims, and that must have gone a good way towards healing the bitter memories of the hopes betrayed in the 1549 commotions.

Admittedly, tensions between mainstream evangelicals and radicals remained high despite their common suffering. Several people who were burned were too original in their theology for John Foxe, who in his *Acts and Monuments* either ignored them altogether or sanitized their opinions. Imprisoned church leaders devoted a lot of energy to bitter arguments with the anti-predestinarian Freewillers, arguments to which Foxe first gave minimum coverage and then later omitted, as they had given ammunition to Catholic polemicists. One of Archdeacon John Philpot's last literary works before he went to the flames was the memorably titled 'An apology for spitting upon an Arian', a tract which was far from the modern sense of apologetic.[33] This bitterness was reciprocated by radicals. Miles Huggarde has left us a wonderfully graphic eyewitness description of a clandestine congregation meeting at an

73. *The burning of Archbishop Cranmer: (above) from the Latin edition of John
Foxe*, Rerum in ecclesia gestarum commentarii *(Basel, 1559); (opposite) from
John Day's 1563 English edition of Foxe*, Acts and Monuments.

Islington tavern in Lent 1555. Its charismatic leader 'Father Browne'
described the Roman Catholicism represented by Bishop Gardiner as
'nought', but 'Cranmer's, Latimer's and Ridley's religion' was 'not good',
and it was clearly to be distinguished from 'God's religion'.[34] Soon
Mary's officialdom broke up this preacher's meetings, and Browne was
travelling round the country during 1556, presumably spreading the
same message. How did such roving radical evangelism affect those who
we know were still secretly using the 1552 Prayer Book and the 1553 catechism? We can get some hint from the story of a Cambridgeshire
yeoman called Henry Orinel. Orinel witnessed the arrival in Marian
England of that most mysterious and exotic variety of Tudor religious
dissidence, the Family of Love, at the moment at which Familists began

recruiting the dispersed faithful of the Edwardian Church for the message of their Dutch founder-mystic Hendrik Niklaes. Twenty years afterwards, Orinel recalled his state of confusion and alarm at hearing the new ideas of the Familists in a Colchester pub: he was so upset that he nearly travelled all the way from Colchester to Oxford to consult the imprisoned Cranmer, Latimer and Ridley. However, he listened instead to other voices: he was drawn into the Familist circle, and he continued in that association for the rest of his life.[35]

So Mary's persecution pushed those loyal to the official Reformation into the same dissidence and concealment as the radicals whom they had lately persecuted. This produced a confused spectrum of belief and practice that would have important implications for any future restoration of Protestantism. Developments within Marian Protestant dissidence also revealed that Edward's death had not halted the dynamic of change for mainstream evangelicals. An obvious recent model for Christians now forced to worship outside the parish system was

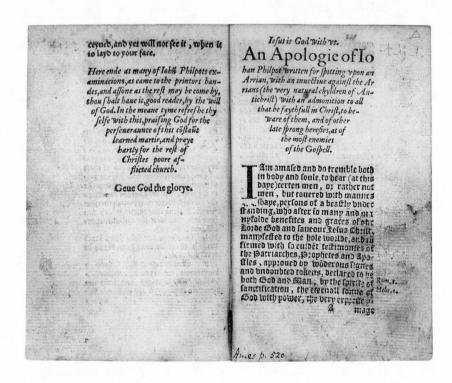

74. First page of the martyred Archdeacon John Philpot's tract explaining
why he had felt it necessary to spit on a unitarian radical fellow-prisoner: the exile
press which published this pamphlet appended it to the account of Philpot's cross-
examinations by the Marian authorities which preceded his burning at the stake.

Edwardian London's Stranger Church. This self-governing body for
refugees had emphasized congregational democracy, but it had been led
by its Polish superintendent Jan Łaski with all the episcopal chutzpah of
Calvin in Geneva. Naturally Queen Mary dispersed the Strangers to
fresh refuges abroad, but we now know, thanks to one casual reference
in a letter of 1559, that a nucleus of the church secretly carried on in
London up to and beyond her death.[36]

In 1555 Łaski published a description of the church order he had
developed in Edward's reign for his London congregation, the *Forma ac
Ratio*. This was as much a public advertisement for the virtues of presby-

terian order as anything the Genevans could do. Its example was felt both in Marian England and abroad. Brett Usher has discovered that English Protestants in their underground congregation in London ordained at least one man, on the authority of the church's superintendent and governing council of elders; this was exactly the form of church government which Łaski's church had taken under Edward.[37] Indeed, it may seem surprising at first sight that even John Knox's doubly exiled English-speaking church in Geneva followed the Łaski model more closely than that of its sympathetic Genevan hosts when it decided on a method for electing ministers. In view of the cool state of relations between Łaski and Calvin, this is a particular testimony to the Polish reformer's influence, as is the fact that Knox, in his post-1560 career in the Scottish Reformation, went on directly borrowing from Łaski's *Forma*. Equally significant is a tribute to Łaski from the church in Wesel, where the congregation's sympathies were wholly with Knox's opponents in the Frankfurt dispute: they too adopted Łaski's form of church polity.[38]

What was happening in these varied cases should not be anachronistically interpreted as a vote in favour of presbyterianism against Anglican episcopacy. The heirs of the Edwardian Church, it cannot be too often stressed, had no notion of Anglican episcopacy. Long ago Gordon Donaldson suggested very plausibly that the persecuted English and Scottish congregations of the mid-1550s, the 'churches under the cross', had a distinctive view of church polity: in the sort of emergency which they faced, they should operate by rules different from those which applied in an established state church.[39] The office of bishop, far from being the linchpin of apostolic order for Edwardian evangelicals, had secular and not sacred overtones. Bishops were governors in a settled society: JPs, members of the upper house of Parliament – in other words, great magnates of the realm. In exile, none of these roles were relevant: so former bishops served happily as pastors or superintendents alongside other ministers. What more natural than for English Stranger churches, like those at Wesel, Emden, Frankfurt or Geneva, to look to the very successful precedent of the Stranger Church in London with its superintendency, ministers and elders?

75. *Jan Łaski: a seventeenth-century English version of the portrait published
by Theodore Beza in a series of pictures of leading reformers.*

And the same pragmatism in an emergency applied to liturgy as to
polity. Cox and his friends at Frankfurt may have defended the Prayer
Book against utter dissolution, but even they were ready to drop parts
of the Prayer Book in order to compromise with their opponents, and
so were other communities.[40] Equally, the exiles at Wesel, thoroughly
and explicitly approving of Knox's defeat at Frankfurt, nevertheless
resolved only 'to retain so much of the book heretofore in our own
country received as now most fitly standeth with this time, places and
persons'. In other words, they were going to make their own cuts in the
text, and they also added some material of their own provided by their
former pastor, one of the veteran liturgists and hymnodists of the
English Reformation: a distinctive general confession 'used sometime
among us by our late worthy pastor Mr Coverdale'. This was a congregation, one should note, led successively by three bishops of

the Edwardian Church, Miles Coverdale, William Barlow and John Scory.[41]

Then, in 1558, came the unlooked-for deliverance: Mary's death and Elizabeth's accession to the English throne. From the outset, there was every reason to suppose that the new reign would be some sort of sequel to the Edwardian adventure. The two principal advisers who drew up Elizabeth's church settlement, the brothers-in-law William Cecil and Nicholas Bacon, were former Edwardian royal servants. Elizabeth's first favourite, Robert Dudley, was equally a symbol of the Edwardian era in which his father the Duke of Northumberland had played such a crucial role, and throughout his Elizabethan career Dudley was a constant patron of clergy who had launched their career in the Edwardian Church.[42] Naturally, however, nothing was quite the same. The new regime would have to take note of the rapid changes in the continental Reformation which had taken place in Mary's reign, not least the new prominence of John Calvin. However, fatally for relations between Geneva and London, the face of Calvinism for Elizabeth was that of John Knox. His famous tract of 1558 against female monarchs, *The first blast of the trumpet against the monstrous regiment of women*, came out just in time for Elizabeth's accession. The immediate consequences in London were arrests and house-to-house searches for the offending book: Elizabeth's fury at Knox meant that, even in the longer term, any clergyman with the slightest hint of Genevan connections was excluded from the most influential positions in the Church in the vital formative years of the new settlement.[43]

But apart from this literary accident, the prime agent making for change in the settlement was the queen herself. Elizabeth kept a low profile in Edward's reign, desperately concerned to avoid the taint of scandal which had come from her traumatic teenage involvement with Lord Thomas Seymour, last husband of Queen Catherine Parr, during the eighteen months which she had spent living in their household in 1547–8. Her profile was lower still under Mary, when she might easily have faced execution, since she was a potential focus for treasonable Protestant hopes.[44] What was the nature of Elizabeth's religious beliefs?

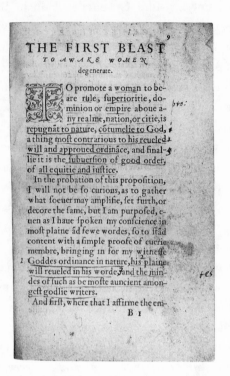

76. *The first page of John Knox's disastrous* The first blast of the trumpet against the monstrous regiment of women *(1558). Its uncompromising opening sentences set the agenda for a work which infuriated Queen Elizabeth, though it clearly fascinated an early owner of this copy, who underlined and numbered the principal propositions.*

Sometimes she has been seen as a Henrician Catholic, pushed into a more Protestant settlement by those around her. This is a clear mistake. Elizabeth was an evangelical, but of a distinctive and (in the conditions of the late 1550s) an extremely old-fashioned variety. She disliked the marriage of clergy and enjoyed more ceremonial and decoration in worship than her half-brother would have considered tolerable. If we want to place her beliefs, we should do so not at the court of Edward, but at the court of Henry VIII and Catherine Parr in the mid-1540s. This was the era when Elizabeth had first been given a role of dignity, when she became one of the élite of children who enjoyed an exceptionally rich and privileged education. It would not be surprising if these years, and her time in the Seymour/Parr household, became a formative experience for her piety, just as the subsequent unfortunate attentions from Lord Thomas affected her entire emotional life.

There are remarkable similarities between the religious peculiarities which Elizabeth displayed throughout her adult life and the picture of a royal evangelical convert painted in Queen Catherine's devotional work *The Lamentations of a sinner*. Catherine wrote this penitential tract while King Henry was alive, but she had the good sense to wait for his death before she ventured into print. Reading it, there is no doubt that we are hearing the testimony of one who has pushed aside an old devotional world and left it for a new. We hear the familiar great evangelical themes: justification by faith alone, sneers at the cult of the saints and attacks on unwritten verities, besides the inevitable abuse of the Bishop of Rome. This is very different from the religious mix prescribed for Henry's Church in the 1543 King's Book, where the 'new learning' is held at arm's length.[45] Yet there are also individual touches in Catherine's work which sound an oddly old-fashioned note in the evolving church of autumn 1547. Catherine clearly envisaged a celibate clergy, discussing the vocation of ministers separately before she went on to the vocation of lay people to marriage and the bringing up of children.[46] She also derived deep consolation from the contemplation of Christ on the cross. In itself this was an evangelical theme, but Catherine described it in markedly visual terms, and she did not shrink from repeatedly terming her vision as that of the 'crucifix'. Here is Catherine warming to her theme: 'This crucifix is the book, wherein God hath included all things, and hath most compendiously written therein ... let us endeavour ourselves to study this book.' One can imagine what Catherine's stepson Edward might have thought of this a year or two later, given his worries about retaining even the plain cross of St George in the insignia of the Garter when he was revising the Statutes of the Order (above, p. 32). More remarkable still is the literary scholar Janel Mueller's discovery that Catherine was redeploying the strange oxymoronic

metaphor of 'the book of the crucifix' from a sermon by that arch-enemy of the 'new learning', Bishop John Fisher.[47] And then one thinks of Elizabeth's obstinate retention of a very physical silver crucifix on the altar of her Chapel Royal, to the horror of her most loyal clergy.[48]

There was another important aspect of Queen Catherine Parr's outlook which may well have impressed the young Elizabeth: she was what John Calvin repeatedly and pejoratively dismissed as a 'Nicodemite'. Nicodemus for fear had visited Christ only by night, and, in the same way, Catherine failed publicly to stand up for her evangelical faith against religious error during the life of her formidable royal husband. In the reign of Queen Mary, Elizabeth also became a Nicodemite, dissembling her undoubted evangelical sympathies and attending mass. So did her old tutor Roger Ascham. Moreover, when Elizabeth came to the throne, she modelled her new church structure with the aid of former Edwardian politicians who had done the same thing: Bacon and Cecil. Even more strikingly, her first Primate of All England, Matthew Parker, had somehow managed to survive in the England of Queen Mary without joining the exile. The same was true of her first Dean of the Chapel Royal, her Edwardian chaplain George Carew. The Elizabethan Settlement was a Nicodemite settlement.

After experiencing the relentless, single-minded advance of Edwardian religious policy, these leaders of the newly conceived Elizabethan Church had been involved in the muddle and humiliation of compromise in order to survive under Mary. It was unlikely that they would feel the same fervour for religious revolution as those who had made a different sacrifice and kept their consciences clean from Marian taint by finding refuge abroad. Moreover, even among the exiles, there were those who had hesitated for a while in Mary's England, and made untidy

*77. Catherine Parr about the time of her marriage to Henry VIII in 1543: attributed to the artist known as Master John. She is wearing a girdle of antique cameos, apparently converted to secular ornament from a rosary which had belonged to Queen Catherine Howard. This picture, in the National Portrait Gallery, was formerly thought to be of Lady Jane Grey.*

# Elizabeth<sup>e</sup> Regina.

2. PARALIPOM, 6.

¶ *Domine Deus Iſrael, non eſt ſimilis tui Deus in cœlo & in terra,*
*qui paƈta cuſtodis & miſericordiam cum ſeruis tuis, qui ambu-*
*lant coram te in toto corde ſuo.*

compromises with the regime before fleeing abroad – for example, the future literary defender of the Elizabethan Settlement, John Jewel. This hesitation had been an issue in the Frankfurt stirs in 1555, when John Knox and his party had attempted to discredit some of Richard Cox's supporters precisely because of their tarnished records.[49] Now it was the likes of Cox and Jewel who would find career opportunities in Elizabeth's church, not Knox's unsullied comrades. The trauma of the Marian experience cast a long shadow over the Elizabethan Church, and within that Church, there sounded an uncertain note which had not been heard in Edward's reign.

Altogether there were many reasons why the Elizabethan Settlement should take a different course from the Edwardian Reformation, despite the formal near-identity of its church polity, liturgy and doctrinal statement. This was a unique way to bring confessionalization to a Reformed Church, a 'Second Reformation' like no other in Reformed Europe. In form it represented a restoration of Edward's Church, but curiously not as it had stood at his death: the moment in time resurrected in 1559 was September 1552. Thus the 1552 Prayer Book was deprived of its 'black rubric', that last-minute addition from autumn 1552 explaining that kneeling for communion did not imply adoration of the bread and wine. Likewise, there was no restructuring of canon law (the scheme killed off by Northumberland in spring 1553) nor reformed catechism and primer (actually published later that same spring).[50] Why was this?

It is certainly true that the black rubric and the catechism and primer had all been presented to the Church with rather unsatisfactory legal backing, but a broader explanation might be found in Elizabeth's bitter memory of the Lady Jane Grey adventure of July 1553. We tend to forget, because of the Roman Catholicism of Mary's regime, that Jane's accession had been as much of a blow for Elizabeth's claim to the throne as for Mary's: during the crisis, no less an Edwardian hero and Marian

78. *Elizabeth I openly valued prayer more than preaching. John Foxe's publisher John Daye used this image of her in two different books of private devotions. She has laid aside the sword of justice in order to concentrate on her prayers.*

martyr than Bishop Nicholas Ridley of London had repeatedly used the pulpit to proclaim Elizabeth's illegitimate status.[51] The depths of Elizabeth's fury at John Knox's scorning of female governors in 1559 are a reminder of just how sensitive she was about her royal title. So however personally fond she may have been of her dead half-brother, the policies of his last tumultuous months may have been associated in her mind with the attempt to ruin her life and thwart God's will for her succession to the Crown. They were not to be revived.[52]

Whatever the details of the 1559 Settlement, all those around the queen with any part in leading the new Church expected that further change would come in due course. Yet Elizabeth was to confound them all, defending her ageing snapshot of Edwardian religious practice for forty-four more years, until many had forgotten the purposes for which Edward's policies had been designed. During the 1560s her bishops, mostly survivors of Edward's clerical leadership, went on struggling to promote further reformation. We now know, thanks to the research of David Crankshaw, that it was the bishops who in 1562–3 sought to use the Convocation of Canterbury to launch sweeping reform proposals, changes which would have continued the trajectory of Edwardian reform well past the 1553 benchmark. Crankshaw has identified Archbishop Parker himself as at the heart of this project.[53] The queen stopped their reform programme in its tracks. Temporarily cowed at that stage, the church leadership tried again in 1566, this time backing a series of reform bills in Parliament; but once more these met with royal sabotage. It was the end of reform from the top. The queen's stance was uncomplicated: she had decided to allow neither Convocation nor Parliament to indulge in any further meddling with what she had achieved in 1559. Let us recall those words of the royal favourite Sir Christopher Hatton to Parliament in 1589: at the beginning of her reign, said Hatton, she had

79. *Design for a monument to King Edward VI, c. 1570. In the end Elizabeth failed to provide monuments for either her father or her sister or brother, and Edward was never to receive one. A simple modern slab in the Henry VII Chapel, Westminster Abbey, marks his grave.*

63

'placed her Reformation as upon a square stone to remain constant'.[54] And so, with the twenty-year interval of the seventeenth-century British Civil Wars, it has proved.

Elizabeth deliberately sought to take the spirit out of the Edwardian Church at the same time as she restored its husk. Symbolic of this is her attitude to preaching and the twelve Edwardian homilies, which were not only brought back, but supplemented with a second set of twenty-one in 1563. Elizabeth subtly redefined the relationship between preaching and homilies. The Edwardian regime had explained in the 1547 royal injunctions that the homilies were a response to the lack of preachers in the Church, providing reliable substitute teaching for the people; but the official aim was also to complement them and to some extent render them redundant by the extension of preaching. Elizabeth felt no such need: too much preaching outside the homilies could be a dangerous thing. The historian William Camden's admiring description of the queen's piety reveals her showing an alarming disregard for the new dawn of the Reformation when she recalled words attributed to her papist predecessor Henry III, 'that he would rather devoutly address his own prayers to God than hear others speaking eloquently about God'.[55] Her attitude crystallized in her loathing of prophesyings, that misleadingly dramatic term for the locally arranged clerical seminars designed to improve preaching standards in her Church: notoriously, in 1577, she ruined the career of Edmund Grindal, her Archbishop of Canterbury, rather than yield to his entreaties to preserve the prophesyings.

Playing to a more sympathetic audience, Grindal's successor as archbishop, John Whitgift, the queen scorned the idea that every parish should have a preaching minister, and she declared that wayward preachers ought to be forced to read the homilies: 'there is more learning in one of those than in twenty of some of their sermons'.[56] This was to praise the Edwardian Reformation in order to subvert it. When the Church of England came near to a universal preaching ministry by the early seventeenth century, it was little thanks to Elizabeth. It was her successor King James, freshly arrived from a national Church in Scotland which made preaching a priority, and himself a major aficionado of the pulpit, who announced that rather than granting his Archbishop's request for more homilies, he intended to plant preachers. Only then was the official prohibition on prophesyings and combination lectures finally lifted.[57]

John Knox had therefore proved prophetic in the 1555 troubles at Frankfurt in singling out the matters which fired up Protestant activists under Elizabeth. He castigated Nicodemites: her Church was led by them. He deplored the lack of discipline in the Edwardian Church: she did nothing to change the system. He called to mind John Hooper's defeat by Cranmer and Ridley on clerical dress: a uniform clerical dress code became a preoccupation of Elizabeth, forcing her bishops into a constant state of disciplinary guerrilla warfare with some of her most conscientious clergy. Pluralism of ecclesiastical benefices and lay financial exploitation of the Church flourished as much as in Edwardian days. Small wonder that under Knox's influence, the Protestants of Scotland looked with rapidly increasing suspicion on Elizabeth's sorry caricature of the Edwardian Church – a Church which, for all its faults, had been such an inspiration to them in their own struggles against the papal Antichrist. In the Scottish national revolution of 1559, the 1552 Prayer Book was gladly used in the parish kirks of Edinburgh, Glasgow and Perth. By contrast, only three years later, the Scottish Protestant leadership had taken the measure of Elizabeth's foot-dragging, and there was general fury among the ministers at a suggestion that Mary Queen of Scots should adopt the English liturgy for use in Scotland.[58] Just as significant was the fact that the Scots took a benevolent interest in one other fragment of the Edwardian Reformation which Elizabeth had chosen to reject: in 1571, both John Knox and the Scottish Privy Council were scrutinizing the recently published edition of the abortive Edwardian reform of canon law (styled by its editor, John Foxe, the 'Reformatio legum'), which in that same year English enthusiasts for change had unsuccessfully offered to the Westminster Parliament.[59]

In such circumstances, it became a moot point as to who was being truly loyal to the memory of the Edwardian Reformation. Was it the conformist clergy like Whitgift, or the activists whom they abusively labelled Puritans or precisians? Through the 1570s, John Whitgift conducted a long battle of the books with his former Cambridge colleague Thomas Cartwright, following the publication of the Puritan *Admonition* to Parliament: an indictment of the Elizabethan Church which Cartwright heartily endorsed and went on to amplify. In this argument about conformity to Elizabeth's settlement, with Whitgift defending the new status quo, and Cartwright insisting on its unacceptability, there were close echoes of the arguments about conformity to vestiarian norms which had pitted Nicholas Ridley and Cranmer against John Hooper in 1550. Whitgift actually possessed a manuscript of Ridley's reply to Hooper's arguments, and his polemic against Cartwright owes much to Ridley's: equally, Cartwright occupied the same ground of argument about conscience and things indifferent as Hooper had done.[60] But although Whitgift and Ridley both argued that one should not question higher authority in matters indifferent, their proclamation of authority was made against two very different backgrounds. The England of 1550 was engaged in a revolution on the march, led by that authority which commanded obedience: the disagreement between Hooper and Ridley had been on the pace of change, not on whether or not it was necessary. In the *Admonition* controversy, Whitgift's argument for obeying authority was a call to Cartwright and his fellows to obey Elizabeth's unchanging settlement.

During the Marian years, the presbyterian polity imitated from Łaski's London Stranger Church had been the common property of the whole English Church under the cross – including those who had been bishops in the Church of Edward VI. By the 1570s, after the *cause célèbre* of Thomas Cartwright's Lady Margaret lectures at Cambridge, discussing church government in the book of Acts, presbyterianism became a symbol of discontent with Elizabeth's bishops. Very many of her bishops had experienced the freedom of exile and the presbyterianism of the 'Church under the cross', but now they found themselves defending the immobility which they themselves personally deplored. Already in the 1560s, former members of the underground church in Marian London began meeting again outside the parish system, outraged by the renewal of official requirements on clerical dress. This in turn infuriated the former exile Bishop Grindal of London: the underground church had been a godly enterprise under Mary, and he himself had retrospectively confirmed a non-episcopal ordination of Thomas Simpson which the church had carried out. Now, however, it was in vain that he reproached his former fellow-victims of persecution: 'you condemn not only us but also the whole state of the Church reformed in King Edward's days ... There be good men and good martyrs that did wear these things in King Edward's days. Do you condemn them?'[61] But the congregation persisted, and a new separatism grew among some mainstream Protestants: even though they abhorred radical sectaries, they imitated their separation because they found Elizabeth's incomplete settlement intolerable. Was this condemnation or fulfilment of the Edwardian revolution? It was no accident that when John Foxe wrote up his account of the Marian London congregation in *Acts and Monuments*, he was extremely circumspect about the way in which it had been run; in fact, in later editions after his 1563 text, he drastically cut back what he had to say about this heroic group.[62]

This was by no means Foxe's worst problem in praising the Edwardian legacy. In glorifying the witnesses to Edwardian truth furnished by the Marian holocaust, he had to face the fact that Edward's Church had itself persecuted and burnt heretics, albeit on a much smaller scale than Mary. This was something which the Elizabethan and Jacobean heirs of the persecuted radicals frequently and bitterly reminded mainstream Protestants, but it was a particularly acute issue for Foxe himself, for he strongly disapproved of all executions for religion. His solution was steadily to cut down his own material on the persecutions, so that in the later English editions, all that the reader could learn of the deaths of Joan Bocher and George van Parris was that they 'died for certain articles not much necessary here to be rehearsed'.[63] Equally problematic in a different way was Foxe's large mass of documentary material about the career of Robert Ferrar, a leading evangelical who, after he was made Bishop of St David's in 1548, had been sucked into a complicated feud with a clerical clique in his diocese. It was a depressing tale of

*Colligit ut* FOXUS *fanctorum gefta virorum*
*Digna facit fanctis plurima Martyribus.*

bb 2.

80. *John Foxe: the portrait type which Boissard derived from the picture in later editions of* Acts and Monuments.

prolonged warfare between evangelical clergy who ought to have been using their energies to further Welsh reformation rather than attacking each other. One of Foxe's friends complained that the Ferrar documents were perfect ammunition for papist sniping, but the martyrologist resisted the call to get rid of them altogether, deciding to name and shame some of the clergy who had harassed the future martyr, and who now held high office in the Elizabethan Church. Nevertheless, he kept tinkering unhappily with the text which he included on Ferrar, and he never integrated it into his main narrative of the Edwardian years: instead he appended it to his account of Ferrar's Marian martyrdom, and thus gave the impression that it was really an anticipation of the later atrocities suffered by the unfortunate prelate.[64]

Despite all such problems, Foxe's account of the Edwardian Church was overall designed to praise a solid record of achievement. There were plenty of commentators who, like him, could treasure their personal golden memories of Edward's reign and wax eloquent about the boy-king. Richard Curteys, Elizabethan Bishop of Chichester, had begun his climb up the church's career ladder as a successful young Cambridge don in Edward's reign, before some very quiet years under Mary. In a Lenten sermon at Richmond Palace in 1575 he made King Edward the centrepiece of his unfolding tale of Reformation triumph, told in Old Testament terms before the queen herself. Henry VIII as Moses had led his people from the Pope's Egypt of superstition into a Reformation Promised Land, 'but did not go over Jordan to it, but died in the land of Moab'. Edward was therefore Joshua who had completed the job, before the backsliding of Israel under Mary. Yet that sad period when the people had 'forgat the Lord their God' had been succeeded by the 'gracious Debora, by whom God ... caused his Church of England to prosper in health, wealth, peace, policie, learning, religion, and many good gifts and graces'.[65] Elizabeth may have enjoyed basking in the heroine's role in the Chapel Royal on this particular day, yet such flattery was not quite what it seemed. Curteys was one of that group of evangelical bishops, led by Archbishop Grindal, who were highly disturbed by her suppression of the prophesyings the year after Curteys's sermon at Richmond. He suffered a strikingly similar fate to Grindal, for he would end his diocesan career suspended from his duties, after causing fury in Sussex by his aggressive confrontation with traditionalist gentry.[66] Curteys might show a smooth tongue at court, but in his role as a bishop his activist evangelical agenda diverged sharply from that of his royal Deborah, and it would have found a more appropriate setting in the time of her half-brother, standing in for Joshua.

Curteys's example thus reminds us that anyone who laid emphasis on praising what had been accomplished in Edward's six years was implicitly judging the lengthening years of Elizabeth's unfinished

Reformation. What are we to make, for instance, of the remarkably persistent rumours early in Elizabeth's reign that Edward VI was still alive and imprisoned in the Tower of London? Such stories were understandable when they emerged in the reign of Catholic Mary, but what did they signify in the time of her Protestant successor? Perhaps some of this rumour-mongering was inspired by the feeling that it was unnatural to have a woman sovereign and that God must have a convincing male waiting in the wings; but it may also reflect a populist Protestantism which dwelt with nostalgia on the memory of Edward VI's religious adventure in less actively godly times. One of those promoting the idea of Edward's survival as late as the reign of James I, a Suffolk clergyman named Gervase Smith, was certainly an enthusiastic Puritan who deplored the way in which the Elizabethan Settlement was operating.[67]

The most graphic example of such oblique criticism is the National Portrait Gallery's celebrated tableau of the young King Edward in the presence of his Privy Council and of his dying father King Henry. Its true importance as a critique of the Elizabethan church has only recently been revealed by Margaret Aston's detective work: she has unexpectedly re-dated to the late 1560s a picture which portrays in very precise detail characters from 1547.[68] What is the meaning of this complex if rather graceless work? Themes abound within it, some very explicit, some submerged. Most obvious is the destruction of the Pope and his associates, trodden underfoot by the young king. They are placed in the lower part of the picture where sin lurks, along with Edward's more conservative Privy Councillors. One of the Pope's names is 'idolatry', and this relates to a scene of iconoclasm inset in the upper part of the picture, where purity reigns. So idolatry and its destruction are major emphases in this representation of the transition from Henry to Edward.

The inset on idolatry is balanced or complemented at the other side with a view of the bedchamber of King Henry: Aston has revealed that his posture and even his bed are derived from a Dutch drawing and engraving of 1563–4 which illustrate stories from the Old Testa-

81. *Henry VIII, Edward VI and the Privy Council: a tableau of the late 1560s by an unknown artist.*

ment Book of Esther. In the original, the Persian King Ahasuerus was gesturing to a book: this had reminded him of the good deeds of the Hebrew Mordecai which he had left unrewarded and, in Esther's story, this recognition of the truth would lead to a happy ending.[69] In the adaptation, King Henry is pointing more directly than in the original to a double repository of truth: his son Edward, at whose feet lies the open book inscribed 'The Word of the Lorde endureth for ever.' The implication is that the full realization of the truth could only come with the new reign. This was precisely the message of the introduction to Edward's reign in the 1563 edition of Foxe's *Acts and Monuments*. Henry had only 'cracked the Pope's crown', and 'that which the father, either could not, or durst not bring to perfection, that the son most worthily did accomplish'. Foxe, who was sometimes amenable to pressure from disapproving outside comment, removed this comparison from his 1570 recasting of his work, but we have already heard Richard Curteys

82. (above) *Drawing of King Ahasuerus of Persia, by Maarten van Heemskerck, 1563; (*opposite) *Engraving from van Heemskerck's drawing of Ahasuerus, published 1564.*

creating his own version of the same relationship between Henry and Edward in his sermon to the queen in 1575.[70] Edward was thus singled out as an example to follow: the boy who could see further and achieve more than his own father. Elizabeth should take note.

Who might have been the intended spectators for this tableau? Dr Aston has suggested two possibilities: Thomas Howard, Duke of Norfolk, and Queen Elizabeth herself. Of the two, Elizabeth might be the more plausible target, but the problems inherent in the picture suggest that it was not intended for her eyes. The picture is very odd in genre. It was uncommon in the England of the 1560s to paint a tableau precisely depicting characters from history twenty years before, let

Conſulit annales, fido prærunte anagnoſte,                    Rex, ubi non habitum virtuti diſcit honorem.

alone to make an attempt to depict them in the costumes of their time. The assembly of portraits of the early Edwardian Privy Council indeed suggests that the artist had some prototype picture in front of him, perhaps with a different original purpose in mind. The nearest parallel type is that of the multi-generational royal family portrait, such as the mural which Henry VIII had placed in the Privy Chamber at Whitehall, or a number of dynastic group pictures which were made in Elizabeth's reign.[71] But this picture of Edward was different: if it was a family picture, the family was incomplete. It showed two Tudors who had furthered reformation, yet it was painted in the reign of another reforming Tudor, without any apparent allusion to her. Nevertheless it contained the ghost of an allusion to a godly queen, so private that no observer could see it without being primed: the figure of Henry VIII has been located through its iconography within the story of good Queen Esther, and Henry is standing in for the Persian King Ahasuerus, husband of Esther, as he comes to a greater knowledge of truth.

In the late 1560s, as this picture was being painted, it was painfully obvious to the godly that the queen needed the same sort of insight. She needed to change roles: at the moment, she was more Ahasuerus than Esther. Her Chapel Royal was infested with the silver crucifix, her Church was frustrated at her obstruction of godly reformation. It is unlikely that the queen was ever intended directly to see the picture, which is in any case unfinished: its full meanings are too hidden, and Elizabeth was notorious for not taking kindly to instruction. The most obvious candidate for a patron is someone who would enjoy a godly joke in private, and the most likely candidate is not the Howard Duke of Norfolk, but a member of the Howards' longstanding rivals the Seymour family. Perhaps the work is a family picture in that sense, rather than a Tudor family portrait. Protector Somerset shares the central position in the picture with King Edward, with his brother Lord Thomas Seymour sitting beside him. One might point to Anne Stanhope Seymour, the widow of the Duke of Somerset himself. Widely regarded as the cause of the duke's downfall through her aggressive personal style, this formidable enthusiast for full-blooded Edwardian evangelicalism survived until 1587, and she would have had every reason to celebrate the dead king in order to sneer at his successor. However, the presence of her egregious brother-in-law Lord Thomas Seymour, quite prominent beside her former husband, might not have appealed to the duchess. Next in line as a possible patron is Somerset's son and heir, the Earl of Hertford: he experienced a particularly troubled relationship with his cousin the queen, after his marriage to another of their cousins from the Grey family line. Given the right sort of instruction in the painting's significance, Hertford would no doubt have enjoyed its tart criticism of Elizabeth's religious backsliding.

However, a very different approach to such celebrations of the Edwardian period emerged among those who wished to defend the Church which Elizabeth had created. Their strategy was not just to admit that Edward's Reformation had had its faults, but to go much

83. *Tomb of Edward Seymour, Earl of Hertford, d. 1621, Salisbury Cathedral. This monstrous monument was clearly meant to remind the Jacobean age of his family's royal connections, and to emphasize that their fortunes had been restored after Edwardian and Elizabethan disgrace.*

further, and deplore its disorder and its shortcomings, in comparison with the settled state of affairs under Elizabeth and her successors. There was a twofold impulse here, one coming from historical writers, the other from theologians and churchmen. First, among the historians, a new vogue for the Roman historian Tacitus at the end of the sixteenth century made the writing of history into an analytical craft, in which cool scepticism, even cynicism, were tools of the trade. John Foxe's commitment to a search for the evidence of God's providence, and his passionate belief that this evidence had been revealed in Edward's proceedings, was a world away from Tacitean history, with its measured and sardonic exploration of power politics: the high-temperature religion of the mid-century revolution was now an embarrassment.[72] During the reign of James I, when Elizabeth's Church may be said to have achieved a peak of self-confidence and effectiveness, this historical stance began emerging into print.

One such historical voice was William Camden, who from 1575 was in a position to disseminate his opinions as a much-admired teacher and headmaster in one of England's most influential schools, Westminster. As a lover of antiquities, Camden deplored the Reformation destruction of beauty. Predictably, he loathed Puritans, for instance sneering in his *Remains*, a discursive analysis of English culture, at Puritans' 'singular and precise conceit' in naming their children. His views may have inspired the memorable stereotypes of Puritans in the plays of one of his most distinguished Westminster students, Ben Jonson, who was also an enthusiast for Tacitus.[73] Camden began his *Annals* of Elizabeth's reign, published in 1615, with a short account of earlier Tudor history, and his miniature summary of the reign of Edward VI is startlingly downbeat in comparison with Foxe. Despite Camden's rather perfunctory round-up list of Edward's religious changes for the better, the bulk of the text emphasizes the greed which destroyed the chantries and other church property, and then aristocratic faction, popular rebellion and the Jane Grey disaster. Camden did not hesitate to paraphrase the biblical text 'woe to you O land, when your king is a child', which long ago had been such an embarrassment to evangelicals in Edward's day.[74] In the English

BRITANNVS. GVLIELMVS CAMDENVS HISTORICVS

DUM laus Britannis sarta mansura est, manet
Aeterna CAMDENI BRITANNIA in libris.

Nnn

84. *William Camden.*

translation of his great topographical tour *Britannia*, Camden, or his translator Philemon Holland, referred angrily to Edward's reign as a 'giddy time', when deploring the destruction of Oxford's medieval university library.[75]

A similar agenda shaped the historian Sir John Hayward's full-scale *Life and Raigne of King Edward the Sixt*, which first circulated in manuscript in the 1620s before its publication in 1630. As Lisa Richardson has demonstrated in her recent study of Hayward, he was soaked in the writing of Tacitus, raiding the ancient text for modes of description for events in his own work, so that he might view the sixteenth century through first-century eyes. Hayward also knew well Foxe's work in *Acts and Monuments*, and used him much elsewhere in his historical work, yet here, in his account of a reign dominated by violent religious change, his only substantial debt to Foxe is in his admiring description of the king himself. Hayward is slightly more forthcoming than Camden about Edward's religious beliefs but, in borrowing material from Foxe on Edward's religion, what interests him most is Foxe's anecdote about the king's supposed efforts at clemency for Joan Bocher and George van Parris, contrasting with the more bloodthirsty attitudes of Edward's advisers.[76] Otherwise, in Richardson's words, Hayward manages to write 'a history of the reign without the Reformation'.[77] It is probably relevant that one of the contemporary sources which Hayward was particularly ready to use was Edward VI's personal Chronicle: as we have observed (above, pp. 21–2), the Chronicle minimizes his preoccupation with religion and gives the impression of a boy-king with primarily secular concerns. Overall, Hayward's distaste for what happened in the Edwardian Reformation is clear. Neither he nor Camden had Catholic sympathies; indeed part of Camden's indictment of the Duke of Northumberland was his hypocrisy in embracing 'popery' at his execution.[78] These historians simply approved of the way that Elizabeth had tidied up the chaos of the earlier Reformation. They represented a new mood in English Protestantism.

A second and different brand of hostility to the Edwardian Church was theological, and it had major consequences for the future character

85. *The entirely secular imagery of the title page of Sir John Hayward's*
Life and Raigne of King Edward the sixt *(1630) is an accurate reflection
of the tone in his text.*

of the English Church. One group of Elizabethan Protestant clergy, a
tiny group at first, began exploring afresh the sacramentalist and cleric-
alist possibilities of the English Church, taking a positive delight in
ceremonial which expressed these interests, and privileging prayer over
preaching. They saw what they were doing as recovering the Catholic
character of the Church. In the writings of their first major spokesman,
Lancelot Andrewes, much of this movement's later thought is already
perceptible by the 1580s.[79] Andrewes and his fellows affirmed a view of
eucharistic real presence which Thomas Cranmer would have strenu-
ously opposed; they deplored the simplified aesthetic of Edwardian
worship and church decoration, and they rejected the characterization

of the Pope as Antichrist which had been axiomatic for Edwardian reform. Naturally the group became a focus for opposition to the
dominance of English theology by John Calvin and Theodore Beza, a
dominance which for the mainstream of Elizabethan theologians was a
natural consequence of the English Church's Reformed character.[80]

By the 1620s Richard Neile and William Laud had made the
movement into a formidable phalanx of clergy; with the support of
King Charles I, they made a bid for monopoly power in the Church of
England, and they liked to make out that their views represented the
Church's only authentic identity. At their most extreme, they could
damn the whole Edwardian enterprise. We have already heard the opin-
ions of two high-flyers within the group, John Cosin and Augustine
Lindsell, on Edwardian bishops and their 'Deformation' (above, p. 173).
Similarly, Laud's chaplain, hagiographer and self-appointed literary
hatchet man Peter Heylyn declared in a sermon preached before
Charles that under his predecessor Edward, the foundations of the state
had been almost utterly subverted, and the whole fabric of government
dissolved by potent factions.[81] In Heylyn's history of the English
Reformation, an enterprise of the Restoration years which pioneered
many of the patterns for later High Church historiography, he commented sourly about Edward that in comparison with all his royal fore-
bears, 'their times were for building up, and his unfortunate reign was
for pulling down'.[82]

At first sight there seems to be little in common between the Tacitean
scepticism of late Elizabethan secular historians and the rediscovery of
Catholic spirituality among Andrewes and his friends to produce this
consensus of condemnation. However, one common factor is the vill of
Westminster. Scholarly concentration on anti-Calvinism among Cambridge dons such as Andrewes or John Overall has tended to obscure
this Westminster dimension. While Camden spent most of his career at
Westminster School, the Dean of the Abbey for forty years from 1561
was his friend and collaborator Gabriel Goodman, one of the few
Protestant church leaders to exhibit the same sort of singular theological outlook as Queen Elizabeth. Goodman was followed as Dean of

*86. Archbishop William Laud was radically different in his theological
outlook from the leaders of the Edwardian Reformation, and his admirers were
articulate critics of it.*

Westminster by Lancelot Andrewes, and under their successive leadership, the Abbey became a self-conscious showcase of liturgical and
choral excellence, as well as a self-conscious tourist attraction. The
Westminster clergy were keenly aware that in their daily worship they
were making statements about the English Church for the benefit of foreign ambassadors and other visitors from abroad, as well as presenting a
particular vision of the Church to the crowds who came up from the
provinces for lawsuits, or business at court or in Parliament.[83] One of
the boys who grew up in the sympathetic Westminster parish of St
Margaret was Richard Neile, future Archbishop and patron of another
Archbishop, William Laud. Just as the nineteenth-century Church of
England experienced the Oxford Movement, we might almost style this
Elizabethan drive for religious renewal the Westminster Movement. In
the period before 1600, that term would make more sense than using

87. *The interior of St Margaret's Church, Westminster, essentially the structure which the future Archbishop Neile would have known in his boyhood. St Margaret's, in the shadow of Westminster Abbey, reflected the ceremonialist churchmanship of the Abbey itself during Elizabeth's reign.*

anachronistic labels like 'Arminian' or 'Laudian', which draw their meanings from the early seventeenth century.

Now it is important to note that the patron for Westminster Abbey and School alike, and also the patron of Camden, Goodman and Neile, was William Cecil, Lord Burghley, who passed on his multiple leading role in Westminster (as he did his role in national government) to his son Robert.[84] William Cecil had been at the heart of the Edwardian Reformation. The Cecils and their changing sympathies make an instructive contrast with that other long-term survivor from Edwardian politics, Robert Dudley, Earl of Leicester: Cecil and Dudley are symbolic of the differing development from the Edwardian inheritance. William Cecil in his old age became disillusioned with Calvinism; he found theologians of the style of Goodman and Andrewes increasingly congenial, and he became a generous patron to the anti-Puritan William Camden. His son Robert became an enthusiastic supporter of ceremonialist worship and of the clergy who expounded it, and the private chapel that Robert built at Hatfield House boasted a startlingly novel assemblage of pictures and stained glass, to emphasize that God should be worshipped in the beauty of holiness.[85] Leicester, on the other hand, became the patron of English Puritans, a discreet opponent of the conformist Archbishop Whitgift and a flamboyant military commander whose service abroad was a living symbol that England was part of militant Calvinist international. Revealingly, Cecil's client Camden portrayed Leicester as that 'new upstart' whom Elizabeth had 'raised out of the dust' – a piece of snobbery which in fact would have applied more accurately to the Cecils than the Dudleys.[86] It was also a far cry from the heady days of Edwardian Reformation, when the young William Cecil had been the go-between for Archbishop Cranmer and Leicester's father John Dudley, Duke of Northumberland.

The Westminster Movement gained recruits and confidence in the reign of James I. Soon, in reference to disputes in the Dutch Reformed Church over its Calvinist inheritance (which had resulted in 1618–19 in the humiliation of revisionist admirers of the academic Jacobus Arminius), the opponents of the English anti-Calvinists labelled them 'Arminians'. The use of a foreign label was not accidental: the views of ceremonialists and sacramentalists like Andrewes, Neile and Laud were seen as alien by the Reformed mainstream clergy who had come to dominate the Elizabethan Church, and who now looked in horror on the antics of the sacramentalist and ceremonialist clerical grouping. The leading mainstream clergy did not fail to challenge the new Arminian development. Peter McCullough's study of court preaching, and of the chaplains who sustained it, has brilliantly revealed how these theological tensions became institutionalized in the courts of James I and his family. Andrewes and his friends established a bridgehead in the King's

Chapel Royal, where James deliberately maintained a religiously inclusive atmosphere, while their opponents rallied to the chapel establishment in the household set up for the king's eldest son, Prince Henry; this was much more self-consciously Reformed in its character. As Henry grew up, he proved very receptive to this distinct agenda: he rallied those who wanted to see England champion the Protestant cause in Europe, as it had done in the reigns of Edward and Elizabeth, in deliberate contrast to his father's search for a universal peace and a reconciliation with the old ideological enemy Spain. Such militancy embraced the struggle to maintain the Reformation at home as well: the teenage Henry's chapel resounded with denunciations of the ills of Jacobean

88. *Robert Dudley, Earl of Leicester, c. 1575, by an unknown artist. His swaggering stance, rich clothes and sword proclaim him as a nobleman and a courtier, the royal favourite par excellence.*

89. *William Cecil, Lord Burghley. Although Cecil proudly displays the*
*Order of the Garter encircling his coat of arms, like Leicester, in all other respects*
*his image is an emphatic contrast: his dress has the discreet dignity appropriate to a*
*royal servant (although he has the badge of the Garter on his chain), and he rides*
*on a mule, symbol of unheroic steadfastness.*

society which recalled the angry preaching of Edward VI's reign, particularly in that fraught last winter of 1553 before the boy-king's death. It
was a far cry from the smooth oratory which was the preferred diet in
the King's Chapel Royal, and its critique included warnings of the dangers which faced England's Protestant religion. Henry's chaplain, Daniel
Price, was not afraid to speak openly in 1613 of the damage done by
'Priests . . . of our own Temple, who wish Rome in the Land, who often
offer strange fire upon the altar even in Bethel.' The Andrewes grouping
was not difficult to discern in this melodramatic description.[87]

In the middle of a developing confrontation, the early death of Prince Henry in 1613 was a shock to the forward Protestants, and it was also bitterly reminiscent of that Reformer boy-king of a half-century before, who had come back to life in Prince Henry, only to die once more. Price made the point explicit in his sermon bitterly lamenting Henry's loss: Jacobean England's manifold social and spiritual ills now deserved no less than the oppression of the reign of Mary, when 'blessed Edward must first be received into Abraham's bosom'.[88] The obvious question was who would now take the part of Edward and Henry to rescue England from looming disaster, and there was an obvious candidate: Henry's younger brother Charles, only twelve years old when Henry died. Several of Henry's chaplains insinuated themselves into Charles's service. Among other newcomers who shared their agenda was the Oxford champion of the Church of England's Reformed identity, Dr George Hakewill, his Reformed credentials honed by study in that stronghold of Calvinist scholarship, the University of Heidelberg. Preaching before Charles, Hakewill resurrected both King Edward and Prince Henry as examples for the new heir to the throne, building a succession of victorious and reforming monarchs: if Charles heeded good advice, he would be 'another Charlemagne, or rather the perfections of all the Edwards and Henries, and Jameses your renowned progenitors united in one Charles'.[89] There were plenty of Edwards, Henries and Jameses to choose from in the English and Scots royal lines, but there can be small doubt that Hakewill was drawing particular attention to the last three royal princes who successively bore those names.

Unlike his brother, Charles proved to be a recalcitrant pupil to such instruction. By the early 1620s, with a good deal of help from the cronies of Lancelot Andrewes, a master of discreet manoeuvres in court politics,

90. *Portrait of Prince Henry attributed to Robert Peake, before and after alteration. The picture has recently been restored (*lower image*) to reveal that it was modelled after Albrecht Dürer's* The knight, death and the devil; *evidently the image of evangelical militancy which the Prince was seeking to project did not commend itself to a later generation.*

he had escaped the influence of his militantly Protestant chaplains, and he began developing the close alliance with the Arminians which in the 1630s brought them control of the commanding heights of the Church of England.[90] Yet still in their years of triumph under Charles, the big problem for the Arminians remained the very immobility of the Elizabethan Settlement. Although the Elizabethan lack of change after 1559 had first given their sacramentalist views the opportunity to emerge, the Church created by the Settlement still contained the fossilized shapes of the Edwardian church polity. The practice and beliefs of the Church were regulated by the virtually unchanged Edwardian Prayer Book and the 1547 Homilies (albeit supplemented in 1563), and the largely Edwardian Thirty-Nine Articles. The theology contained within all these documents was a powerful constraint on any reinterpretation of doctrine in a Catholic direction. Opponents of Laud's policies, such as Bishop John Williams of Lincoln, well appreciated this when arguing with Laud on such contentious issues as the status of communion tables or altars in liturgical furnishing.[91] The 'spiritual presence' eucharistic theology of the 1552 communion rite was a particular embarrassment, even considering the slight moderations which had been made both in its 1559 adaptation, and in the eucharistic statements of the doctrinal articles in 1563.[92] Yet it was difficult to make public criticisms of what was after all the public liturgy of the Church. Bishop Andrewes's solution in his private chapel, to judge from his own annotations on the Prayer Book, was to exploit the fact that the rubrics (liturgical instructions) of the 1559 communion rite were sufficiently brief to leave a good deal of discretion in its performance: he could thus add ceremonial and even private prayers from a variety of older western and eastern sources, the better to express his view of what the eucharist signified.[93]

Another possible escape route for Laudians was to appeal to the Edwardian Reformation against itself: to take the 1549 Prayer Book as a model for liturgical revision of the 1552 rite. This involved, as we have seen, making the assumption that there was a clear distinction in theology between the two books, and further, that the difference was accounted for by interference from the likes of Bucer and Calvin.[94] For example William Forbes, the Scottish High Churchman and Charles I's first bishop in the newly founded diocese of Edinburgh, did his best in his eirenical writing of the early 1630s to seek out moderate opinion in the Church of Rome in the pursuit of reunion. Determined to separate the practice of prayers for the dead (of which he approved) from the doctrine of purgatory (which he regarded as non-scriptural), he approvingly quoted the 1549 Prayer Book for its recognition of the value of prayers for the dead. He spoke with corresponding regret of how Bucer and others had persuaded the bishops of Edward's reign to get rid of 'these most ancient and pious prayers' and to restructure the liturgy in ways 'redolent of modern novelty'.[95] Naturally, those who thus exalted the 1549 rite ignored the possibility that Cranmer needed little prompting from foreign divines to change it, never intending it to be more than a stopgap.

Admirers of the 1549 liturgy (if they had wished to or had possessed the knowledge) could have pointed to the book's own afterlife. Queen Elizabeth seems to have had hankerings after using it: Roger Bowers has recently provided evidence that the queen started her reign by using the 1549 liturgy in the Chapel Royal, before she recognized in spring 1559 that she must bow to political realities and abandon it for a version of the 1552 Prayer Book. Moreover, 1549 had been used in the Irish Church right up to King Edward's death, and there had even been a Dublin printing of it in 1551, a year after any English edition.[96] Although this may not have been known in the 1630s, it was in fact in Ireland that practical action to revive the first Prayer Book was first contemplated. In 1634 the new Lord Deputy, Sir Thomas Wentworth, steamrollered through a reconstruction of the Irish Church in consultation with Archbishop Laud, intended among other things to put it on an Arminian path. John McCafferty's researches on the early Stuart Church of Ireland have revealed that when the Lord Deputy's chaplain, Bishop John Bramhall, drew up proposals for reform on Wentworth's behalf, he tentatively proposed to Laud the reintroduction of the 1549 Book, but Bramhall then thought better of his suggestion, and nothing was done.[97]

It may have been Laud himself who shrank from taking such a radical step; he was on occasion less extreme than his colleagues and henchmen. Certainly three years later Laud tried to exercise a moderating influence in a new scheme: the creation of a new Prayer Book for Scotland. Here his initial idea was simply to introduce the existing English liturgy to Charles's northern kingdom: a different initiative for adapting substantial aspects of the 1549 rite came not from him, but from an advanced fellow-travelling enthusiast among the Scottish bishops, James Wedderburn of Dunblane. Wedderburn did not disguise his motives: for him, as for Bishop Forbes, 1552 was an imperfect rite, including for instance a formula of administration which 'may seem to relish somewhat of the Zwinglian tenet, that the sacrament is a bare sign taken in remembrance of Christ's passion'.[98] Wedderburn did not get away with his most radical suggestions for a return to the liturgical shape of the earlier Prayer Book, but when the new liturgy was published, there were alterations enough to amount for the first time to an official move away from the 1552 book towards the earlier rite.[99] Any moderation which Laud had shown could not save the 1637 Prayer Book from the anger which followed in Scotland; nor could it save Charles I from war with his subjects, first in Scotland, then throughout the British Isles.

So, like the tilt of Cleopatra's nose, Cranmer's 1549 Prayer Book plunged the entire British Isles into two decades of war; and the Church of England which had been shaped by the Edwardian Reformation fell to destruction. One anecdote about those civil wars, whether true or not, encapsulates the unfairness of games of historical consequences. When soldiers of the Parliamentarian general William Waller wrecked Chichester Cathedral in 1642 in the name of godly Reformation, among their targets was a picture of King Edward VI. The perpetrator of this vandalism poked out the king's eyes, saying 'That all this mischief came from him, when he established the Book of Common Prayer.'[100] Such iconoclasm against a devout iconophobe was sadly unhistorical. But after such trauma, it was hardly surprising that when the pre-war Church of England was resurrected at Charles II's Restoration in 1660, it had a vengeful spirit against those who had torn down its polity and its liturgy in the 1640s. The Church's leadership and the Cavalier Parlia-

91. *Seventeenth-century stool in the Museum of Antiquities, Edinburgh. It is said to have been hurled in fury by Jenny Geddes at the Dean of St Giles Cathedral as he tried to read the service from the 1637 liturgy for the first time. Even if Jenny Geddes never existed, the symbolism of the stool remained permanently associated in Scots mythology with the attempt to introduce the new liturgy.*

ment chose to narrow the Church's identity, excluding Presbyterians and those who objected to being told exactly how to use the Prayer Book. For the sake of uniformity, the victors of 1660 were now ready to exclude sections of the Protestant population of England who would have felt very happy in the Church of Cranmer, Latimer and Ridley, but who were henceforth to form a nonconformist religious identity within English society. The victors also modified the 1552 Prayer Book in order to remove the worst of its Reformation angularity, creating the 1662 Book of Common Prayer, which remains the official standard of the Church of England's worship today.

In this work of re-creation and subtle adaptation, the Church of England created a new theological synthesis called Anglicanism. It is a creation which has had some happy and fruitful results, but it is something that Cranmer, Latimer and Ridley would have deplored. In return, there is much that we may deplore about their six-year adventure under the boy-king: much that was negative, destructive and cynical in the revolution which they unleashed. However, we will misread their work and do injustice to their memories if we do not listen out for the genuine idealism, the righteous anger and the excitement which were essential components of the play of King Edward. The ghost of the Edwardian Reformation has continued to haunt Anglicanism: all this mischief did indeed come from the boy-king, even if his long-lived half-sister decisively turned the story to her own purposes. Perhaps the Anglican Communion, most enigmatic member of the Christian family of Churches, might show more gratitude for Edwardian mischief – or at the very least, some remembrance and understanding.

92. *A portrait of the fifteen-year-old Edward VI, depicted in the year of his death, still ornamented the title-page of Elizabeth's official 'Bishops' Bible' in its 1595 edition.*

# *Notes*

## Chapter 1. Dramatis Personae

1. See the listings for Henry VIII's funeral at PRO, SP 10/1, f.69v (*CSP, Domestic, Edward VI*, no. 16, p. 6) and cf. *CSP, Spanish 1547–49*, p. 49. Coronation: Bodley MS Ashmole 817 f. 1v.

2. Likewise, I will be using the terms 'conservative' or 'traditionalist' to describe those who defended the theology and practice of the medieval Western Church. Cf. MacCulloch, *Thomas Cranmer*, pp. 2–3.

3. For a more extended treatment of Henry's views, see my discussion in MacCulloch, ed., *Henry VIII*, pp. 176–80.

4. For detailed analysis and narrative of the 1540s to justify this paragraph, see MacCulloch, *Thomas Cranmer*, Ch. 8 and pp. 351–61. An important recent addition to debate is McDiarmid, 'John Cheke's Preface to *De Superstitione*', providing evidence of the way in which evangelicals could survive at court in Henry's last years.

5. The membership of the Privy Council is usefully discussed and tabulated in Hoak, *King's Council*, Ch. 2.

6. Not all historians would be as positive as I have been about the evangelical agendas of the leaders of the first Edwardian regime. However, for my extended account of events around Henry's death with substantiating references, see MacCulloch, *Thomas Cranmer*, pp. 358–69.

7. The jury is still out on the nature of Edward's fatal illness. A gathering of expert medical opinion from Professor Paul Beeson and Dr Trevor Hughes by the late Jennifer Loach for her study of the reign questions the usual suggestion of tuberculosis, and suggests complications brought on by pyogenic

pneumonia, or bronchopneumonia which led to general septicaemia: Loach, *Edward VI*, pp. 161–2.

8. Folger MS V.b.303, pp. 183–6, qu. Collinson, 'Puritans, men of business and Elizabethan Parliaments', p. 192.

9. On Ireland, see the excellent summary discussion in Bradshaw, 'Edwardian Reformation in Ireland'. For another idiosyncratic Edwardian Reformation, Ogier, *Reformation and Society in Guernsey*, Ch. 3.

10. For useful summary discussion of maritime projects, see Loades, *Northumberland*, pp. 244–7.

11. Moody et al. eds., *New History of Ireland*, p. 78; Brady, *Chief Governors*, p. 52.

12. On the ballads, cf. the dedication to Edward by Thomas Sternhold, qu. Nichols, ed., *Literary Remains of Edward VI*, p. lvi.

13. P. Tudor-Craig, 'Henry VIII and King David', in D. Williams, ed., *Early Tudor England* (1989), pp. 183–206. On Henry as Solomon, see Ives, 'Queen and the painters', pp. 38–9.

14. A useful treatment of this is Bradshaw, 'David or Josiah?'.

15. Cf. e.g., Aston, *The King's Bedpost*, pp. 26–53. Nichols, ed., *Literary Remains of Edward VI*, p. cciv, usefully rounds up references to Edward as Josiah.

16. For some contemporary references to Edward as Solomon, see Bindseil, ed., *Melanchthonis Epistolae*, p. 351 (Cranmer, 1553); *CSP, Foreign 1547–1553*, p. 217 (D'Albiac, 1552); Corrie, ed., *Latimer's Sermons*, pp. 114–16 (1549); Lever, *Sermons*, p. 90 (1550); Nichols, ed., *Literary Remains of Edward VI*, p. ccii (Bibliander), ccxlix (Thomas Cooper, 1548).

17. Lord Stafford's preface to Somerset in his translation of Edward Foxe's *De vera differentia* [*RSTC*, 11220], qu. Nichols, ed., *Literary Remains of Edward VI*, p. lxiii.

18. Lever, *History of the Defendors of the Catholique Faith*, p. 85; Hakewill, *Answere*, p. 181; and on Hakewill, see below, p. 217.

19. Nichols, ed., *Literary Remains of Edward VI*, p. cccxix. Alexandre: CCCC, 126 f. 88v: he completed his lectures on 27 July 1553 (ibid., f. 155v).

20. Bond, ed., *Homilies*, p. 214.

21. Muller, ed., *Letters of Gardiner*, p. 310; cf. ibid., pp. 265–7, 286, 290–91, 295, 299, 310–14, 352, 399, 422.

22. Carr, S., ed., *Early Writings of Bishop Hooper*, p. 439.

23. Vinay, 'Riformatori e lotte contadine', p. 228n.

24. The text is Eccl. 16. For useful discussion of evangelical defences against this text, see King, *English Reformation Literature*, pp. 161–2.

**25.** Nichols, ed., *Literary Remains of Edward VI*, p. 93. The *orationes* are to be found in BL, Harley MS 5087, ff. 78–89, and Additional MS 4724. Jordan, *Edward VI: The Threshold of Power*, Ch. II, provides some basic discussion of Edward's education.

**26.** Nichols, ed., *Literary Remains of Edward VI*, pp. 110–12: 'num mors in bello sit mors praeclarissima et pulcherima [*sic*]' (21 July 1549; BL, Harley MS 5087, ff. 85r–86v); 'Dulce bellum inexpertis' (28 July 1549; BL, Harley MS 5087, ff. 86v–89v). On Cheke to Somerset, see ibid., pp. ccxlv.

**27.** Cf., e.g., Jordan, ed., *Chronicle of Edward VI*, p. xxii. Jennifer Loach advanced the same argument in a rather more nuanced way: Loach, *Edward VI*, especially p. 181.

**28.** Nichols, ed., *Literary Remains of Edward VI*, pp. i–ii.

**29.** *CSP, Spanish 1550–52*, p. 63, though a bad mistranslation or confusion in the Calendar seems to suggest that Edward was writing the sermons himself.

**30.** Nichols, ed., *Literary Remains of Edward VI*, p. clxxx, qu. Grafton's Chronicle; see P. Slack in Loach and Tittler, eds., *Mid-Tudor Polity*, pp. 110–11.

**31.** McCullough, *Sermons at Court*, pp. 42–3, convincingly disproves the common assumption that the Privy Garden pulpit was built in Edward's reign. If it was indeed inaugurated on a 17 March which was a Wednesday (cf. ibid., p. 42), then the most likely date for its building is 1540: the politics of that year would be appropriate, and in 1535 and 1546, the only other possible years, the court was respectively at Hampton Court and Greenwich on that day.

**32.** McCullough, *Sermons at Court*, p. 93; on the medieval Lenten custom, see ibid., pp. 52–3.

**33.** Cf. Anglo, *Spectacle*, p. 296.

**34.** Muller, ed., *Letters of Gardiner*, pp. 161–2.

**35.** Maddison, ed., *Lincolnshire Pedigrees*, I, p.6. Belmain also translated the 1552 Prayer Book into French, finishing it by 18 April 1553, in some haste, which no doubt reflected his fears for the king's life: cf. preface in Nichols, ed., *Literary Remains of Edward VI*, pp. cccxxxvi-cccxxxviii, from BL, Royal 20 A.XIV.

**36.** Nichols, ed., *Literary Remains of Edward VI*, pp. 145–55, from BL, Additional MS 9000 (dated Westminster, 2 December 1548) and Trinity College Cambridge MS R.7.31 (und.). An unfinished copy of the preface is tipped into BL, Additional MS 5464.

**37.** MacCulloch, *Thomas Cranmer*, index s.v. Cranmer, Thomas: canon law collections; 'Great Commonplaces'.

**38.** Nichols, ed., *Literary Remains of Edward VI*, pp. cccxx-cccxxiiii.

**39**. Nichols, ed., *Literary Remains of Edward VI*, p. 205: 'le vray filz du diable, homme mauvais, un Antichrist, et tiran abominable'.

**40**. Cf. the introduction to the 1682 edn, repr. in Nichols, ed., *Literary Remains of Edward VI*, pp. 176–80.

**41**. Nichols, ed., *Literary Remains of Edward VI*, pp. 173–205, from the fair autograph copy, Cambridge UL, MS Dd 12.59 and the draft autograph copy, BL Additional MS 5464. The corrections in the latter seem compatible with Belmain's secretary hand in BL, Royal 20 A.XIV, but the identification cannot be certain. Another hand, in a different italic hand from that of Belmain, adds on the latter 'Car des ce qu'il commenca a escrivre ledict livre et jusques a ce qu'il l'eust achevé, ledict livre a tousjours esté en ma garde jusques a present' (ibid., p. 174).

**42**. BL, C.37.e.23 (formerly 484.a.15), a mid-Tudor royal library binding, with the signature 'gwalter lynne' inside the back cover. This cannot be the edition from which the king worked for his treatise, since the second edition came out after Somerset's fall and deleted the flattering references to him. It has no annotations.

**43**. Ochino, *Dialoge*, sigs. Zia-Bbiia. Ochino may also have been indebted to conversations with Cranmer for his discussion of the pseudo-Clementine epistles, ibid., sig. Qiva.

**44**. Cf. Edward's text at Nichols, ed., *Literary Remains of Edward VI*, p. 199 with Ochino, *Dialoge*, sigs. Qiiia-Qiva: see also MacCulloch, *Thomas Cranmer*, pp. 489–90.

**45**. Cf. Edward, p. 181, with Ochino, sigs. Ciibf.

**46**. Cf. Edward, p. 191, with Ochino, sig. Kiva; Edward, p. 186, with Ochino, sig. Bbiia; for other correspondences, Edward, pp. 198, 200, with Ochino, sigs. Givbf, Ziva.

**47**. Nichols, ed., *Literary Remains of Edward VI*, p. 196 (Cambridge UL, MS Dd 12.59, f. 33rv): 'Aussy s'ilz ne font ses preceptes, c'est adire adorer des ymages, offrir aux ydoles et diables, il les brule, ou leur fait faire amende honorable [the king in his draft, BL, Additional MS 5464, f. 26v, had written 'il nous brusle et nous fair porter un fagot' – his master altered it as in the main text], ou les gehenne et tourmente. Du temps du feu roy mon pere ['Aux jours de mon pere' in king's draft] quand son nom fut effacé de livres, il estouppa les bouches des Chrestiens avec ses six articles, comme avec six poins' ['siz points' in king's draft].

**48.** For useful discussion, see Thompson, 'Order of the Garter' and Strong, *Cult of Elizabeth*, Ch. 6.

**49.** Thompson, 'Order of the Garter', p. 198.

**50.** Edward's joke about St George was at Lord Treasurer Winchester's expense: Townshend and Cattley, eds., *Foxe*, VI, pp. 351–2. St George's day was abolished by Parliament in 1552, Bishop Ridley of London additionally ordering that it should henceforth not be observed in his diocese: Nichols, ed., *Grey Friars*, p. 74.

**51.** Nichols, ed., *Literary Remains of Edward VI*, pp. 511–38. Cecil was made Chancellor of the Order, no doubt as a reward for his work, on 12 April 1553: *CPR, Domestic, Edward VI 1553*, p. 39.

**52.** Nichols, ed., *Literary Remains of Edward VI*, p. 522.

**53.** Thompson, 'Order of the Garter', p. 179.

**54.** On the term 'holy communion', cf. e.g. the proclamation of 25 December 1549, Hughes and Larkin, eds., *Tudor Royal Proclamations*, I, no. 352.

**55.** For all refs. in this paragraph, Nichols, ed., *Literary Remains of Edward VI*, pp. 528, 530, 538. On Hooper, see *ET*, p. 51 (*OL*, p. 81). See also Edward's remarks to his friend Barnaby Fitzpatrick on avoiding mass-going in France, and Fitzpatrick's iconophobic anecdotes, ibid., pp. 69–73.

**56.** Murphy in Starkey, ed., *English Court*, p. 128. On the events of autumn 1549, see MacCulloch, *Thomas Cranmer*, pp. 443–51.

**57.** *ET*, p. 274 (*OL*, pp. 415–16); for context, see MacCulloch, *Thomas Cranmer*, pp. 471–3.

**58.** *CSP, Spanish 1550–52*, pp. 258–60 (a meeting of 17 March 1551).

**59.** Pr. Nichols, ed., *Literary Remains of Edward VI*, pp. ccxxiv-ccxxxiv, from BL, Harley 353, ff. 130–138v, Ralph Starkey's transcript of a discourse of Sir Richard Morison. Cecil was by now in effect private secretary to both Northumberland and Edward, and he was Morison's close friend and regular correspondent at this time (cf. Read, *Mr. Secretary Cecil*, p. 70; Starkey, ed., *English Court*, p. 130).

**60.** Nichols, ed., *Literary Remains of Edward VI*, p. ccxxvii. For Ambassador Scheyfve's comments a year later on the king's precocity, see *CSP, Spanish 1550–52*, p. 437. It is interesting that William Thomas did indeed set up a private briefing system for Edward as part of his education, perhaps with Northumberland's connivance, in September 1551: Loades, *Northumberland*, pp. 201–2.

61. Cf. the bishops' statement of 20 March 'to suffer and wink at it for a time might be borne, so all haste possible might be used' (Jordan, ed., *Chronicle of Edward VI*, p. 56) with the Council's phrase 'should be suffered and winked at . . . for a season': Cox, ed., *Works of Cranmer*, II, p. 526.

62. There is a vexing chronological inconsistency here. Edward quotes Ps. 78, which is set in the 1549 Calendar for evensong on 16 March (reckoned in the March psalter cycle as the 15th evening). He says nevertheless that 'it is not two daies since' Ps. 78 had occurred; but the Emperor's warning was delivered, according to Edward, on 19 March (Jordan, ed., *Chronicle of Edward VI*, pp. 55–6), and his conversation with the bishops must have been on 20 March.

63. John Foxe's account of the same incident tidies up the story, but it does not represent the king as winning his point: Townshend and Cattley, eds., *Foxe*, V, pp. 700–701.

64. MacCulloch, *Thomas Cranmer*, pp. 495–6. For Edward's later consistency about Mary, see *CSP, Spanish 1550–52*, pp. 435–8. On August 1551, Jordan, ed., *Chronicle of Edward VI*, pp. 76–8.

65. *CSP, Spanish 1550–52*, p. 293.

66. Murphy in Starkey, ed., *English Court*, pp. 135–40. Dr Murphy misquotes the PRO call number of Peter Osborne's warrant-book at ibid., p. 139n.: the warrants are PRO, E 101/546/19, ff. 62, 64, 66, 68, 72. The first warrant signed solely by the king, for £600 in prest for livery coats is ibid., f. 69 (30 May 1552).

67. Loades, *Northumberland*, p. 231, plausibly sees Edward as initiating plans for the succession, as did W.K. Jordan: Jordan, *The Threshold of Power*, pp. 513–17.

68. Ponet, *Treatise of politike power*, sig. Iiiia, for both phrases.

69. Jordan, *The Threshold of Power*, p. 109.

70. Bush, *Government Policy of Protector Somerset*, NB especially index references to Pollard and Jordan. Review of Bush by Elton in *Times Literary Supplement*, 6 Feb. 1976, p. 130, repr. in Elton, *Studies*, 3, pp. 460–64.

71. Jordan, *The Threshold of Power*, p. 109. Cf. Bush, *Government Policy of Protector Somerset*, Ch. 5, esp. pp. 103–4.

72. BL, Additional MS 48018, ff. 388r–391v. I myself must confess to having skimmed this MS a quarter of a century ago without noting the 1549 material, and I am exceedingly grateful to Dr Shagan for alerting me to its significance, and for generously sharing with me his transcripts of the material in advance of its publication. See Shagan, 'Protector Somerset'.

73. Cf. MacCulloch, *Thomas Cranmer*, pp. 432–8, and below, Ch. 3.

74. Pr. Townshend and Cattley, eds., *Foxe*, VI, pp. 290–91: 14 October 1549.

75. BL, Additional MS 48018, f. 390r. Cf. CCCC, MS 102, f. 325, where the English translation of Ochino's 'Dialogue betwene the kinge and his people' stresses the king's clemency, 'sending you pardons even home to your doores'.

76. BL, Additional MS 48018, ff. 389v, 390v, 391r.

77. BL, Additional MS 48018, f. 390v; cf. Hughes and Larkin, eds., *Tudor Royal Proclamations*, I, no. 338; *CSP, Domestic, Edward VI*, no. 307. This is not a proclamation: see Bush, *Government Policy of Protector Somerset*, pp. 46–7 and n. 38, although his statement that the commission was issued in 'a temporary lull in the peasant risings' is the reverse of the real situation. Cf. no. 11 of the October 1549 charges against Somerset, Townshend and Cattley, eds., *Foxe*, VI, p. 291.

78. BL, Additional MS 48018, f. 389v. On Somerset's lease from the Duchy of Lancaster, see Bindoff, ed., *House of Commons 1509–1558*, I, p. 199.

79. Fletcher and MacCulloch, *Tudor Rebellions*, p. 146.

80. BL, Additional MS 48018, ff. 388v, 389v. These letters were dated 17 and 18 July 1549, and formed part of a wider government move to seize the initiative: see MacCulloch, *Thomas Cranmer*, pp. 434–5.

81. Pr. Strype, *Ecclesiastical Memorials*, II, ii, pp. 429–37; Jack and Beer, eds., 'Letters of Paget', p. 54.

82. *CSP, Domestic, Edward VI*, no. 330.

83. PRO, SP 10/8/56, f. 103r (*CSP, Domestic, Edward VI*, no. 356). Cf. Aucher's second letter: Beer and Nash, eds., 'Latimer and the lusty knave of Kent', pp. 176–7.

84. BL, Additional MS 48018, f. 388r.

85. Tytler, *England under Edward VI and Mary*, I, p. 114; and cf. Tyacke, ed., *England's Long Reformation*, pp. 17–18.

86. Contrast Bush, *Government Policy of Protector Somerset*, p. 161: 'Absent were unfamiliar principles or extraordinary personal qualities'.

87. Modernized edition in Gorham, ed., *Gleanings*, pp. 128–40. Norton was then tutor to Somerset's children.

88. For an extended discussion of the high politics/low politics theme, see Fletcher and MacCulloch, *Tudor Rebellions*, Ch. 10.

89. *CSP, Domestic, Edward VI*, nos. 378–80, 400; cf. ibid., no. 379 with *APC 1547–49*, p. 330–31.

90. For Somerset's part in neutralizing commotions in 1550 and 1551, see Jordan, ed., *Chronicle of Edward VI*, pp. 41–2, 78; for his lieutenancy in Buckinghamshire and Berkshire, BL, Royal MS 18 C XXIV, f. 88v. For his political antics in 1550–51, MacCulloch, *Thomas Cranmer*, pp. 484, 486, 495–6. Loades,

*Northumberland*, p. 182, is rather sanguine in saying that Somerset had given up his political ambitions by 1551, and he probably therefore lays too much stress on Warwick's manipulation of the situation: ibid., pp. 180–87.

91. *CSP, Spanish 1550–52*, p. 452; cf Townshend and Cattley, eds., *Foxe*, VI, p. 293; Nichols, ed., *Diary of Machyn*, p. 14.

92. Nichols, ed., *Queen Jane and Queen Mary*, p. 21, and refs. there.

93. *CSP, Domestic, Edward VI*, no. 779.

94. Bourbon, *Nugarum libri octo*, pp. 252, 385; note particularly the evangelical flavour of the ending to the latter poem. For discussion of Bourbon, see MacCulloch, *Thomas Cranmer*, p. 136.

95. The inventory is Bodl., Add. C. 94, f. 13r.

96. Bale, *Expostulation*, sig. Aviib.

97. On Edward's Council attendance, Jordan, ed., *Chronicle of Edward VI*, p. 76, and *CSP, Spanish 1550–52*, p. 493. On his relations with Dudley, ibid., pp. 435–7, and cf. sensible discussion in Loades, *Northumberland*, pp. 192–4, 233–4. For the self-interested side of Dudley's strategy, MacCulloch, *Thomas Cranmer*, p. 497.

98. Creation: *CPR, Edward VI, 1550–53*, p. 115. For the maps at Durham Place, PRO, LR 2/118 f. 80r; LR 2/119 ff. 10v, 23r.

99. For popular reaction to the loss of Boulogne, see *CSP, Spanish 1550–52*, pp. 47, 93, 177. Cf. the part played by threats to Boulogne in raising anger against Somerset in September 1549: MacCulloch, *Thomas Cranmer*, p. 444.

100. Starkey, ed., *English Court*, pp. 136–8.

## Chapter 2. King Josiah: Purifying the Realm

1. *CSP, Spanish 1547–49*, pp. 187, 205.

2. Cranmer: Townshend and Cattley, eds. *Foxe*, V, p. 563; Bucer, *Gratulation*, sigs. Biva-Bva.

3. Zürich Staatsarchiv, E II 345a, f. 422rv (*ET*, p. 26; *OL*, p. 41).

4. *CSP, Spanish 1547–49*, pp. 15, 38.

5. Read, *Mr. Secretary Cecil*, p. 68 and see n. 30, p. 474. Professor Simon Adams in a private letter to me redates this memorandum to the end of 1551. William Paget expressed very similar fears to Somerset in 1549: Jack and Beer, eds., 'Letters of Paget', p. 23.

6. Townshend and Cattley, eds., *Foxe*, V, p. 563.

7. Corrie, ed., *Latimer's Sermons*, pp. 121–3. Cf. also the attack on the conservative

bishops in William Samuel, *The Practice, Practised by the Pope and His Prelates* (1548), esp. sig. Aiv, qu. Davies, 'Towards a Godly Commonwealth', p. 102.

8. Cranmer's speech is in Cox, ed., *Works of Cranmer*, 2, pp. 126–7. The text has no definite pedigree before the time of John Strype, and contains one oddity in referring to Paul III as 'late bishop of Rome'. It is not described in the contemporary accounts of the coronation, but may correspond to the exchange between Edward and Cranmer after the anointing, recorded by Ludovico Montio: *CSP, Venetian*, 6, pt. 3, p. 1638. For expenses for the revels, see Folger MS L.b.8, f. [4r].

9. Anglo, *Spectacle, Pageantry and Early Tudor Policy*, pp. 283–95, esp. pp. 286, 294, 354.

10. Loach, 'Ceremonial in the reign of Henry VIII', pp. 56–68.

11. Somerset to Pole: Pocock, ed., *Troubles*, p. viii. On the cult of Henry, Duffy, *Stripping of the Altars*, p. 195, and see index refs. s.v. Henry VI. The comparison between Somerset and Gloucester was taken up by Foxe: cf. Townshend and Cattley, eds., *Foxe*, VI, p. 296. It had the additional resonance that both Protectors had enemies who were Bishops of Winchester.

12. Nichols, ed., *Narratives*, p. 68; Bodl. MS Tanner 90 no. 40, f. 144 (4 May 1547).

13. Pr. in extract form from Bonner's Register in Townshend and Cattley, eds., *Foxe*, V, App. XX. For instances of new cases against evangelicals, see ibid., VIII, p. 715; MacCulloch, *Thomas Cranmer*, pp. 370–71; and Tyacke, ed., *England's Long Reformation*, pp. 95–6.

14. Bodl. MS Tanner 90 no. 41, f. 145 (11 May 1547); Muller, ed., *Letters of Gardiner*, p. 301, and generally pp. 296–406. On 22 April Richard Grafton and Edward Whitchurch had been granted a privilege to print the homilies and other liturgical books 'that shall be used, suffered or authorised' (*CPR, Edward VI, 1547–48*, p. 100), but the homilies were not published until 31 July. On the visitation, see MacCulloch, *Thomas Cranmer*, pp. 369–70.

15. Cf. text in Townshend and Cattley, eds., *Foxe*, VI, p. 217.

16. Hughes and Larkin, eds., *Tudor Royal Proclamations*, I, no. 281; Muller, ed., *Letters of Gardiner*, p. 287.

17. Bodl. MS Tanner 90 no. 44, f. 150. The printed editions of the *Exoneratorium* between 1516 and 1530 are *RSTC*, 10627.5–10634.3.

18. MacCulloch, *Thomas Cranmer*, p. 370; *CSP, Spanish 1547–49*, p. 106; Lefèvre-Pontalis, ed., *Selve*, pp. 151–2.

19. Jordan, *Edward VI: The Young King*, pp. 249–53.

20. *CSP, Spanish 1547–49*, pp. 92, 103; on France, Loades, *Northumberland*, p. 95.

21. For discussion, MacCulloch, *Thomas Cranmer*, pp. 372–5.

22. We await the conclusions of Mr Alec Ryrie in his doctoral research on the outlook of evangelical opinion-formers in the England of the 1540s.

23. For Cranmer and Ridley, MacCulloch, *Thomas Cranmer*, pp. 354–5, 379–83. On Latimer, Corrie, ed., *Sermons and Remains of Latimer*, pp. 265–6.

24. Christmas, ed., *Works of Ridley*, pp. 259–60, 264–5; MacCulloch, *Thomas Cranmer*, pp. 378–9.

25. Cf. *CPR, Edward VI 1548–9*, p. 406 (12 April 1549), *CPR, Edward VI 1549–51*, p. 347 (18 January 1551).

26. *Regiae Maiestatis mandatorum epitome*: the second edition is dated 1548.

27. Townshend and Cattley, eds., *Foxe*, V, p. 563. Duffy, *Stripping of the Altars*, pp. 449–53.

28. *CSP, Spanish 1547–49*, p. 148.

29. *CSP, Spanish 1547–49*, pp. 219, 222. The English translation suggests that the crosses were on church altars, but it is quite clear that in fact the text refers to figures above rood screens.

30. Hamilton, ed., *Wriothesley*, II, p. 1; *CSP, Spanish 1547–49*, pp. 219–20. On restraints, Lefèvre-Pontalis, ed., *Selve*, pp. 210–11.

31. M. McLendon in Tyacke, ed., *England's Long Reformation*, p. 96.

32. Much Wenlock register, s.v. 7 November 1547 (I am grateful to Dr Will Coster for allowing me to see his forthcoming edition of this fragmentary MS). Leighton, ed., 'Early Chronicles of Shrewsbury', p. 258: the bonfire is described immediately following a note of the provisions of the 1547 visitation injunctions. Fowler, ed., *Rites of Durham*, pp. 69, 108: the 'Dr Harvey' responsible was probably Dr Henry Harvey, whom Nicholas Ridley would make Archdeacon of Middlesex in 1551. He and his fellow-commissioner Dr Whitby are not among those named as principal visitors; alternatively the names might be garbled from two of the visitors, Sir John Herseley (perhaps for Sir John Hercy) and Edward Plankney. See list in Strype, ed. Barnes, *Memorials of Cranmer*, i, p. 209.

33. Shepherd, *John Bon and Mast Person*, f. [1r]. Cf. King, *English Reformation Literature*, pp. 258–9.

34. AST, 40, f. 839r, Martyr to Dryander, Strassburg, 5 October 1547: 'Ex Anglia litteri sunt allati, quibus Christi negotium significatur mirabiliter progredi, et comitia sunt habenda paulo post kalendas novembris, in quibus complura christiane constituentur.'

35. MacCulloch, *Thomas Cranmer*, pp. 377–8.

36. Lefèvre-Pontalis, ed., *Selve*, p. 258.

37. Thomas, 'Tunstal', pp. 342–3.

38. Jordan, *The Young King*, p. 309.

39. MacCulloch, *Thomas Cranmer*, pp. 361, 492.

40. Loach, *Parliament under the Tudors*, pp. 17, 80–81; *CSP, Spanish 1547–49*, p. 222, and cf. ibid., p. 230. I do not see religious motives as fuelling the Commons' successful opposition to the bill depriving Bishop Tunstall in 1552; this is likely to have been a protest against the manifest unfairness of accusing Tunstall of misprision of treason.

41. Gorham, ed., *Gleanings*, p. 38.

42. *CSP, Spanish 1547–49*, p. 299.

43. I am deeply grateful to Dr Paul Ayris for drawing my attention to this letter of 27 January 1547[8] from Bonner's Register, London Guildhall Library MS 9531/12 pt 1, f. 117r. Bonner put up a vigorous though unsuccessful rearguard action to the accompanying order about ceremonies: cf. Ayris and Selwyn, eds, *Thomas Cranmer*, p. 143, and London, Guildhall Library MS 9531/12 pt 1, f. 117v.

44. For examples of the 1549 Prayer Book as 'the King's Book', see Nicolas, ed., *Testamenta Vetusta*, p. 727; 1550 Norwich Visitation articles (see below, p. 235, n. 74); Bruce, ed., *Works of Hutchinson*, p. 231; Christmas Ed., *Works of Ridley*, p. 322; *CSP, Spanish 1550–52*, p. 591. For hat-doffing, Pearson, ed., *Remains of Coverdale*, p. 6.

45. CCCC, MS 106 f. 493A (4 September 1548); cf. the comments in Gasquet and Bishop, *Edward VI and the Book of Common Prayer*, p. 147. It is interesting that in this letter Somerset referred to the eucharist as 'the mass': a further example of the double-message gambit.

46. Bodl. MS Ashmole 1123 no. II, f. 41r (cf. Frere and Kennedy, eds., *Visitation Articles and Injunctions*, 2, pp. 254f). On the destruction of the Windsor organs, see Bodl. MS Ashmole 1123, f. 187v.

47. See MacCulloch and Hughes, 'Chronicle from Worcester', especially p. 246.

48. Christmas, ed., *Works of Ridley*, p. 331 (23 July 1551).

49. Frere and Kennedy, eds., *Visitation Articles and Injunctions*, 2, p. 133.

50. See Benson's will, PCC, 38 Populwell (made 10 September 1549, proved 23 September 1549). On the Henrician origins of the Privy Garden pulpit, see above, pp. 23–4 and p. 225, n. 31.

51. Cooper, *Cooper's Chronicle*, f. 342r; King, *English Reformation Literature*, pp. 88–9.

52. See the successive 1548 preaching restrictions in Hughes and Larkin, eds.,

*Tudor Royal Proclamations*, I, nos. 303, 313; for a useful summary of preaching regulations, see Frere and Kennedy, eds., *Visitation Articles and Injunctions*, 2, p. 232.

53. PRO, SP 10/2/34 f. 116 lists preachers licensed under the ecclesiastical seal from July 1547 to June 1552. A whole series of these from 1550 can be found in BL, Royal MS 18 C XXIV f. 17f. The last page of the SP 10 list appears to be lost, as the correspondence between the two lists ends abruptly in June 1552.

54. Wilson, ed., *Sermons by Edgeworth*, p. 338: a reference which seems to date from spring 1553, and therefore puts his five- or six-year ban back to 1548.

55. MacCulloch, *Thomas Cranmer*, p. 398.

56. For a summary of the important discussion of the MS concerned in Selwyn, 'Vernacular tract' and Selwyn, 'The "Book of Doctrine"', see MacCulloch, *Thomas Cranmer*, pp. 397–8.

57. King, *English Reformation Literature*, p. 89. For narrative, see MacCulloch, *Thomas Cranmer*, pp. 399–403. Paul Ayris points out to me that Richard Bonner, Martin Bucer's correspondent at this time and self-styled author of a treatise incorporating discussion by Bucer on eucharistic adoration, did have a real if shadowy existence – as incumbent of St Tricat in Calais, a royal benefice (admission in Lambeth, Cranmer's Register, f. 380v, 6 June 1541). This makes it less likely that the treatise was given his name in order to annoy Bishop Bonner, as I suggested in *Thomas Cranmer*, p. 402; nevertheless, Richard Bonner, as an incumbent in Calais, was ideally placed to be an unobtrusive postman and front-man for Cranmer and Bucer at a diplomatically awkward time.

58. Shepherd, *John Bon and Mast Person*, f. [4v]. King, *English Reformation Literature*, p. 258, misses the dating clue provided by mention of the catechism: the pamphlet must relate to late summer 1548 and the issuing of the catechism, not to the feast of Corpus Christi (31 May 1548). On the catechism fiasco, see MacCulloch, *Thomas Cranmer*, pp. 386–91.

59. The Martyr tract, dedicated to Somerset, is BL, Royal MS 17C V; Selwyn, 'The "Book of Doctrine"', p. 460n, notes another copy at CUL, MS Ff 5 14. Annotations on the Royal MS are in the same hand as minutes of the Lords' debate (BL, Royal MS 17 B XXXIX, ff. 1–31); that hand also corrects the English translation of Calvin's letter to Somerset, PRO, SP 10/5, f. 25r.

60. For discussion, MacCulloch, *Thomas Cranmer*, pp. 403–7. On the bishops' divisions, see Dryander's comments, *ET*, p. 232 (*OL*, p. 351). The inconclusive result of the debate is presumably the reason for the disappearance into obscurity of the document discussed in Selwyn, 'Vernacular tract' and Selwyn, 'The "Book of Doctrine"'.

61. MacCulloch, *Thomas Cranmer*, pp. 412–14, 462–9, 505–8.

62. Brightman, *English Rite*, p. cxxii. NB also a curious statement in the injunctions for All Souls College, Oxford, put out in May or June 1549: they were told to teach the catechism 'quem publica regni concilia, Rex, senatus populusque Britannicus, *consenserint*' [my italics] (Frere and Kennedy, eds., *Visitation Articles and Injunctions*, 2, p. 197). If the verb tense is correct, this does not sound like a vote of confidence in the current catechism in the Prayer Book.

63. Bradshaw, 'Edwardian Reformation in Ireland', esp. pp. 94–6.

64. *Disputatio de eucharistiae sacramento*, sig. A7b. Edward's copy, of the London edition, is BL, C.37.e.2; NB his enthusiastic marginal distortion of William Tresham's conservative argument, ibid., f. 12v.

65. *Disputatio de eucharistiae sacramento*, p. 296: 'Caeterum de hisce controversiis sententiam ferre, et litem prorsus dirimere, modo non decrevimus. Tum autem decernetur, cum regiae maiestati, et ecclesiae Anglicanae proceribus visum fuerit.' Cf the translation of Vermigli, *Common Places*, 3rd pagination p. 249, for the praise of Martyr, and on this passage: 'wee are not now minded to give judgement of these controversies, and utterlie to breake the strife. But then shall it be determined, when it shall seeme good unto the Kings Maiestie, and the Estates of the church of England.'

66. MacCulloch, *Thomas Cranmer*, pp. 462–3.

67. MacCulloch, ibid., pp. 614–17.

68. For detailed argument to substantiate this account of the coup, see MacCulloch, ibid., pp. 444–8; Hughes and Larkin, eds., *Tudor Royal Proclamations*, I, no. 352.

69. *ET*, p. 233 (*OL*, p. 353).

70. Hughes and Larkin, eds., *Tudor Royal Proclamations*, I, no. 353, though this is not in fact a proclamation. For narrative, see MacCulloch, *Thomas Cranmer*, pp. 450–53.

71. MacCulloch, ibid., pp. 454–9. There were in fact 26 dioceses after 1550, given the dissolution of the see of Westminster on Thirlby's translation.

72. On ecclesiastical politics in Norwich at this time, see MacCulloch, 'A Reformation in the balance'.

73. Lambeth, Cranmer's register, f. 105rv.

74. The Norwich articles and injunctions, printed by Cranmer's preferred printer Reyner Wolfe, are discussed in Tabor, 'Additions to STC', pp. 194–5; the injunctions survive only in a unique copy at the Folger Library (Folger, STC 10285.8, which originally formed a single copy with the copy of the

articles at the Huntington Library, San Marino). I am most grateful to Dr Paul Ayris for supplying me with a complete text of them from his forthcoming edition of Cranmer's Register. On traditionalist adaptations of the 1549 book, see MacCulloch, *Thomas Cranmer*, pp. 461–2.

75. For Cranmer's 1548 articles, see Cox, ed., *Works of Cranmer*, 2, pp. 154–9. The unattributed articles, headed 'Articles to be followed and observed, according to the King's Majesty's Injunctions and Proceedings', are preserved only in a copy by Gilbert Burnet: Burnet, *History of the Reformation*, II, pt ii, pp. 226–7; Frere and Kennedy, eds., *Visitation Articles and Injunctions*, I, p. 136, plausibly suggest that they are the articles sent by Edward VI to Cranmer on 4 March 1550 by a letter pr. Wilkins, ed., *Concilia*, IV, p. 38; but NB also the citation for a royal visitation of London diocese, Lambeth, Cranmer's Register, f. 117r (... February 50; noted during Cranmer's formal *sede vacante* business for London). This latter set talks of 'the Lord's table', and is therefore likely to be slightly later than the Norwich set, which uses the word 'altar'. Both should be compared with Ridley's adaptation (which is often seen as the original source): Frere and Kennedy, eds., *Visitation Articles and Injunctions*, II, pp. 230–45. On Cranmer and London, see MacCulloch, *Thomas Cranmer*, p. 455.

76. Frere and Kennedy, eds., *Visitation Articles and Injunctions*, 2, pp. 262–6. Bulkeley's articles were described by Browne Willis, *Survey of the Cathedral Church of Bangor* (1721), pp. 331, as 'holden in 1551 in the month of May preceding his death'. However, Bulkeley died on 14 March 1553.

77. MacCulloch, *Thomas Cranmer*, pp. 479, 501–3, 518, 520.

78. MacCulloch, ibid., pp. 493–7.

79. On Cecil, see esp. MacCulloch, ibid., p. 500.

80. For discussion of the delays and the confrontation with Knox, MacCulloch, ibid., pp. 512–13, 517, 525–30.

81. MacCulloch, ibid., pp. 531–5, and see below, Ch. 3, pp. 154–5.

82. Nichols, ed., *Literary Remains of Edward VI*, p. ccxxxiv.

83. MacCulloch, *Thomas Cranmer*, pp. 522–3.

84. Ponet, *Treatise of politike power*, sig. Iiiib.

85. Laing, ed., *Works of Knox*, IV, p. 419.

86. For examples, see MacCulloch, *Thomas Cranmer*, p. 630.

## Chapter 3. King Solomon: Building the Temple

1. Frere and Kennedy, eds., *Visitation Articles and Injunctions*, 1, p. 143.

2. Binney, ed., *Accounts of Morebath*, p. 200; Duffy, 'Morebath'. I judge Duffy to be mistaken in his argument (ibid., p. 30) that entries in the 1549 accounts should be interpreted as meaning that the village loyally sent troops to suppress the Western rebels, rather than joining the rebel camp at St David's, Exeter. The crux of his argument, based on a previous entry referring to 'the furst communion book', is that the accounts were written up after the issue of the 1552 Book, so they misleadingly telescope much earlier events. Yet this is much less likely to be a retrospective reference to the 1549 Prayer Book, than a reference made in 1549 to the 1548 Order of Communion. So the entries about the camp are from 1549, and mean what they say. There is another instance of rebel actions being recorded in parish accounts: see Fletcher and MacCulloch, *Tudor Rebellions*, p. 73.

3. The standard treatment is now Kümin, *Shaping of a Community*.

4. A. Foster in French, Gibbs and Kümin, eds., *The Parish in English Life*, pp. 80–82: Foster's is an admirably balanced survey of the problems and possibilities of churchwardens' accounts, albeit concentrating on a slightly later period.

5. See the Uniformity Act, Ketley, ed., *Two Liturgies*, p. 213; Canterbury articles, Cox, ed., *Works of Cranmer*, II, p. 158; Nevinson, ed., *Later Writings of Hooper*, pp. 140–41.

6. Corrie, ed., *Latimer's Sermons*, p. 204, and cf. pp. 121–2; Cox, ed., *Works of Cranmer*, II, p. 158; 1550 Norwich Articles (see above, p. 235, n. 74), art. 28; Christmas, ed., *Works of Ridley*, p. 321.

7. Hughes and Larkin, eds., *Tudor Royal Proclamations*, I, no. 353.

8. Frere and Kennedy, eds., *Visitation Articles and Injunctions*, 2, art. 20, p. 234; and on frequent communion, inj. 11, p. 245 (repeating 1550 Norwich visitation articles, inj. 7). For a disapproving comment from Easter 1552 about once-a-year communion, see Bruce, ed., *Works of Hutchinson*, pp. 215–16.

9. Williams, ed., *English Historical Documents 1485–1558*, p. 208; *CSP, Venetian*, V, p. 556.

10. Huggarde, *Displaying of the Protestantes*, f. 93v.

11. *CSP, Spanish 1547–49*, pp. 46, 52, 205, 222, 230, 462–3.

12. Houghton, ed., *Cranmer's Recantacyons*, p. 25.

13. Huggarde, *Displaying of the Protestantes*, f. 95rv; Christopherson, *Exhortation*, sig. Eeiva.

14. *CSP, Spanish 1547–49*, pp. 298, 148.

15. I am very grateful to the late Professor Fines for sharing his unpublished findings with me; I have used the version of his research current in 1991.

16. BL, Royal MS 17B XXXV, f. 8rv, 10v; the author of this treatise has not been identified. The original of the quotation, at f. 10v, has 'knoweth not the gospell', which in context is clearly a slip of the pen.

17. Above, Ch. 2, pp. 71 [glass] and 82–4 [city-state].

18. The standard treatment is now Brigden, *London and the Reformation*.

19. McConica, ed., *Oxford*, pp. 152–3; ibid., p. 144 has smaller totals of evangelicals, derived from an earlier version of Fines's research.

20. MacCulloch, 'A Reformation in the balance'.

21. Bale, *Expostulation*, sig. Ciiib, and cf. his bitter comments on the combination of local senior clergy, ibid., sig. Ava.

22. Aston, *King's Bedpost*, p. 193 and n.

23. Houlbrooke, *Church Courts and the People*, p. 246, and cf. ibid., p. 243.

24. On Calais, MacCulloch, *Thomas Cranmer*, pp. 110–11. Dickens, 'Early expansion of Protestantism', pp. 11–13.

25. Wilson, ed., *Sermons by Edgeworth*, p. 197.

26. Ayr and Kyle: Cowan, *Scottish Reformation*, pp. 89, 92; Sanderson, *Mary Stewart's People*, p. 159–63. On Dumfries, Bush, *Government Policy of Protector Somerset*, p. 21. On the western Highlands, Kirk, *Patterns of Reform*, p. 454.

27. *CSP, Spanish 1550–52*, p. 122.

28. See especially Duffy's discussion of East Anglian rood-screens in French, Gibbs and Kümin, eds., *The Parish in English Life*, pp. 133–62.

29. Caraman, ed., *John Gerard*, p. 33.

30. Proctor, *Fal of the late Arrian*: see esp. sigs. Aiia-Aiva, Biib-Biiia [text quoted], Dviiib, Svibf. The 'Arian' was probably the priest John Ashton, who recanted his opinions before Cranmer in December 1548.

31. On Mary, cf. e.g. Ellis, ed., *Original Letters*, 3rd ser., pt 1, p. 162.

32. On Smith, Marshall, 'Fear, purgatory and polemic', p. 163, n. 11. Joliffe and Johnson, *Responsio*, f. 90r: 'De nomine Purgatorii nullum nobis negocium'. Crowley, *Confutation of Shaxton*, sig. Hvib.

33. *CSP, Venetian*, V, p. 346. Cf. Roger Edgeworth's embarrassed editing of his Henrician attack on papal primacy: Wilson, ed., *Sermons by Edgeworth*, pp. 193–4.

34. Joliffe and Johnson, *Responsio*, ff. 80v–81v, and cf. ibid., f. 189v.

35. *Disputatio de eucharistiae sacramento*, pp. 89–90; cf. exchanges at pp. 28, 76.

36. *Disputatio de eucharistiae sacramento*, pp. 259–60: 'sed nunc Roffen., non suscipio defendendum'. For examples of silent plagiarism of Fisher, see Rex, *Theology of Fisher*, pp. 90–91, and MacCulloch, *Thomas Cranmer*, p. 344. On Day, BL, Royal MS 17B XXXIX, f.26v. For similar problems about using the writings of Thomas More, cf. comments in Wilson, ed., *Sermons by Edgeworth*, pp. 55, 61.

37. Fletcher and MacCulloch, *Tudor Rebellions*, Ch. 5, and see Youings, 'South-Western Rebellion', pp. 121–2.

38. Oxfordshire: *CSP, Domestic, Edward VI*, no. 329. Yorkshire: Townshend and Cattley, eds., *Foxe*, V pp. 738–41. Hampshire: *CSP, Domestic, Edward VI*, no. 338.

39. Bond, ed., *Homilies*, p. 244.

40. BL, Additional MS 48018, f. 391r. For a marshalling of other evidence, MacCulloch, *Thomas Cranmer*, pp. 432–8.

41. BL, Additional MS 48018, ff. 388r, 389v.

42. Pocock, ed., *Troubles*, p. 24: the Council to Russell, 10 July 1549. This was not merely an empty report designed to keep Russell's spirits up, because only a day or two before, the Council had written in warm terms to the Hampshire insurgents after their submission: BL, Additional MS 48018, f. 391r, dated by reference to Hughes and Larkin, eds., *Tudor Royal Proclamations*, I, no. 337 (8 July 1549).

43. See discussion and references, MacCulloch, *Thomas Cranmer*, p. 432, and for 'Captain Commonwealth', Davies, ed., 'Boulogne and Calais from 1545 to 1550', p. 60.

44. Cf. the remarks on Robert Crowley and other Commonwealth writers by Nicholas Tyacke: Tyacke, ed., *England's Long Reformation*, pp. 15–20.

45. BL, Royal MS 17 B.XXXV. The dating is after the 1543 Act restricting the reading of the Bible on the basis of social status (ibid., f. 8r), but the treatise is clearly written before the resumption of burnings for evangelical belief in spring 1546 (cf. marginal note, ibid., f. 8v). Once more I have to thank Dr Shagan for pointing out the existence of this MS to me.

46. Cf. BL, Royal 17B XXXV ff. 13r–14r, 19v, 20rv with Fletcher and MacCulloch, *Tudor Rebellions*, p. 146, and the set of Norfolk demands now lost but glimpsed in Edward VI's 18 July letter to the Norfolk rebels, BL, Additional MS 48018, f. 388rv.

47. PRO, E. 163/16/14. I am most grateful to Prof. Hoyle for drawing my attention to this document. For discussion of a very late example of the same

commonwealth rhetoric, in the Chorographies of Norfolk and Suffolk *c.* 1600, see D. MacCulloch, 'Power, privilege and the county community: county politics in Elizabethan Suffolk' (unpublished Cambridge PhD thesis, 1977), pp. 248–51. By then the rhetoric had anti-Puritan and clerical associations.

48. Elton, G. R., 'Reform and the "Commonwealth-men" of Edward VI's England', in Elton, *Studies*, III, pp. 234–53.

49. Fletcher and MacCulloch, *Tudor Rebellions*, p. 26, and cf. further use of the word in 1536, ibid., pp. 31, 37.

50. Elton, *Policy and Police*, especially on the universities, pp. 29–33.

51. Cox, ed., *Works of Cranmer*, II, p. 157.

52. BL, Additional MS 48018, f. 388r.

53. Mason, ed., *Scotland and England 1286–1815*, pp. 67–81, 85–99.

54. BL, Additional MS 48018, f. 391r.

55. Read, *Mr. Secretary Cecil*, pp. 34–5.

56. Brigden, 'Youth and the English Reformation': above, pp. 108–9.

57. e.g. Richard Cox in June 1549: *Disputatio de eucharistiae sacramento*, p. 299.

58. Huggarde, *Displaying of the Protestantes*, ff. 116–17. Calvin's discussion of liberty: McNeill and Battles, eds., *Calvin: Institutes*, pp. 833–49 (Bk III, xix, 1–16).

59. Huggarde, *Displaying of the Protestantes*, ff. 114v, 30v.

60. Wilson, ed., *Sermons by Edgeworth*, p. 364, and cf. Edgeworth's earlier comments, ibid., pp. 127–8, with a useful listing of further examples of the usage, p. 379. See also John Morwen's revival of the complaint in 1561, with James Pilkington's response, Scholefield, ed., *Works of Pilkington*, pp. 486, 614.

61. Williams, *Welsh Reformation Essays*, p. 52. Contrast the lack of Marian deprivations for marriage in conservative areas of England, e.g. Cumbria: Clark, 'Lake Counties', p. 84.

62. Bond, ed., *Homilies*, p. 180; Hughes and Larkin, eds., *Tudor Royal Proclamations*, I, no. 303.

63. On Parr and Ayscough, MacCulloch, *Thomas Cranmer*, pp. 352, 367–70, 383, 420–21, 455, 498–9, 534, 630; for Parr's outburst, *APC 1547–50*, p. 164. Christopherson, *Exhortation*, sig. Sviiiab.

64. Bullinger, *Christen State of Matrymonye*, ff. 88r–91r. Edns are *RSTC*, 4045–53, beginning with an Antwerp edn of 1541; the thirteenth edn came out in 1575. Ketley, ed., *Two Liturgies*, p. 127.

65. Huggarde, *Displaying of the Protestantes*, ff. 22–3. The passage is 1 Tim. iv, 3–5.

66. Christopherson, *Exhortation*, sig. Tvib.

67. *Disputatio de eucharistiae sacramento*, p. 302: 'Possumus ex authoritate vobis imperare, et pervicacibus meritum supplicium comminari, malumus tamen pro dilectione nostra erga vos, rogare, et exhortari.'

68. The Cecil/Morison debates are noted in Strype, *Life of Cheke*, pp. 70. On Feckenham, *DNB*, s.v. Feckenham, John; and cf. Joliffe and Johnson, *Responsio*, ff. 5rv, 41v.

69. Cf. excellent discussion in Marshall, 'Debate over "unwritten verities" '.

70. *APC 1550–51*, p. 224. McConica, ed., *Oxford*, p. 466. The argument for the burning of the library, as opposed to its dispersal and sale, rests on the extraordinarily small survival rate of known books from the medieval Oxford collection.

71. See discussions of reuses in Hutchinson and Egan, 'Fermer Workshop', esp. pp. 148–50, 358–9.

72. On France, *CSP, Spanish 1550–52*, p. 323; Barnaby Fitzpatrick seems to be reporting the same incident to Edward VI in his letter of 28 December 1551, denying English involvement: Nichols, ed., *Literary Remains of Edward VI*, p. 73. Portugal: Freeman and Borges, 'William Gardiner's desecration'.

73. Cox, ed., *Works of Cranmer*, II, p. 119, p. 351 [latter text corrected from the original, PRO, SP 6/2, ff. 86–92]. Bucer, *Gratulation*, sig. Kviib.

74. Patterson, 'Sir John Oldcastle', p. 7.

75. Dickens, 'Shape of Anticlericalism and the English Reformation', pp. 153–5.

76. *RSTC*, 25590, 25590.5, 25591, 25591a (1546–48). The two versions of the Bible prologue are [Wyclif], *Dore of holy Scripture* and [Wyclif], *True copy of a Prolog.* King, *English Reformation Literature*, pp. 12, 71, 97–100, 255.

77. MacCulloch, 'Archbishop Cranmer: consensus and tolerance', pp. 209–11.

78. MacCulloch, *Thomas Cranmer*, p. 436.

79. Fletcher and MacCulloch, *Tudor Rebellions*, pp. 72–3, 118–21, and cf. Ellis Gruffydd's comment on the rebels' honesty: Davies, ed., 'Boulogne and Calais from 1545 to 1550', p. 60. I have always been sceptical about attempts to make direct connections between the Mousehold demand for the freeing of serfs and the German Peasant Articles of 1525: for a different view, see Tyacke, ed., *England's Long Reformation*, p. 14.

80. Davies, 'Edwardian concepts of the Church', pp. 11, 89–91. See also Davies and Facey, 'Reformation dilemma'.

81. Rodgers, *John à Lasco in England*, p. 67. On the Stranger Church and radicalism, see MacCulloch, *Thomas Cranmer*, p. 477. It also cooperated with the burning of radicals in Elizabeth's reign: Grell, 'Exile and tolerance', pp. 180–81.

82. Ketley, ed., *Two Liturgies*, pp. 38, 229.

83. Davies, 'Edwardian concepts of the Church', esp. pp. 86–7, and Davies, 'Towards a Godly Commonwealth', p. 403.

84. Wright, ed., *Martin Bucer: Reforming Church and Commonwealth*, pp. 89–92, 129–30, 133.

85. Cole, *A godly and frutefull sermon*, sig. Aii; cf. Wilson, ed., *Sermons by Edgeworth*, p. 281.

86. For examples from a wearisomely numerous genre, Bruce, ed., *Works of Hutchinson*, p. 202; Corrie, ed., *Latimer's Sermons*, pp. 121–3; Ponet, J., *A notable sermon*, sigs. Fviiib-Gib.

87. BL, Royal MS 17B XXXV, f. 14v.

88. Olde, *Acquital*, sig. A3a; cf. sig. A3b. Cf. the index in e.g. Foxe, *Acts and Monuments* (1570), s.v. 'Bonner'; the illustration of Bonner scourging a Protestant is at ibid., p. 2242. For useful discussion of the deviant sexuality theme in relation to Rome, see King, *English Reformation Literature*, pp. 377–84.

89. Huggarde, *Displaying of the Protestantes*, f. 74r.

90. Huggarde, *Assault of the sacrament*, sig. Eiia; cf. Huggarde, *Displaying of the Protestantes*, f. 80v.

91. Houlbrooke, *Church Courts and the People*, esp. Conclusion.

92. Ayre, ed., *Works of Becon*, II, p. 600 (*The Fortress of the Faithful*, dedicated to Sir John Robsart, whose daughter Amy married Robert Dudley). Cf. ibid., III, p. 24, and useful discussion in Davies, 'Towards a Godly Commonwealth', p. 260.

93. Bond, ed., *Homilies*, pp. 169, 171–2. I am grateful to Prof. John Wall for sorting out the various editions of the homilies for me. The Grafton edition in which the missing paragraph uniquely appears is *RSTC*, 13638.5, from Bodley shelfmark 4° 1.6(2) Th. Seld.; the Whitchurch edition with signs of disturbance is *RSTC*, 13641 (Bodley shelfmark Tanner 216).

94. Tyacke, ed., *England's Long Reformation*, pp. 12–19.

95. Fletcher and MacCulloch, *Tudor Rebellions*, pp. 77, 125.

96. Warwick emblem: Tawney and Power, eds., *Tudor Economic Documents*, I, p. 49: a deposition about a conversation in January 1550. Speech of James Fuller of Lavenham, *Calendar of Patent Rolls, Elizabeth I, 1569–72*, no. 1818.

97. Lever, *Sermons*, p. 104; Ayre, ed., *Works of Becon*, II, p. 601, both from 1550 (though for an earlier, Henrician, example of an evangelical using the phrase, see Parr, *Lamentacion of a sinner*, sig. Fib). On the background of this phrase, Wilson, ed., *Sermons by Edgeworth*, p. 379. Cf. also Ponet's discussion of how

Anabaptists perverted the concept of Christian liberty into antinomianism: Ponet, *Treatise of politike power*, sig. Cviiib.

**98**. Lever, *Sermons*, p. 79.

**99**. Cox, ed., *Works of Cranmer*, II, pp. 190–202; and cf. discussion, MacCulloch, *Thomas Cranmer*, pp. 434–7.

**100**. Cf. Corrie, ed., *Latimer's Sermons*, pp. 246–8; Ayre, ed., *Works of Becon*, II, p. 617; Lever, *Sermons*, p. 37; Philip Gerrard, 'An exhortation unto the Kynges Maiestie' (1553), BL, Royal 17 B XL, f. 6v; Anthony Gilby in Laing, ed., *Works of Knox*, IV, p. 565.

**101**. Lever, *Sermons*, pp. 56, 65, and see Davies, 'Towards a Godly Commonwealth', pp. 357–60.

**102**. Lever, *Sermons*, p. 23; Bruce, ed., *Works of Hutchinson*, p. 338; Davies, 'Edwardian concepts of the Church', p. 86.

**103**. *APC 1550–52*, p. 318, and text in Cox, ed., *Works of Cranmer*, II, p. 531. For Northumberland's own anticlerical application of the covetousness theme, see *CSP, Domestic, Edward VI*, no. 799.

**104**. Christmas, ed., *Works of Ridley*, pp. 331–5.

**105**. Lanquet, *Epitome of Chronicles*, sig. Eeee 2v. Cooper, *Cooper's Chronicle*, f. 351r; Ponet, *Treatise of politike power*, sig. Mi.

**106**. Laing, ed., *Works of Knox*, IV, p. 565.

**107**. Lever, *Sermons*, p. 61.

**108**. MacCulloch, *Thomas Cranmer*, pp. 520–23, 531–3.

**109**. Ellis, ed., *Original Letters*, 3rd ser., pt 3, p. 311; cf. anon., *Retrospective Review*, p. 504. For commonwealth rhetoric in Mary's support, PRO, E. 163/16/14; see discussion of the popular elements in Mary's coup, MacCulloch, ed., '*Vita Mariae*', pp. 214–15, 263–4.

## Chapter 4. The Afterlife of the Edwardian Reformation

**1**. H. Whistler, *False Alternatives at the Reformation*, SPCK, 1957, p. 24. I am grateful to Simon White for drawing this pamphlet to my attention.

**2**. For purchase of 'printed papers that hangeth upon the walls' in 1553, see Masters and Ralph, eds., *Church Book of St. Ewen's Bristol*, p. 188.

**3**. Cf. the extended discussion of this theme in the 1547 royal injunctions, in the order to set up poor boxes: Cox, ed., *Works of Cranmer*, II, p. 498, and above, p. 125 and p. 240, n. 51.

4. There is commonly an understandable confusion between the beads of the rosary and the prayers known as the bedes (from which the word 'bead' is derived), but there is no necessary liturgical connection between the two forms of devotion.

5. *Disputatio de eucharistiae sacramento*, p. 296.

6. MacCulloch, *Thomas Cranmer*, pp. 536–7.

7. For discussion, see MacCulloch, *Thomas Cranmer*, pp. 452, n. 112; 504–5; the 1550 fragment was preserved by Peter Heylyn. For other evidence of Convocation meetings at this time, see a slightly obscure reference to Richard Cox leaving for Oxford at the ending of a 'council' ('Dimisso itaque concilio'): *ET*, p. 307 (*OL*, p. 465; 28 February 1550); this can only have been a meeting of convocation in parallel with Parliament. See also the informed reference to Convocation in *CSP, Venetian*, V, p. 343 (May 1551). However, the reference to a convocation on 12 December 1551 ('Synodus jussu regiae majestatis') in *ET*, p. 293 (*OL*, p. 444) can only be to some ad hoc drafting committee.

8. For Hooper's use of drafts of the articles, see MacCulloch, *Thomas Cranmer*, p. 504. Hooper also used drafts as the basis of the 19 articles which he presented as doctrinal tests to the conservative canons of Worcester in 1552: his articles correspond in different ways to both draft and final versions of the 42 Articles text. See Joliffe and Johnson, *Responsio, passim*.

9. MacCulloch, *Thomas Cranmer*, pp. 525–8.

10. Grisbrooke, *Anglican Liturgies*, p. 40.

11. The best summary account of the Swiss background and aftermath of the *Consensus* negotiations is Gordon, 'Calvin and the Swiss Reformed Churches'. For the warm welcome accorded the *Consensus* in Łaski's London Stranger Church, see Pettegree, *Foreign Protestant Communities*, p. 70.

12. Pettegree, *Marian Protestantism*, Ch. 3, esp. p. 82.

13. Pettegree, 'Reception of Calvinism', pp. 276–7, 280.

14. MacCulloch, *Thomas Cranmer*, pp. 539–40. On Melanchthon's belief in his horoscope prediction that he would suffer shipwreck in the Baltic Sea, see Cameron, 'Melanchthon', pp. 711–12. Presumably his English chaperone John Abell was hoping to lead him back on a southerly route across the English Channel, to avoid the threatened doom.

15. Pettegree, *Marian Protestantism*, p. 80. However, Melanchthon did urge Frankfurt city council not to expel the French and English congregations in the 1557 crisis: Cameron, 'Melanchthon', p. 720.

16. Cf. for instance, Parsons, *Third part of a treatise*, Calendar, s.v. 19 October

(Ridley); 21 October (John Webb and Geo Roper); 24 October (Mark Burgess); 9 November (John Kerby); 23 December (Martin Bucer). The totals are at ibid., p. 456.

17. Grisbrooke, *Anglican Liturgies*, pp. 40–41. For a classic statement of 'Zuinglian or Calvinian' infiltration of anti-vestiarian opinions into the Edwardian Church from Heylyn the Laudian arch-polemicist, see Heylyn, ed. Robertson, *Ecclesia Restaurata*, I, pp. 193–5.

18. Smyth, *Cranmer and the Reformation*.

19. Gerrish, *Grace and Gratitude*, esp. pp. 166–7; and cf. also Gerrish, 'Lord's Supper in the Reformed confessions', esp. p. 128; on Zwingli, Gerrish, *Continuing the Reformation*, pp. 64–75.

20. Cf. Lewis, ed., *Sander*, pp. 182–3, 194, 196, 207–8, 211, and on Bocher, ibid., p. 191. Cf. Parsons, *Review*, p. 94, for a characterization of the official Edwardian changes as Calvinist. On Cosin and Lindsell, Milton, *Catholic and Reformed*, p. 334. For the use of the 'deformation' pun by Bonner's chaplain John Morwen in 1561, see Scholefield, ed., *Works of Pilkington*, p. 485.

21. Cf. Gorham, ed., *Gleanings*, pp. 55–71 (wrongly dated 1548: it is from 1549); *OL*, p. 704 (spring 1550); *ET*, p. 456 (*OL*, p. 704; Spring 1550); *ET*, p. 466 (*OL*, p. 707; 1 January 1551); Schickler, *Eglises du Refuge*, III, p. 6 (7 April 1551); Gorham, ed., *Gleanings*, p. 267 (15 June 1551); Gorham, ed., *Gleanings*, p. 269 (25 July 1551).

22. *ET*, pp. 478–9 (*OL*, pp. 737–9): Vallerand Poullain to Calvin, 7 March 1552.

23. Guggisberg, *Basel in the Sixteenth Century*, p. 41. For English relations with Bullinger, see index entries in MacCulloch, *Thomas Cranmer*. For useful comments on Calvin and Edwardian England, Pettegree, *Foreign Protestant Communities*, pp. 71–3, and Pettegree, *Marian Protestantism*, p. 83; for Calvin's place in Elizabethan England, Pettegree, 'Reception of Calvinism', esp. pp. 274–80.

24. For Christopher Carleill's references to Cheke's admiration, see Buisson, *Castellion*, pp. 415, 459 [I owe these references to John McDiarmid].

25. Gorham, ed., *Gleanings*, pp. 245, 264. On relations between Łaski and Calvin, Pettegree, *Foreign Protestant Communities*, pp. 70–71.

26. *Biblia interprete Castalione*, sigs. Aii–Av; see also Guggisberg, *Basel in the Sixteenth Century*, pp. 60–63. On the 1549 biblical translation project, MacCulloch, *Thomas Cranmer*, pp. 426–9.

27. On the ascription of the pamphlet to Thomas Wood and discussion of context, see Collinson, 'Authorship of *A Brieff Discours*'.

28. Pettegree, *Marian Protestantism*, pp. 73–7.

29. Arber, ed., *Brief discourse*, p. 75 (the report of a 'Master H.' who cannot be more definitely identified among the exiles; it may have been Christopher Hales, see Garrett, *The Marian Exiles*, pp. 171–2). See also Arber, ed., *Brief discourse*, pp. 37, 45.

30. Arber, ed., *ibid.*, pp. 42, 52–3.

31. Arber, ed., ibid., pp. 44–9, 54–5, 62.

32. Pettegree, *Marian Protestantism*, p. 161.

33. Penny, *Freewill or Predestination*, Chs. 4–7; Eden, ed., *Writings of Philpot*, pp. 293–318. On Foxe and the Freewillers, Freeman, 'New perspectives on an old book', p. 322.

34. Huggarde, *Displaying of the Protestantes*, f. 124v, and generally, ff. 121r–125v.

35. Marsh, *Family of Love*, pp. 54–64, 285–6. On Prayer Book and catechism use, see Christopherson, *Exhortation*, sig. Bbii.

36. Pettegree, *Marian Protestantism*, pp. 197–8.

37. Usher, 'In a time of persecution', esp. pp. 238–9.

38. On Wesel and Geneva, Pettegree, *Marian Protestantism*, pp. 19–22, 32–3, and on Wesel also Bill, ed., *Catalogue of Lambeth MSS. 2341–3119*, pp. 22–3 (calendaring Lambeth MS 2523). On Knox's later borrowings, Rodgers, *John à Lasco in England*, pp. 163–4.

39. Donaldson, *Scottish Reformation*, pp. 50, 80, 107–8.

40. Arber, ed., *Brief discourse*, p. 77.

41. Bill, ed., *Catalogue of Lambeth MSS. 2341–3119*, pp. 22–3.

42. We await Simon Adams's forthcoming biography of the Earl of Leicester which will substantiate these points. I am very grateful to Prof. Adams for our discussions.

43. Pettegree, *Marian Protestantism*, pp. 144–8, 197–9.

44. MacCaffrey, *Elizabeth*, Chs. 1 and 2, and note esp. p. 11.

45. e.g., for solifidianism, Parr, *Lamentacion of a Sinner*, sig. Biiib; for saints, sig. Giva; for unwritten verities, sigs. Eib, Fiva.

46. Parr, *Lamentacion of a Sinner*, sig. Giab.

47. Parr, *Lamentacion of a sinner*, sig. Ciiab: the passage continues to sig. Diiiab. Cf. Mueller, 'Katherine Parr', pp. 20–22.

48. On Elizabeth's crucifix, Aston, *England's Iconoclasts*, pp. 306–14, and public perceptions of her devotion to the cross, Aston, *King's Bedpost*, pp. 101–3.

49. Arber, ed., *Brief discourse*, p. 55. For examples of compromisers among the

exiles, Pettegree, *Marian Protestantism*, pp. 25–6, and see his excellent discussion of Nicodemism, ibid., Ch. 4.

50. MacCulloch, *Thomas Cranmer*, pp. 620–21.

51. For Ridley's preaching, Nichols, ed., *Grey Friars*, p. 78; Kingsford, ed., 'Two London Chronicles', p. 26: V., *Historical Narration of certain events in 1553*, sigs. Biiii–Bv, makes clear that Ridley preached more than once. Foxe is notably silent on these sermons.

52. On Elizabeth's feelings for Edward, Aston, *King's Bedpost*, p. 134.

53. Crankshaw, 'Preparations for the Canterbury Provincial Convocation of 1562–63'. I am most grateful to David Crankshaw for sharing his findings with me in advance of publication.

54. Folger MS V.b. 303, pp. 183–6, qu. Collinson, 'Puritans, men of business and Elizabethan Parliaments', p. 192. On the 1566 bills, Elton, *Parliament of England*, pp. 205–7.

55. My translation of Camden, *Annales*, p. 40: 'se malle devote precibus Deum alloqui quam alios de Deo diserte loquentes audire'.

56. Neale, *Elizabeth I and Her Parliaments*, 2, pp. 69–71. On the prophesyings affair, Collinson, *Archbishop Grindal*, Ch. 13.

57. Bond, ed., *Homilies*, p. 11. For James's enthusiasm for preachers, see McCullough, *Sermons at Court*, pp. 125–6.

58. Kirk, *Patterns of Reform*, pp. 102–3, 339.

59. Donaldson, *Scottish Reformation*, p. 178. Donaldson missed the point that in English terms the *Reformatio* was by this stage a symbol of opposition to the stasis brought to the Church by the Queen.

60. Perrott, 'Richard Hooker and the Elizabethan Church', pp. 39–40.

61. Collinson, *Grindal*, pp. 177–81.

62. Freeman, 'New perspectives on an old book', pp. 321–2, and cf. Usher, 'In a time of persecution', pp. 239–41, 243.

63. Townshend and Cattley, eds., *Foxe*, V p. 704. For further discussion of Foxe, radicals and persecution, see MacCulloch, *Thomas Cranmer*, pp. 474–6.

64. Brown, *Robert Ferrar*, pp. 247–9. Foxe also invented (apparently inadvertently) a spurious Edwardian imprisonment for Ferrar: ibid., pp. 216–18.

65. Curteys, qu. in McCullough, *Sermons at Court*, p. 82.

66. McCullough, ibid., pp. 83–4. On Curteys's turbulent career at Chichester, see Manning, *Elizabethan Sussex*, Chs. 4–6.

67. Thomas, *Religion and the Decline of Magic*, pp. 498–501, and Fox, 'Rumour and popular political opinion', p. 614.

68. The following description is greatly indebted to Aston, *King's Bedpost*. Interpretation is largely my own. Jennifer Loach, in a review of Dr Aston's book in *EHR*, III (1996), pp. 704–5, attempted to reassert an Edwardian date for an original version of the picture. While the question of the portraits of Privy Councillors does suggest some Edwardian prototype, Loach's particular arguments, and her other objections to Dr Aston's thesis, seem to me to be unconvincing. I am, however, grateful to Professor Eric Ives for our conversations and genial disagreements about the picture.

69. Aston, *King's Bedpost*, pp. 67–70. The story is at Esther vi, 1–3.

70. Foxe, *Acts and Monuments* (1563), p. 675 (*recte* 684). On Foxe in 1563 and 1570, Aston, *King's Bedpost*, pp. 158–9. On Curteys, above, p. 199.

71. Aston, *King's Bedpost*, pp. 128–34.

72. Smuts, 'Court-centred politics'.

73. Worden, 'Ben Jonson among the historians'; also Worden, 'Camden and Jonson'. Cf. Camden, *Remains*, p. 58.

74. Camden, *Annales*, pp. 21–4: the marginal comment is '*Infaelix sub puero Rege regnum*'. Camden's immediately sequential material on Elizabeth's studies, derived from Ascham, was mistakenly copied and reapplied to Edward's education in Henry Holland's *Heroologia Anglica* (1620; cf. text qu. Nichols, ed., *Literary Remains of Edward VI*, pp. ccx-ccxi). Holland should therefore not be used as a source on Edward.

75. Camden, *Britaine*, p. 382. I owe my references to *Britannia* to the kindness of Professor Blair Worden.

76. Beer, ed., *Edward VI by Hayward*, p. 37.

77. Richardson, 'Hayward and historiography', I, p. 218. I am very grateful to Dr Richardson for generously sending me extracts from her work, and for giving me permission to quote from it.

78. Camden, *Britaine*, p. 822.

79. See Lossky, *Lancelot Andrewes the Preacher*.

80. The literature on anti-Calvinism is now extensive. Central texts are Tyacke, *Anti-Calvinists*, and Milton, *Catholic and Reformed*.

81. Qu. by Milton, *Catholic and Reformed*, p. 333.

82. Heylyn, ed. Robertson, *Ecclesia Restaurata*, I, p. 300.

83. Cf. the letter of Dean Andrewes and the Chapter to Robert Cecil, HMC, *Salisbury* 12, pp. 142–3, 5 May 1602 (I am grateful to Dr Marianne Dorman for drawing my attention to this letter). On Westminster Abbey and the parallel

theological stance of the parish church of St Margaret, we await the publication of Julia Merritt's important research.

84. Croft, 'Camden, Westminster and the Cecils'.

85. Croft, 'Religion of Robert Cecil'. On William Cecil's revulsion against Calvinism, see Collinson, 'Sir Nicholas Bacon', p. 267.

86. Qu. by Worden, 'Ben Jonson among the historians', p. 77. Leicester's patronage could be interestingly eclectic, particularly in his role as Chancellor of Oxford: see McConica, ed., *Oxford*, pp. 423–31. Nevertheless, his status as chief patron of the Puritan movement during his lifetime can hardly be overlooked.

87. Qu. by McCullough, *Sermons at Court*, p. 194, and on Henry's chaplains generally, see ibid, pp. 183–94.

88. Qu. by McCullough, ibid., pp. 189–90.

89. McCullough, ibid., p. 198.

90. McCullough, ibid., pp. 204–9.

91. On Williams and the altar controversy, see MacCulloch, *Thomas Cranmer*, p. 626. Cf. Milton, *Catholic and Reformed*, p. 332. Dr John McCafferty points out to me that, interestingly, the Laudian-inspired canons for the Church of Ireland promulgated in 1634 did not require reading of the Homilies.

92. For summary discussion, MacCulloch, *Thomas Cranmer*, pp. 621–2.

93. Andrewes, *Works*, XI, pp. 151–8, 335; cf. also the plan of Andrewes's private chapel, with notes, ibid., facing p. xcvii, and pp. xcvii–xcix.

94. Above, pp. 171–2; Milton, *Catholic and Reformed*, pp. 332, 497

95. Forbes, *Considerationes*, II, pp. 92–5. I am most grateful to Joyce B. Martin for pointing me to this reference.

96. We await the publication of Dr Bowers's research on Chapel Royal music in 1558–9. Bradshaw, 'Edwardian Reformation in Ireland', pp. 85–6, 90, 94–5, 98. The Dublin printing of the 1549 Prayer Book is *RSTC*, 16277.

97. McCafferty, 'Bramhall, Laud and the Church of Ireland', quoting Strafford Papers, vol. XX, no. 149. I am very grateful to Dr McCafferty for sharing his discovery with me.

98. Grisbrooke, *Anglican Liturgies*, pp. 15–16.

99. Grisbrooke, *Anglican Liturgies*, pp. 2–4: for the text of the eucharistic rite, see ibid., pp. 163–82.

100. Aston, *England's Iconoclasts*, p. 94.

# *Bibliography*

All printed works are published in London unless otherwise stated.

## PRIMARY SOURCES IN MANUSCRIPT
### Cambridge: Corpus Christi College

MS 126: lectures on matrimony by Pierre Alexandre

### Cambridge University Library

MS Dd 12.59: Edward VI's treatise on the papal supremacy

### London: British Library

Cottonian MSS
Harleian MSS and Charters
Lansdowne MSS and Rolls
Royal MSS
Sloane Charters
Stowe MSS

### London, Guildhall Library

MS 9531/12 pt 1: Bonner's Register

## London: Lambeth Palace Library

Cranmer's Register (no class reference)

## London: Public Record Office

E.101: Exchequer, miscellaneous books
E. 163/16/14: petition of Norfolk yeomen to Queen Mary, *c.* 1553–4
L.R.2/118; L.R. 2/119: inventories of attainted persons, 1553
SP6; SP10; SP46: State Papers, Theological tracts, and Domestic, Edward VI

## Oxford: Bodleian Library

Ashmole MSS
Tanner MSS

## Strasbourg: Archives Municipales

MSS Archives du Chapître de St Thomas de Strasbourg, vols. 40, 41, 153, 157: collected letters and transcripts

## Washington, DC: Folger Shakespeare Library

L.b.8: Loseley MSS: accounts for the revels, coronation of Edward VI

## Zürich, Staatsarchiv

E II 345a: correspondence of the Reformers (I am very grateful to Dr Hirofumi Horie for supplying me with this reference, and to Dr Bruce Gordon for arranging for photocopies to be sent to me.)

## PRIMARY (PRE-1640) SOURCES IN PRINT

Andrewes, L., ed. J. P. Wilson and J. Bliss, *Works* (11 vols., LACT, 1851–4)

Anon, *Retrospective Review*, 2nd ser. 1 (1827), pp. 503–5: notices of documents from the reign of Queen Jane

Arber, E., ed., *A brief discourse of the troubles at Frankfort 1554–1558 A.D.* ... (Elliot Stock, 1908)

Ayre, J., ed., *The Works of Thomas Becon* (3 vols., PS, 1843–4)

Bale, J., *An Expostulation or complaynte agaynste the blasphemyes of a franticke papyst of Hamshyre* (J. Daye, ?1552), RSTC, 1294

Beer, B. L., ed., *The life and raigne of King Edward the Sixth by John Hayward* (Kent State UP, 1993)

Beer, B. L., and Nash, R. J., eds., 'Latimer and the lusty knave of Kent', *BIHR*, 52 (1979), pp. 175–8

*Biblia interprete Sebastiano Castalione una cum eiusdem annotationibus* (Basel, J. Oporinus, 1551)

Bill, E. G. W., ed., *A Catalogue of Manuscripts in Lambeth Palace Library: Lambeth MSS. 2341–3119 (excluding MSS. 2690–2750)* (Oxford UP, 1983)

Bindseil, H. E., ed., *Philippi Melanchthonis epistolae, iudicia, consilia, testimonia aliorumque ad eum epistolae quae in Corpore Reformatorum desiderantur* ... (Halle, G. Schwetschke, 1874)

Binney, E. J., ed., *The Accounts of the Wardens of the parish of Morebath, Devon, 1520–1573* (Exeter, James G. Commin, 1904)

Bond, R. B., ed., *Certain Sermons or Homilies (1547) and A Homily against Disobedience and Wilful Rebellion (1570)* (Toronto UP, 1987)

Bourbon, N., *Nugarum libri octo* (Lyon, S. Gryphius, 1538); BL shelfmark 1213 b. 24

Bruce, J., ed., *The Works of Roger Hutchinson* ... (PS, 1842)

Bucer, M., *The Gratulation of the most famous Clerk M. Martin Bucer* ..., tr. and with preface by T. Hoby (R. Jugge, 1548), *RSTC*, 3963

Bullinger, H., tr. M. Coverdale, *The Christen State of Matrymonye* (Nicholas Hill, 1552) *RSTC*, 4049

*Calendar of State Papers, Domestic, Edward VI, Philip and Mary, Elizabeth* (9 vols., HMSO, 1856–72. A supplementary volume ed. by C. S. Knighton, 1992, replaces the older Calendar for Edward VI, 1547–53)

*Calendar of State Papers, Foreign* (23 vols., HMSO, 1863–1950)

*Calendar of State Papers, Spanish,* ed. P. de Gayangos, G. Mattingly, M. A. S. Hume and R. Tyler (15 vols. in 20, HMSO, 1862–1954)

*Calendar of State Papers, Venetian,* ed. R. Brown, C. Bentinck and H. Brown (9 vols., HMSO, 1864–98)

Camden, W., *Annales rerum Anglicarum, et Hibernicarum regnante Elizabetha ad annum salutis M. D. LXXXIX* ... (Frankfurt am Main, J. and P. Ruland, 1616) [2nd edn of *RSTC*, 4496]

Camden, W., tr. P. Holland, *Britaine, or a chorographicall description of England, Scotland and Ireland* ... (G. Bishop and J. Norton, 1610) *RSTC*, 4509

Camden, W., *Remains concerning Britain* (John Russell Smith, 1870)

Caraman, P., ed., *John Gerard: the Autobiography of an Elizabethan* (Longmans, 1951)

Carr, S., ed., *Early Writings of Bishop Hooper* ..., (PS, 1843)

Christmas, H., ed., *The Works of Nicholas Ridley, D. D.* .... (PS, 1843)

Christopherson, J., *An exhortation to all menne to ... beware of rebellion* (John Cawood, 1554) *RSTC*, 5207: repr. The English Experience no. 1580 (Amsterdam and New York, Da Capo Press, 1973)

Cole, T., *A godly and frutefull sermon, made at Maydestone* ... (Reyner Wolfe, 1553) *RSTC*, 5539

Cooper, T., *Cooper's Chronicle* ... (T. Powell, 1560) *RSTC*, 15218. See also Lanquet

Corrie, G. E., ed., *Sermons by Hugh Latimer* ...; *Sermons and Remains of Hugh Latimer* ... (PS, 1844, 1845)

Cox, J. E., ed., *Works of Archbishop Cranmer* (2 vols., PS, 1844 [Vol. 1 in two paginations], 1846)

Cranmer, T., *A Defence of the true and catholike doctrine of the sacrament* ... (R. Wolfe, 1550) *RSTC*, 6000, 6001

Crowley, R., *The Confutation of xiii Articles, wherunto Nicolas Shaxton, late byshop of Salisborye subscribed and caused to be set forth in print the yere of our Lorde M. C. xlvi, [sic]* ... (J. Day and W. Seres, 1548) *RSTC*, 6083

Crowley, R.: see also Lanquet

Dasent, J. R., ed., *Acts of the Privy Council of England* (32 vols., 1890–1907)

Davies, M. B., ed., 'Boulogne and Calais from 1545 to 1550', *Bulletin of the Faculty of Arts, Fouad I University, Cairo,* 12 (1950), pp. 1–90

*Disputatio de eucharistiae sacramento habita in celeberr. Universitate Oxonien. in Anglia, antea quidem illic excusa, iam vero denuo cum triplica indice in lucem edita* (Zürich, C. Gesner, 1552) [2nd edn of *RSTC*, 24763]

Eden, R., ed., *The Examinations and Writings of John Philpot* ... (PS, 1842)

Ellis, H., ed., *Original Letters Illustrative of English History . . . from Autographs in the British Museum and . . . Other Collections* (11 vols. in 3 series, Harding, Triphook and Lepard, 1824, 1827, 1846)

*Epistolae Tigurinae de rebus potissimum ad ecclesiae Anglicanae Reformationem pertinentibus . . .* (PS, 1848)

Forbes, W., ed. G. H. Forbes, *Considerationes modestae et pacificae controversiarum de Justificatione, Purgatorio, Invocatione sanctorum, Christo mediatore et eucharistia* (2 vols., LACT, 1850–56)

Fowler, J. T., ed., *Rites of Durham . . .* (Surtees Society, 107, 1902)

Foxe, J., *Acts and Monuments of these latter and perilous days . . .* (J. Day, 1563) *RSTC*, 11222

Foxe, J., *Acts and Monuments of these latter and perilous days . . .* (3 vols., J. Day, 1570) *RSTC*, 11223

Frere, W. H., and Kennedy, W. M., eds., *Visitation Articles and Injunctions: 1. Introduction; 2. 1536–1558* (Alcuin Club 14, 15, 1910)

Gasquet, F. A., and Bishop, E., *Edward VI and the Book of Common Prayer* (J. Hodges, 1890)

Gorham, G. C., ed., *Gleanings of a Few Scattered Ears, during the Period of the Reformation in England . . .* (Bell & Daldy, 1857)

Hakewill, G., *An Answere to a Treatise written by Dr. Carier . . .* (John Bill, 1616) *RSTC*, 12610

Hamilton, W. D., ed., *A Chronicle of England . . . by Charles Wriothesley, Windsor Herald* (2 vols., CS, 2nd ser. 11, 20, 1875, 1877)

Historical Manuscripts Commission, Reports: *Manuscripts . . . Preserved at Hatfield House* (24 vols., ser. 9, 1883–1976)

Houghton, R., Lord, ed., *Bishop Cranmer's Recantacyons*, with introd. by J. Gairdner (Philobiblon Society Miscellanies 15, 1877–84)

Huggarde, M., *The assault of the sacrament of the Altar containyng as well six severall assaultes made from tyme to tyme against the sayd blessed sacrament: as also the names and opinions of all the heretical captaines of the same assaultes: Written in the yere of our Lorde 1549, by Myles Huggarde, and dedicated to the Quenes most excellent maiestie, beyng then Ladie Marie: in whiche tyme (heresie then raigning) it could take no place. Now newly imprynted this present yere* (R. Caly, 1554) RSTC, 13556

Huggarde, M., *The displaying of the Protestantes . . . Newly imprinted agayne, and augmented, with a table in the ende, of all suche matter as is specially contained within this volume* (R. Caly, 1556) RSTC, 13558

Hughes, P. L., and Larkin, J. F., eds., *Tudor Royal Proclamations* (2 vols., New Haven, Yale UP, 1964, 1969)

Jack, S. M., and Beer, B. L., eds., 'The Letters of William, Lord Paget of Beaudesert, 1547–1563', *Camden Miscellany* 25 (CS, 4th ser. 13, 1974), pp. 1–142

Joliffe, H., and Johnson, R., *Responsio venerabilium sacerdotum, Henrici Joliffi et Roberti Jonson, sub protestatione facta, ad illos articulos Ioannis Hoperi, Episcopi Vigorniae nomen gerentis, in quibus a Catholica fide dissentiebat, una cum Confutationibus eiusdem Hoperi, et Replicationibus reverendiss. in Christo patris, bonae memoriae, Stephani Gardineri, Episcopi Wintoniensis, tunc temporis pro confessione fidei in carcere detenti* (Antwerp, Chr. Plantin, 1564)

Jordan, W. K., ed., *The Chronicle and Political Papers of King Edward VI* (George Allen & Unwin, 1966)

Ketley, J., ed., *The Two Liturgies ... Set Forth by Authority in the Reign of King Edward VI ...* (PS, 1844)

Kingsford, C. L., ed., 'Two London Chronicles from the collections of John Stow ...', *Camden Miscellany* 4 (CS, 3rd ser. 18, 1910), pp. iii–59

[Lanquet, T.], *An Epitome of Chronicles conteyninge the whole discourse of the histories as well of this realme of England as al other countreys ... gathered ... first by Thomas Lanquet ... secondely to the reigne of our soveraigne lord king Edward the sixt by Thomas Cooper, and thirdly to the reigne of our soveraigne Ladye Quene Elizabeth, by Robert Crowley* (W. Seres, 1559) [pirated edn of *Cooper's Chronicle*, q.v.] *RSTC*, 15217.5

Lefèvre-Pontalis, G., ed., *Correspondance politique de Odet de Selve ...* (Paris, 1888)

Leighton, W. A., ed., 'Early Chronicles of Shrewsbury, 1372–1606', *Transactions of the Shropshire Archaeological and Natural History Society* 3 (1880), pp. 239–352

Lever, C., *The History of the Defendors of the Catholique Faith. Wheareunto are Added Observations Divine, Politique, Morrall ...* (Geo. Miller, for Nicholas Fussell and Humphrey Moseley, 1627), *RSTC* 15537

Lever, T., *Sermons* (Edward Arber reprints, 1870)

Lewis, D., ed., *Rise and Growth of the Anglican Schism by Nicholas Sander* (Burns & Oates, 1877)

MacCulloch, D., ed., 'The *Vita Mariae Angliae Reginae* of Robert Wingfield of Brantham' (*Camden Miscellany* 28, CS, 4th ser. 29, 1984), pp. 181–301

MacCulloch, D., and Hughes, P., 'A bailiff's list and chronicle from Worcester', *Antiquaries Journal* 75 (1995), pp. 235–53

McNeill, J. T., and Battles, F. L., eds., *Calvin: Institutes of the Christian Religion*

(2 vols., Philadelphia, Westminster Press, Library of Christian Classics 20I, 21, 1960)

Maddison, A. R., ed., *Lincolnshire Pedigrees*, (4 vols., Harleian Society 51–3, 55, 1902–4, 1906: continuous pagination)

Martyr: see *Disputatio*, Vermigli

Masters, B. R., and Ralph, E., eds., *Church Book of St. Ewen's Bristol*, (Bristol and Gloucestershire Archaeological Society, Records Section 6, 1967)

Muller, J. A., ed., *The Letters of Stephen Gardiner* (Cambridge UP, 1933, repr. Greenwood Press, Westport, Conn., 1970)

Nevinson, C., ed., *Later Writings of Bishop Hooper* ... (PS, 1852)

Nicolas, N. H., ed., *Testamenta Vetusta* ... (2 vols. [continuous pagination], Nichols & Son, 1826)

Nichols, J. G., ed., *The Diary of Henry Machyn, Citizen and Merchant-taylor of London, 1550–63*, (CS, 1st ser. 42, 1848)

Nichols, J. G., ed., *The Chronicle of Queen Jane, and of Two Years of Queen Mary* (CS, 1st ser. 48, 1850)

Nichols, J. G., ed., *Chronicle of the Grey Friars of London* (CS, 1st ser. 53, 1852)

Nichols, J. G., ed., *Literary Remains of King Edward the Sixth* (2 vols., Roxburghe Club, 1857)

Nichols, J. G., ed., *Narratives of the Reformation* (CS, 1st ser. 77, 1859)

Ochino, B., *A tragoedie or dialoge of the uniuste usurped primacie of the Bishop of Rome, and of all the iust abolishynge of the same, made by master Barnadine Ochine an Italian, and translated out of Latine into Englishe by Master John Ponet Doctor of Divinitie, never printed before in any language*, [N. Hill for W. Lynne] 1549. *RSTC*, 18770. *RSTC*, 18771, is a second edition of 1549, censoring out references to the Duke of Somerset: the signatures are virtually identical for the actual text.

[Olde, J.], *The acquital or purgation of the moost catholyke Christen Prince, Edwarde the VI, Kyng of Englande, Fraunce, and Irelande &c, and of the Churche of Englande refourmed and governed under hym, agaynst al suche as blasphemously and traitorously infame hym or the sayd Church, of heresie or sedicion* (Waterford, i.e. Emden, G. van der Erve, 1555) *RSTC*, 18797

Parr, C., *The lamentacion of a sinner, made by the most vertuous Ladie, Quene Caterin, bewayling the ignoraunce of her blind life; set furth and put in print at the instaunt desire of the righte gracious ladie Caterin Duchesse of Suffolke, and the earnest requeste of the right honourable Lord, William Parre, Marquesse of Northampton* (E. Whitchurch, 1547) *RSTC*, 4827

[Parsons, R.], *The third part of a treatise intituled of three conversions of England conteyning an examen of the Calendar or Catalogue of Protestant Saintes, Martyrs and Confessors, devised by Fox . . . the last six monethes, Wherunto is annexed in the end, another severall Treatise, called: a re-view of ten publike Disputacions, or conferences, held in England about matters of religion, especially about the sacrament and sacrifice of the Altar, under King Edward and Queene Mary,* ([St Omer, F. Bellet] 1604) *RSTC*, 19416 and 19414 [the annexed book]

Pearson, G., ed., *Remains of Myles Coverdale . . .* (PS, 1846)

Pocock, N., ed., *Troubles Connected with the Prayer Book of 1549 . . .* (CS, 1st ser. 37, 1884)

Pollard, A. W., and Redgrave, G. R., eds., *A Short Title Catalogue of Books Printed in England, Scotland, and Ireland and of English Books Printed Abroad before the Year 1640*, rev. W. A. Jackson and F. S. Ferguson and completed by K. F. Pantzer (The Bibliographical Society, 3 vols., 1976–91)

Ponet, J., *A notable sermon concerninge the ryght use of the lordes supper and other thynges very profitable for all men to knowe preached before the kynges most excellent Mayestye and hys most honorable counsel in hys courte at Westmynster the 14 daye of Marche* (S. Mierdman, for Walter Lynne, 1550) *RSTC*, 20177

Ponet, J., *A shorte treatise of politike power, and of the true Obedience which subiectes owe to kynges and other civile Governours, with an Exhortacion to all true naturall Englishe men, Compyled by D.I.P.B[ishop of]. R[ochester and]. W[inchester]. ([Strassburg, heirs of W. Kopfel], 1556) RSTC*, 20178

[Proctor, J.], *The fal of the late Arrian* (W. Powell, 1549) *RSTC*, 20406

*Regiae Maiestatis Angliae etc. mandatorum epitome, ex praescripto, ad subditos suos, tam sacris addictos, quam laicos, ex Anglico sermone in Latinum converso* (?pr. abroad, 1547, 1548) *RSTC*, 10094

Robinson H., ed., *Original Letters Relative to the English Reformation . . .* (2 vols., PS, 1846–7)

Scholefield, J., ed., *The Works of James Pilkington . . .* (PS, 1842)

?Shepherd, L., *John Bon and Mast Person* (J. Daye at Wm Seres, [1548]) *RSTC*, 3258.5 [No signatures or foliation]

Tawney, R. H., and Power, E., eds., *Tudor Economic Documents* (3 vols., Longman, 1924)

Townshend, G., and Cattley, S. R., eds., *The Acts and Monuments of John Foxe* (8 vols., 1837–41)

V., P., *Historical Narration of certain events that took place in the Kingdom of Great Britain in the month of July, in the year of our Lord, 1553*, ed. J. P. Berjeau (Bell & Daldy, 1865)

Vermigli, P. Martyr, *The Common Places of the most famous and renowmed Divine Doctor Peter Martyr . . . translated and partlie gathered by Anthonie Marten, one of the Sewers of hir Maiesties most Honourable Chamber* (H. Denham and H. Middleton, [1583] *RSTC*, 24669

Wilkins, D., ed., *Concilia Magnae Britanniae et Hiberniae* (4 vols., 1737)

Williams, C. H., ed., *English Historical Documents 1485–1558* (Eyre & Spottiswoode, 1967)

Wilson, J., ed., *Sermons Very Fruitfull, Godly and Learned by Roger Edgeworth: Preaching in the Reformation c. 1535-c. 1553* (Woodbridge, D. S. Brewer, 1993)

[Wyclif, John], *The dore of holy Scripture . . .* ( J. Gowgh, 1541) *RSTC*, 25587.5

[Wyclif, John], *The true copy of a Prolog wrytten about two C. yeres paste by John Wycklife (as maye iustly be gatherid bi that, that John Bale hath written of him in his boke entitled the Summarie of famouse writers of the Isle of great Britan) the Originall whereof is founde written in an olde English Bible bitwixt the olde Testament and the Newe. Whych Bible remaynith now in the kyng hys maiesties Chamber* (R. Crowley, 1550) *RSTC*, 25588

## SECONDARY SOURCES

Anglo, S., *Spectacle, Pageantry and Early Tudor Policy* (Oxford, Clarendon Press, 1969)

Aston, M., *England's Iconoclasts, I: Laws against Images* (Oxford, Clarendon Press, 1988)

Aston, M., *The King's Bedpost: Reformation and Iconography in a Tudor Group Portrait* (Cambridge UP, 1993)

Ayris, P., and Selwyn D., eds, *Thomas Cranmer: Churchman and Scholar* (Woodbridge, Boydell Press, 1993)

Bindoff, S. T., ed., *History of Parliament: The House of Commons 1509–1558* (3 vols., Secker & Warburg, 1982)

Bradshaw, B., 'The Edwardian Reformation in Ireland', *Archivum Hibernicum* 34 (1977), pp. 83–99

Bradshaw, C., 'David or Josiah? Old Testament kings as exemplars in Edwardian religious polemic' in Gordon, ed., *Protestant History and Identity in 16th Century Europe*, pp. 77–90

Brady, C., *The Chief Governors: the Rise and Fall of Reform Government in Tudor Ireland, 1536–1588* (Cambridge UP, 1994)

Brigden, S., 'Youth and the English Reformation', in P. Marshall, ed., *The Impact of the English Reformation 1500–1640* (Arnold, 1997), pp. 55–84; repr. from *PP*, 95 (May 1982), pp. 37–67

Brigden, S., *London and the Reformation* (Oxford and New York, Clarendon Press, 1989)

Brightman, F. E., *The English Rite* (2 vols., Rivingtons, 1915)

Brown, A. J., *Robert Ferrar. Yorkshire Monk, Reformation Bishop, and Martyr in Wales (c. 1500–1555)* (Inscriptor Imprints, 1997)

Buisson, F., *Sébastien Castellion, sa vie et son oeuvre (1515–1563)* (2 vols., Paris, 1892)

Burnet, G., *History of the Reformation of the Church of England* ( J. F. Dove, for Richard Priestley, 3 vols. in 6, 1820)

Bush, M. L., *The Government Policy of Protector Somerset* (Edward Arnold, 1975)

Cameron, E., 'Philipp Melanchthon: image and substance', *JEH* 48 (1997), pp. 705–22.

Chavasse, R., 'Humanism in exile: Celio Secondo Curione's learned women friends and *exempla* for Elizabeth I', in S. M. Jack and B. A. Masters, eds., *Protestants, Property, Puritans: Godly People Revisited, Parergon*, new ser. 14 (1996), pp. 165–86

Collinson, P., 'The authorship of *A Brieff Discours off the Troubles begonne at Franckford*', *JEH* 9 (1958), pp. 188–209, repr. in Collinson, *Godly People*, pp. 191–212

Collinson, P., 'Sir Nicholas Bacon and the Elizabethan *Via Media*', *HJ* 23 (1980), pp. 255–73, repr. in Collinson, *Godly People*, pp. 135–54

Collinson, P., *Archbishop Grindal 1519–1583: the Struggle for a Reformed Church* ( Jonathan Cape, 1979)

Collinson, P., *Godly People: Essays in English Protestantism and Puritanism* (London and Rio Grande, Hambledon Press, 1983)

Collinson, P., 'Puritans, men of business and Elizabethan Parliaments', *Parliamentary History* 7 (1988), pp. 187–211, repr. in Collinson, *Elizabethan Essays* (Hambledon Press, 1994), pp. 59–86

Cowan, I. B., *The Scottish Reformation: Church and Society in Sixteenth Century Scotland* (Weidenfeld & Nicolson, 1982)

Crankshaw, D., 'Preparations for the Canterbury Provincial Convocation of 1562–63: a question of attribution', in S. Wabuda and C. Litzenberger, eds., *Belief and Practice in Reformation England* (Aldershot, St Andrews Studies in Reformation History, 1998), pp. 60–93

Croft, P., 'The religion of Robert Cecil', *HJ* 34 (1991), pp. 773–96

Croft, P., 'Camden, Westminster and the Cecils', *TRHS* [forthcoming]

Davies, C. M. F., ' "Poor persecuted little flock" or "Commonwealth of Christians": Edwardian Protestant concepts of the Church', in P. Lake and M. Dowling, eds., *Protestantism and the National Church in Sixteenth Century England* (Croom Helm, 1987), pp. 36–77

Davies, C. M. F., and Facey, J., 'A Reformation dilemma: John Foxe and the problem of discipline', *JEH* 39 (1988), pp. 37–65

Dickens, A. G., 'The early expansion of Protestantism in England 1520–1558', in Dickens, *Later Monasticism and the Reformation*, pp. 101–31, repr. from *ARG* 78 (1987), pp. 187–222

Dickens, A. G., 'The shape of anticlericalism and the English Reformation', in Dickens, *Later Monasticism and the Reformation*, pp. 151–75, repr. from E. I. Kouri and T. Scott, eds., *Politics and Society in Reformation Europe* (1987), pp. 379–410

Dickens, A. G., *Later Monasticism and the Reformation* (London and Rio Grande, Hambledon Press, 1994)

Donaldson, G., *The Scottish Reformation* (Cambridge UP, 1960)

Duffy, E., *The Stripping of the Altars: Traditional Religion in England 1400–1580* (Yale UP, 1992)

Duffy, E., 'Morebath 1520–1570: a rural parish in the Reformation', in J. Devlin and R. Fanning, eds., *Religion and Rebellion* (*Historical Studies* 20, 1997), pp. 17–39

Elton, G. R., *Policy and Police: the Enforcement of the Reformation in the Age of Thomas Cromwell* (Cambridge UP, 1972)

Elton, G. R., *The Parliament of England 1559–1581* (Cambridge UP, 1986)

Elton, G. R., *Studies in Tudor and Stuart Politics and Government* (4 vols., Cambridge UP, 1974–92)

Fletcher, A., and MacCulloch, D., *Tudor Rebellions* (4th edn, Longman, 1997)

Fox, A., 'Rumour, news and popular political opinion in Elizabethan and early Stuart England', *HJ* 40 (1997), pp. 597–620

Freeman, T. S., and Borges, M. J., ' "A grave and heinous incident against our Holy Catholic Faith": two accounts of William Gardiner's desecration of the Portuguese royal chapel in 1552', *HR* 69 (1996), pp. 1–17

Freeman, T. S., 'New perspectives on an old book: the creation and influence of Foxe's "Book of Martyrs" ', *JEH* 49 (1998), pp. 317–28

French, K. L., Gibbs, G. G., and Kümin, B. A., eds., *The Parish in English Life 1400–1600* (Manchester UP, 1997)

Garrett, C. H., *The Marian Exiles: a Study in the Origins of Elizabethan Puritanism* (Cambridge UP, 1938)

Gerrish, B. A., 'Sign and reality: the Lord's Supper in the Reformed Confessions', in Gerrish, *The Old Protestantism and the New* (Chicago UP, and Edinburgh, T. & T. Clark, 1982), pp. 118–30

Gerrish, B. A., *Continuing the Reformation: Essays on Modern Religious Thought* (Chicago UP, 1993)

Gerrish, B. A., *Grace and Gratitude: the Eucharistic Theology of John Calvin* (Minneapolis, Fortress Press, and Edinburgh, T. & T. Clark, 1993)

Gordon, B., 'Calvin and the Swiss Reformed Churches' in A. Pettegree, A. Duke and G. Lewis, eds., *Calvinism in Europe, 1540–1620* (Cambridge UP, 1994), pp. 64–81

Gordon, B., ed., *Protestant History and Identity in Sixteenth Century Europe* (2 vols., Aldershot, St Andrews Studies in Reformation History, 1996)

Grell, O., 'Exile and tolerance', in O. Grell and B. Scribner, eds., *Tolerance and Intolerance in the European Reformation* (Cambridge UP, 1996), pp. 164–181

Grisbrooke, W. J., *Anglican Liturgies of the Seventeenth and Eighteenth Centuries* (Alcuin Club Collections 40, 1958)

Guggisberg, H. R., *Basel in the Sixteenth Century: Aspects of the City Republic before, during and after the Reformation* (Center for Reformation Research, St Louis, 1982)

Guy, J., ed., *The Reign of Elizabeth I: Court and Culture in the Last Decade* (Cambridge UP, 1995)

Heylyn, P., ed. Robertson, J. C., *Ecclesia Restaurata; or, the History of the Reformation of the Church of England* (2 vols., Cambridge, Ecclesiastical History Society, 1859)

Hoak, D. E., *The King's Council in the Reign of Edward VI* (Cambridge UP, 1976)

Houlbrooke, R. A., *Church Courts and the People during the English Reformation 1520–1570* (Oxford, Clarendon Press, 1979)

Hutchinson, R., and Egan, B., 'History writ in brass – the Fermer Workshop', *Transactions of the Monumental Brass Society* 15 (1992–97), pp. 142–83, 256–81, 355–74, 466–84

Ives, E. W., 'The Queen and the painters: Anne Boleyn, Holbein and Tudor royal portraits', *Apollo* (July 1994), pp. 36–45

Jordan, W. K., *Edward VI: the Young King* (George Allen & Unwin, 1968)

Jordan, W. K., *Edward VI: the Threshold of Power* (George Allen & Unwin, 1970)

King, J. N., *English Reformation Literature: the Tudor Origins of the Protestant Tradition* (Princeton UP, 1982)

Kirk, J., *Patterns of Reform: Continuity and Change in the Reformation Kirk* (Edinburgh, T. and T. Clark, 1989)

Kümin, B., *The Shaping of a Community: the Rise and Reformation of the English Parish c. 1400–1560* (Aldershot, St Andrews Studies in Reformation History, 1996)

Laing, D., ed., *The Works of John Knox* (6 vols., Edinburgh, Wodrow Society, 1846–64)

Loach, J., *Parliament under the Tudors* (Oxford, Clarendon Press, 1991)

Loach, J., 'The function of ceremonial in the reign of Henry VIII', *PP* 142 (February 1994), pp. 43–68

Loach, J., *Edward VI* (London and New Haven, Yale UP, 1999)

Loach, J., and Tittler, R., eds, *The Mid-Tudor Polity, c. 1540–1560* (London and Basingstoke, Macmillan, 1980)

Loades, D. M., *Mary Tudor: a Life* (Oxford and Cambridge, Mass. Basil Blackwell, 1989)

Loades, D. M., *John Dudley, Duke of Northumberland 1504–1553* (Oxford, Clarendon Press, 1996)

Lossky, N., *Lancelot Andrewes the Preacher (1555–1626): the Origins of the Mystical Theology of the Church of England* (Oxford, Clarendon Press, 1986)

McCafferty, J., 'Bishop John Bramhall, Laud and the Church of Ireland in the 1630s' [unpublished paper]

MacCaffrey, W., *Elizabeth I* (Edward Arnold, 1993)

McConica, J., ed., *History of the University of Oxford: III, The Collegiate University* (Oxford, Clarendon Press, 1986)

MacCulloch, D., ed., *The Reign of Henry VIII: Politics, Policy and Piety* (Basingstoke, Macmillan, 1995)

MacCulloch, D., 'Archbishop Cranmer: consensus and tolerance in a changing Church', in O. Grell and B. Scribner, eds., *Tolerance and Intolerance in the European Reformation* (Cambridge UP, 1996), pp. 199–215

MacCulloch, D., *Thomas Cranmer: a Life* (London and New Haven, Yale UP, 1996)

MacCulloch, D., 'A Reformation in the balance: power struggles in the diocese of Norwich, 1533–53', in C. Rawcliffe, R. Virgoe and R. Wilson, eds., *Counties and Communities: Essays on East Anglian History* (Centre for East Anglian Studies, 1996), pp. 97–114

McCullough, P., *Sermons at Court: Politics and Religion in Elizabethan and Jacobean Preaching* (Cambridge UP, 1998)

McDiarmid, J. F., 'John Cheke's Preface to *De Superstitione*', *JEH* 48 (1997), pp. 100–120

McRae, A., *God Speed the Plough: the Representation of Agrarian England, 1500–1660* (Cambridge UP, 1996)

Manning, R. B., *Religion and Society in Elizabethan Sussex* (Leicester University Press, 1969)

Marsh, C., *The Family of Love in English Society, 1550–1630* (Cambridge UP, 1994)

Marshall, P., 'The debate over "unwritten verities" in early Reformation England', in Gordon, ed., *Protestant History and Identity in 16th Century Europe*, pp. 60–77

Marshall, P., 'Fear, purgatory and polemic in Reformation England', in W. G. Naphy and P. Roberts, eds., *Fear in Early Modern Society* (Manchester UP, 1997), pp. 150–66

Mason, R. A., ed., *Scotland and England 1286–1815* (Edinburgh, John Donald, 1987)

Milton, A., *Catholic and Reformed: the Roman and Protestant Churches in English Protestant Thought 1600–1640* (Cambridge UP, 1995)

Moody, T. W., Martin, F. X., and Byrne, F. J., eds., *A New History of Ireland: III, Early Modern Ireland, 1534–1691* (Oxford, Clarendon Press, 2nd edn, 1991)

Mueller, J., 'Complications of intertextuality: John Fisher, Katherine Parr and "The Book of the Crucifix" ', in C. C. Brown and A. F. Marotti, eds., *Texts and Cultural Change in Early Modern England* (Macmillan, 1997), pp. 15–36

Neale, J. E., *Elizabeth I and Her Parliaments* (2 vols., Jonathan Cape, 1953, 1957)

Ogier, D. M., *Reformation and Society in Guernsey* (Woodbridge, Boydell Press, 1996)

Patterson, A., 'Sir John Oldcastle and Reformation historiography' in D. B. Hamilton and R. Strier eds., *Religion, Literature and Politics in Post-Reformation England, 1540–1688* (Cambridge UP, 1996), pp. 6–26

Penny, D. A., *Freewill or Predestination: the Battle over Saving Grace in Mid-Tudor England* (RHS St.Hist., 61, 1990)

Perrott, M. E. C., 'Richard Hooker and the Elizabethan Church', *JEH* 49 (1998), pp. 29–60

Pettegree, A., *Foreign Protestant Communities in the Sixteenth Century London* (Oxford, Clarendon Press, 1986)

Pettegree, A., *Marian Protestantism: Six Studies* (Aldershot, St Andrews Studies in Reformation History, 1996)

Pettegree, A., 'The reception of Calvinism in Britain', in W. H. Neusner and B. G. Armstrong, eds., *Calvinus sincerioris religionis vindex: Calvin as the Protector of the Purer Religion* (Sixteenth Century Essays and Studies, 36, 1997), pp. 267–89

Read, C., *Mr Secretary Cecil and Queen Elizabeth* (Jonathan Cape, 1965)

Rex, R., *The Theology of John Fisher* (Cambridge UP, 1991)

Rodgers, D. W., *John à Lasco in England* (New York, Peter Lang, 1994)

Sanderson, M. B., *Mary Stewart's People: Life in Mary Stewart's Scotland* (Edinburgh, James Thin, 1987)

Schickler, F. de, *Les Eglises du refuge en Angleterre* (3 vols., Paris, Librarie Fischbacher, 1892)

Selwyn, D. G., 'A new version of a mid-sixteenth-century vernacular tract on the eucharist: a document of the early Edwardian Reformation?', *JEH* 39 (1988), pp. 217–29

Selwyn, D. G., 'The "Book of Doctrine", the Lords' Debate and the First Prayer Book of Edward VI: an abortive attempt at Doctrinal Consensus?' *JTS*, NS 40 (1989), pp. 446–80

Shagan, E., 'Protector Somerset and the 1549 rebellions: new sources and new perspectives' *EHR* 144 (1999), pp. 34–63

Sharpe, K., and Lake, P., eds., *Culture and Politics in Early Stuart England* (Basingstoke, Macmillan, 1994)

Smuts, M., 'Court-centred politics and the uses of Roman historians, c. 1590–1630', in Sharpe and Lake, eds., *Culture and Politics in Early Stuart England*, pp. 21–43

Smyth, C. H., *Cranmer and the Reformation under Edward VI* (SPCK, 1926; 2nd edn 1973)

Starkey, D., ed., *The English Court from the Wars of the Roses to the Civil War* (Longman, 1987)

Strong, R., *The Cult of Elizabeth: Elizabethan Portraiture and Pageantry* (Thames & Hudson, 1977)

Strype, J., *The Life of the Learned Sir John Cheke ...* (Oxford, Clarendon Press, 1821)

Strype, J., *Ecclesiastical Memorials ...* (3 vols. in 6, Oxford, Clarendon Press, 1822)

Strype, J., ed. Barnes, P. E., *Memorials ... of ... Thomas Cranmer ...* (2 vols., George Routledge & Co., 1853)

Tabor, S., 'Additions to *STC*', *Library*, 6th ser. 16 (1994), pp. 190–207

Thomas, K., *Religion and the Decline of Magic: Studies in Popular Beliefs in Sixteenth and Seventeenth Century England* (Penguin, 1973)

Thomas, M., 'Tunstal – trimmer or martyr?', *JEH* 24 (1973), pp. 337–55

Thompson, E. M., 'The revision of the Statutes of the Order of the Garter by King Edward VI', *Archaeologia* 54, 1894, pp. 173–98

Tudor-Craig, P., 'Henry VIII and King David', in Williams, D., ed., *Early Tudor England* (Woodbridge, Boydell, 1989), pp. 183–206

Tyacke, N., *Anti-Calvinists: the Rise of English Arminianism* (Oxford, Clarendon Press, revised edn, 1990)

Tyacke, N., ed., *England's Long Reformation 1500–1800* (UCL Press, 1998)

Tytler, P. F., *England under the Reigns of Edward VI and Mary* . . . (2 vols., 1839)

Usher, B., 'In a time of persecution: new light on the secret Protestant congregation in Marian London', in D. Loades, ed., *John Foxe and the English Reformation* (Aldershot, St Andrews Studies in Reformation History, 1997), pp. 233–51

Vinay, V., 'Riformatori e lotte contadine. Scritti e polemiche relative alla ribellione dei contadini nella Cornovaglia e nel Devonshire sotto Edoardo VI', *Rivista di storia e letteratura religiosa* 3 (1967), pp. 203–51

Williams, G., *Welsh Reformation Essays* (Cardiff, University of Wales Press, 1967)

Worden, B., 'Ben Jonson among the historians', in Sharpe and Lake, eds., *Culture and Politics in Early Stuart England*, pp. 67–90

Worden, B., 'William Camden and Ben Jonson', *TRHS* [forthcoming]

Wright, D. F., ed., *Martin Bucer: Reforming Church and Commonwealth* (Cambridge UP, 1994)

Youings, J., 'The South-Western Rebellion of 1549', *Southern History* 1 (1979), pp. 99–122

## Unpublished Dissertations

Clark, M., 'The Reformation in the Diocese of Carlisle and the Lake Counties to 1570' (CNAA PhD, 1990)

Davies, C. M. F., 'Towards a Godly Commonwealth: the public ideology of Protestantism, *c.* 1546–1553' (London Ph.D., 1988)

Richardson, L., 'Sir John Hayward and early Stuart Historiography' (Cambridge PhD, 1998)

# Index

Page references in bold denote an illustration.